One of the best guides to h
give ourselves the love we a.. ....aing about
receiving from others.
bell hooks

be gentle with
black girls

Tania De'Shawn

Tania's writing is the essence of a Black feminine warrior wolfing off the pages. She uses her wordsmithing to surely capture and paint powerful depictions of what it is to grow up in the body of a girl identified as full-grown before womanhood— using her storytelling capabilities to challenge the narrative placed on Black girls; her poetry reclaims the righteousness that is Black femininity. Tania is a true champion and protector of Black girlhood and womanhood.

-Nubia Adisa

Contents

3

In 2017 the Georgetown Law Center on Poverty and Inequality published a study called Girlhood Interrupted: The Erasure of Black Girls' Childhood. It is the first study of its kind to provide scientific evidence that black girls are perceived to require less nurturing, protection, and support. Black girls were also perceived to be more independent, know more about adult topics, and know more about sex. Adultification bias or contributing adult behaviors to children is the common thread in these false presumptions. This chapbook is a reminder to be gentle with the black girls.

Psychology of Maturation

adulthood ravished my girlhood like a relaxer on
virgin hair / this world can break you down until
you are unrecognizable and structurally different /
and some might even open their mouths to call your
deterioration beauty / did you know / that you lose
approximately five brain cells every time you relax
your hair / wise up while you can / there is always
someone counting on your insecurities and need for
conformity to make you look dumb

the brain doesn't reach full maturity until it's 25-
years-old / specifically / the pre-frontal cortex also
known as the decision-making center of the brain /
so / forgive yourself / for the drunken nights / for
not understanding that nice men can be nice
narcissists / for not believing in your dreams the
first time it sparked within you / and on the days /
when your skin is a minefield of triggers / breathe

you are grown and safe, and your body is the best
place to be right now / your mind is a center for
restoration / rest / did you know that the brain has
its own cleansing system that's only active when you
sleep / scientists believe that the buildup of proteins
that can only be removed by the lymphatic system /
is the leading cause of Alzheimer's

which is to say/ it's the things that keep you up at
night that will make you forget yourself
forget the people who love you most or your
favorite song that makes you smile / I'm happy to
be grown in mind - not just body / someone asked
me when I first felt like an adult / I was 25 / and it
tasted like lavender and honey tea in the morning /
praying away the demons / and they actually fled /
and I was no longer afraid

Be /bē/
Verb

Definition: to remain unmolested, undisturbed, or uninterrupted

Black girlhood be valued here

Black womanhood be sacred here

black girls need less comfort
By The Age of Five

Girlhood is the myth
Enters Deja - smelling of baby magic
She be swaying her head side to side
Ringing a symphony of rainbow-colored beads
she be a musician - Her eyes two small suns
Her voice unpasteurized honey
And at the tender age of five
why would any god disapprove of her

Unless god is a teacher
with dandelion confidence
each inquisitive remark or wind from hair
Eye roll when she couldn't have her way
a threat to the education systems ego
an excuse for parent-teacher meetings
a cause for expulsion

The weight of Deja's world oscillated between girl
and woman
Then stalled on the wrong end of the pendulum
Too soon - for too long
Her words became lemon rinds and raw turnip
greens
Her aura pungent coffee with no cream
The comfort she received was milk curdled
No teacher to say, "Baby, what do you need"
And no family to give her a little sugar to keep her
sweet

Fast /fast/

Adjective

Definition: A girl who is perceived to be engaged in any sexual activities or behaviors

Look at her fast tail, wearing those shorts.

That girl is fast; she knew what she was getting herself into

Puberty

Deja with the strong brown legs and hips to match
switched down hallways and up sidewalks with her
crew a legend in her grade – she taught the girls
about pads
difference between training bras and bra bras
captivation clinging to her strawberry lemonade lip
gloss
neighborhood kids curious about puberty entranced
by her wisdom
Ms. Mae sitting on her front porch dispels Deja's
magic
"Sit your fast tail down. It ain't cute for a lady to
wear shorts like that"
Ms. Mae's indignation is the chitterlings and onions
boiling in a pot
It can be smelled from the front door of her heart
it's easy to recognize the scent of bs when it is not
your own
I wish fast-tailed girls, so quick, they can outrun lust
and the ill-intentioned
Sha'Carri Richardson speed, so angelic, they surpass
preconceptions effortlessly

Deja Speaks of Ms. Mae's Heart

Diabetic Ms. Mae with the decaying leg sits on the
front pew of the church / clapping to the rhythm of
faith without works / She asks for prayers / and the
female elders contort their tongues to speak a holy
language over a dying limb / as a child Ms. Mae was
caught in a man's insatiable hands / too dark and
developed to claim innocence she found / comfort
/ in food

Ms. Mae's ability to manage what entered and left
her mouth became as dead as her self-control / the
congregation is here / at the Sunday fish fry to
mourn accountability / Ms. Mae is ready to inhale
the whitening and white bread maybe a little
poundcake after Sunday service / here lies my body
image / What Ms. Mae fed grew – grew so big it
devoured her / and I am scared

Most days nourishing my body is a throat full of fish
bones / I think it might kill me / I can feel the
corpse of conversation drag its way up my
esophagus / I felt each jagged edge of "Your face is
getting fuller" / "You're doing good on your diet" /
"You've let yourself go" / Ms. Mae whispering "I
don't want you to be like me" / When memories
begin to strangle me, purging seems like the most
sensible act of survival

Nowadays / I go to church and barely stomach the gospel / When I see my elders living like they're waiting to die / When they die / slow / asking for my assistance / more sugar and salt / mobility is referred to in past tense / Can I tell you that sometimes I prefer the sensation of a growling stomach / I still get pissed when I smell hot grease

Where are the sirens for chubby black girls who count the calories in communion / whose fast are more about escaping the mammy archetype than getting closer to God Ms. Mae taught me that food / was / a / love / language / I was in the fourth grade the first time I rejected a meal / I think that's why I haven't been able to hold myself gently since / She drops the fish in a cast iron skillet / and the bubbles swarm / and her smile is big and beautiful / and she made it just for me

And if I refuse it means I do not love her / and if I refuse it means I do not love myself / and when I refuse / we both feel empty and full of why I ain't good enough and I realize we don't understand love but we want to / a few moments ago we were happy in pews singing our hypocritical hallelujahs / Declaring we love a creator / all the while hating the bodies he created

adorn

Deja wore her soft-heartedness like clip-on earrings
Circular white enamel with gold trimming
Passed down from her great grandmother
There is a supernatural coolness that clings to the
metal
Decrescendo the final notes of white diamond
perfume
Deja embraces the clamps pinch as she places one
on each ear
She examines her reflection in the mirror
Wondering if her great grandmother's tenderness
looks good on her
She pretends that she hasn't been pierced so deep
That a part of her never closed
Her earlobes drop carrying the weight

Deja has worn soft-heartedness like her best friends
Heart-shaped bamboo earrings from the corner
beauty supply store
So big they rest on her shoulder - interrupt phone
conversations with clinking
Her sensitivity obvious to anyone who meets her
Dry scales inflame the side of her neck to her ears
She places cream to sooth the irritation
She wears high neck shirts and jackets to limit the
interaction
Until it is impossible to ignore - her biology detects
the fake
No matter how pretty or familiar if it harms it must
go

Deja wears her soft-heartedness like her favorite earrings
They have a black and white checkerboard arch
Primary colors turning into a circle – matches any outfit
They rest on her shoulders - despite their size they are light
They are loud in all the ways she is afraid to be
Strangers want to ask where she got them from
A peculiar aesthetic and not many can pull it off
She is experienced in making what is strange look natural

Pocketbook / pok-it-book /

Noun

Definition: a vagina

Definition: a safe place where you keep your valuables

Don't let anyone touch your pocketbook

Your pocketbook is a gift to your husband

mothers & children

Celeste is a mother and five of her children are dead and three are not/ Iris is a mother to all the children left waiting for unsteady love/ Deja, Jasmine, and Darius are children with no mamas/ Terrence is a baby and every big bellied woman with fleshy back of arms is mama/ Mary has been grieving all her life/ Crying "Nobody will weep for my babies"/ That dead baby was born a Pisces on February 23/ That mama heartbeat stopped in delivery a Pisces on February 23/ This mama with no babies/ That mama with dead babies/ That mama with babies calling everyone mama but her/ That other mama is a baby/ Diamond cried/ "God I'm only a baby I can't have no baby"/ "God I'm only a baby I can't have no baby"/ That mama cries in her driveway and eats/ Ebony don't touch her baby but she feeds it/ Celeste don't let no men touch her no more/ Jada has a revolving door to her bedroom/ Taylor smokes to calm her nerves/ Calm, what the mamas need is calm/ It's hard on a mama you know/ It's hard on the babies/ Mamas and babies just hurting/ Hurting so loudly/ Both wailing with mouths too inexperienced to form foreign words like "Hold me and tell me you love me"

black girls are perceived to know more about adult things

ain't nothing sweet about love to Deja / beginning
with elementary school crush / Delonte with skin
dark as chalkboard / long curly eyelashes / teeth
whiter than the face towels her grandmama bleaches
/ real black boy beauty / except his eyes could only
find disgust in her / Delonte an amateur wizard
whose words attempt a curse / "You ugly fat beast"
/ and her belief in her beauty vanishes / she
questions if she is a real girl / or a monster / if she
should take her nails and peel back his skin /
droplets of his blood become vindication / love is
green honey-suckle plucked from a bush before it
can bloom / like nine years old is too soon to learn
because you are dark or big, then you are less
valuable

how to use a mirror

misuse me - that's what you're going to do anyways / didn't anyone instruct you on how to use a mirror / I am an instrument who is only as skillful as its player / enter into the department store dressing room / full of discounted clothes and hand me down confidence / I've been here so long I've seen generations of self-loathing

12-dollar tops make you feel unworthy / your fingerprint pressed into me to test if the reflection is yours / mistake me for your cellphone / you try unlocking my screen / want to swap your body for the girls who pop up on your Instagram feed / Brazilian butt lifts purchased on sale and prefer incision scars over your scraped knees

your vision distorted / in childhood, you fogged glass with your breath just to draw a heart in it / low self-esteem sours your tongue / that's the mouth you curse yourself with every time you look at me / I am tired of being the one to blame / manic silence between us / if I could, I would destroy myself / contort each piece into a mosaic of you / proximity to perfection does not define us / I cannot define but remind you

that your skin stretched and scared from birthing
tomorrows you thought would not come / is beauty
/ mountains and valleys of acne scars / reminders
to unconditionally maintain self-worth no matter the
terrain you traverse / is beauty / I confess my
deficiency / there are qualities in you I cannot
capture / you are a visionary / loved/ exquisite / I
am an instrument perfectly designed to sing
affirmations sweet love song over you / use me – to
call forth the intangible / this is your instructions

Fannie Pearl

Was a quiet woman
I came to know her long after age melted the fat
from her bones
As a child I don't recall her face
Whenever I do, it was always unsmiling –
unbothered
When the men and boys entered her home
She sliced tomatoes
Spread a perfect layer of mayo on each segment
Sprinkled it with salt and pepper
Placed the plate in their hands
And us girl children watched
The men smile
Wrap their arms around her
Take large bites and wipe the remains from the
corner of their mouths

What I remember most of my great grandmother
were the peach trees
She picked a bucket full
Emptied in the sink
Never looking never advising
She washed them clean
My stomach growled
Reaching peak appetite for
The peach preserve that
Would soon be fried peach pies
She moved not once casting an eye my way
Not a sigh or a mumble
When the boys came

There was a plate ready
With turnip greens, pinto beans, cornbread, a piece
of smoked ham, and sliced tomatoes
And she watched unsmiling and attentive

In my great grandmother's garden
There were rows of cabbages, turnip greens, peach
trees, and green plums
I wonder what makes a woman smile
What makes her silent
What it means for a man to clean his plate

how to heal a black body

Hovering your head above a boiling pot of orange
peels & cloves
If the nose is congested
With sweet oil soaked in cotton and lodged in the
ear
With Robitussin
With Vicks rubs on the chest
With whisky on the babies' gums
Growth hurts when it breaks the softest parts of you
With Toni Morrison / Alice Walker/bell hooks
Women who biopsied an African heart
And drew blueprints to loving ourselves back to life
With an x-ray imagination that can see through
Debt and dead-end jobs
With the knowledge on how to use a mirror
constructively
With endurance to make your character strong
With wide-tooth combs, water, and Softsheen-
Carson Let's Jam
Sitting in between your mama's leg
Your confidence laid perfect in a neat hairstyle
and no one can touch it
With bebops and games you made up with your
cousins
Making use of sunlight
Hula hoop hugging your waist
With elders who tell you that you are unlimited
Daydreams that your children and their children
will never have to deny their humanity to earn a
dollar

With respect & dignity
With kisses on the forehead
With an embrace when your spirit is sick
With the scent of myrrh and olive oil
Pressed to your forehead dripping
Down the arch of your nose
Holy tongue sealing the prayer
A reminder you are not from here
And if all else fails with flirtatious heat of ginger ale
Because to heal, the heart must be open

it be like that

hit snooze six times, late to work, scroll on
Instagram
you breathe in deep as you enter your bedroom

medical bill in pink envelope, friends are not friends,
drink
Silence wraps her loyal arms around your loneliness

voicemail full, ghost the men, daydream about
quitting
too weary to be frightened you abide in solitude

kick off your shoes, pull down your pants, remove
your shirt
perfection sheds like work clothes after a long day

retrace your mistakes, map out the road to here,
re-route
acceptance is a bra removed - breasts hanging low

thank the empty room, linen scented candle, full
bookcase   beads of sweat cool underneath your
chest - you become yourself

gossip about friends, four weeks of dirty laundry, 38
missed calls
your pressure cooker heart implodes inside your
chest

real housewives of potomac, therapy assignment,
jazmine sullivan
tears running down your face is how you blow off
steam

kleenex, just like a woman by nina simone, gentle
hums
practice self-forgiveness - hold yourself in the soft
corners of your mind

Galactic Sisters

you are a prayer passed from your mother
and her mother's mother / plead to God make my
daughter free to love all you've created within her /
sound travels at 767 miles per hour / each syllable
spoken strikes my spirit at high intensity rates /
propelled into the future / I see myself loving this
life / that is enough to get me out of bed when
covers are the only security I have to hold / globally
black womanhood is mispronounced as eternally
strong / spectators apathetically gaze as we balance
worlds on our shoulders

earth is the loneliest planet / for a pre-pubescent
adolescent nurturing siblings / care taking for elders
cleaning up house / preparing dinners and enrolled
in honors courses / as we cleanse the Africanism
from our grammar / fix our hair - graduate with
bachelor's masters doctorates / we descend to the
bottom of our checklists / when the tower of babel
plummeted over man's ego / cinnamon nutmeg
women kept our own language / to remind each
other that we are grand, lovely, protected /
communicate each affirmation with a gentle glance

black women are no small creations / we are
nebulas places stars go to form / in space you
cannot hear a sound / so, every "you ain't nothing
but a fast-tailed girl" / "why you actin' so
masculine" / "put your head down" / "ain't no man
gonna deal with your attitude" / "you should know
better" / "you must not know you black, girl" /
cannot reach us / maybe that's why we're
extraterrestrial in sci-fi movies

my galactic sisters / we are not sub-human / we are
orchards bearing fruits of wisdom and heartache / a
garden full of generational dreams fulfilled /
liberation is a bitter fruit ripe on the vines
pressed into wine / i've acquired the taste for /
never to be constrained by public opinion again

Love's Discernment

pass me not oh gentle Savior / allow your sons to
miss me by lightyears / if they do not have hands
that can handle my heart as readily as they reach for
my body / hear my humble cry /
loneliness rocked me into desperation / there are
dangerous alleyways in my heart i don't want
another man to catch me on / while on others thou
art calling / i've force-fed men my name to leave a
trail in case i go missing / i search all over for love /
settled that it was stolen / i was too careless to keep
it close / love can't be lost/ it's transformed into
fear that makes me flinch at the thought of
relationships getting serious

being called beautiful was *once* fighting words /
violence can fit inside four-letter words like lust / i
break every morning / to build a new self again / it
gets exhausting / the world i made of my own
strength lay wet and wailing on my back / finally
slipped down my spine / dare i wear all my burderns
and be beautiful / *once* / i assumed i was invincible /
i looked to heaven / my soul took this body /
folded it into a suitcase / carried it around like old
baggage / on a journey to self-acceptance / God
leading the way making background music of my are
we there yets / His refusal to answer a just keep
living

you hear me God / i hear you weep / when i do not
see myself / the divine mourns on heavy days /
Holy Spirit mold me from clay every day / there are
certain works of art / only a few people get to place
their hands-on / curate my life God / give me the
discernment to know / who is here to marvel / find
inspiration / seem cultured / be taught / teach /
help me discern who cares about the story behind
my creation / and the one who created me / Savior
don't you dare pass me by /neither the one created
for me / help me find sweet relief / help my
unbelief / Love belongs to Black girls like Me

Acknowledgments

Thank you to my mother and father for providing space for me to be an artist; I love you both. To Jonathan and Jordan, you two are limitless. Thank you to my family for supporting me and making long distance drives to shows. Thank you to my poetry family at Kingdom Inc and The Flourish Alabama for creating an environment that has been pivotal to my development as an artist. Thank you to my favorite black historian Nubia and the woman who birthed her Anita. Thank you to all my friends, mentors, and guides for simply being. Thank you Dr.V for showing me that I am God's greatest miracle.

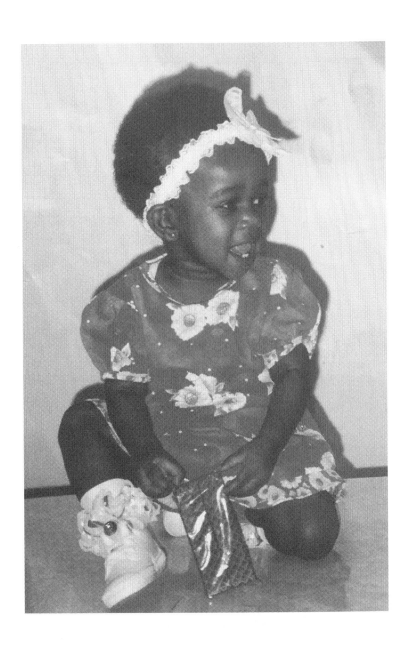

About Tania De'Shawn

Tania De'Shawn is a poet, teaching artist, and psychology enthusiast. She was born and raised in Birmingham, AL, and currently serves as a writer and entrepreneur. She is a first-generation college student who earned her Bachelor of Arts in Psychology.

You can find Tania on the following platforms.
Instagram: @taniadeshawnwrites
YouTube: Tania De'Shawn Writes
Medium: @taniadeshawn
Facebook: Tania De'Shawn Writes

Made in the USA
Las Vegas, NV
20 May 2025

22444760R00023

A God of Death & Rest

Pine Hollow Series
Book 2

K. M. Moronova

Important Notice

Some of the content in this book may be triggering for some readers. The contents of this book contain aspects of depression, mental illness, morally grey characters, death, physical violence, and explicit sexual scenes. Reader discretion is advised.

Also by K. M. Moronova

Pine Hollow Series

A God of Wrath & Lies

A God of Death & Rest

A Goddess of Life & Dawn

Alkrose Academy

Of Deathless Shadows

For those who still make wishes
Even if we no longer believe

Playlist

Can we Kiss Forever - Kina (slow/reverb)
All that really Matters - Illenium
My Love - Sia (slow/reverb)
For her - Adi x Elli
Go Tomorrow - Newton Brothers
Hurts so good - Astrid S (slow/reverb)
Just pretend - Bad Omens
Enough - charlieonnafriday
Crawling in my skin - Linkin Park
Spirits - The Strumbellas
My Blood - Ellie Goulding
Another Love - Tom Odell

One week after they took her

Wren

Miserable doesn't begin to describe the fucking joke of my existence.

I stare hollowly into the dark cup of tea that Moro's forcing me to drink. Says it will make me *feel better*, but I really doubt a cup of bitter water will help. My amber eyes aren't as bright as they used to be and the dark circles under them are enough to make me want to sleep forever. Or have someone hit me with a shovel so I can get a good night's sleep for once.

The Hollow Keeper's been off. Rightfully so—I mean,

he lost everything... Those Hollows were everything to him. His entire purpose is to tend to the beasts but Violet took everything he loves. She took a lot from all of us... I shift my eyes to my leafless hair; now it's just dark and empty. I can't stand the sight of it.

The sad and good news is that there's been a large influx of new Hollows, so at least he's been busy. Thank gods he has Margo to help tame the new rowdy Hollows or he'd probably drag me into helping as well. He claims I have a way with them as he does, but I just can't let my heart open like that again.

Not after Murph.

I angle the small mirror I have set on Moro's kitchen table so I can see my head clearly. I cut my hair with a curved knife. The sides are already shaved and I shorten my hair until it's no more than three inches so I can style it.

I let my head tilt down once I'm done and I sigh.

"Wren, stop wallowing, will you? We're all hurting, okay?" Kastian snaps from beside me—grumpy mother-fucker as always. He misses Elodie more than the sky yearns to touch the stars.

Death calls to life. Endlessly—eternally.

But I miss her too.

I tap my finger on the oak table as I push the loss of Murph from my weary mind. "We can't just leave her there..." I run my hand down my face and take a deep gulp of Moro's nasty tea. It fills my mouth with bitter warmth. I slam the mug back down, wincing like I've just drunk fucking ale. "Did you know about Arulius?"

We all went our separate ways for one week... We agreed we all needed the rest but I don't think any of us got any. It was the longest week of my life. I had to go back home to check in on Marley, and Moro was a head case after all his Hollows were gone. Kastian just spent his time alone in his death glades. One week. Now we're here.

Kastian stands from his seat like a barbarian, nearly knocking over the table and his chair as he growls at me. "How the fuck would *I* have known about Arulius? I live in my glades *alone* and you're the one who served *her highness* and worked beside the golden prick." His eyes are filled with icy fury but I can see the sting in his gaze.

Arulius was a friend to all of us... We lost more than Elodie that day.

I'm about to tell him to piss off but Moro cuts in. "Stop it, you two." He sips his tea like he's got all the time in the world. "It's only been a week. I know this is all... a lot, but we won't get anything done if we're fighting with one another."

Ugh, this guy is sooo *all knowing*. It's annoying as fuck.

"Well, what are we going to do? We can't just do nothing." Kastian crosses his arms and glares at the Keeper.

Moro raises a brow at him and the Eostrix rolls his eyes but sits back down, dipping his head at the Hollow keeper in apology for his attitude. *That's more than I ever get...*

"We're not doing *nothing*. We're recovering and planning. Do you really think we can just storm in there and save her? The three of us?"

I take a deep breath before sighing. "No."

Kastian snorts at me and I glare at him. I know he loves Elodie, but he doesn't know her like I do... I saw how ruined she was during her time in the *in-between*. My chest feels heavy with the thought so I shift back to focusing on the plan, grabbing the joint that rests behind my ear and sparking it with Elodie's pink lighter.

"So what's the plan then?" I mumble with the joint between my lips.

Kastian leans forward. His ebony wings flex behind him as his eyes flicker with an idea. "I can steal her away in the middle of the night."

I shake my head. "She's bonded to Arulius. Even *if* we can get her out of there, Arulius won't let her reincarnate... and I doubt there wouldn't be any repercussions. What if Violet sends her soldiers to kill the Hollows? Why else would she be holding all of them captive?" I cross my arms and lean back in my chair, letting a plume of smoke curl from my lips.

Moro frowns and nods. "I've been worried about that too. Violet has the upper hand and she knows we know it..."

We all fall silent at the table as we think. There has to be some way...

A sharp knock sounds at the door and Moro stands to answer it. Kastian and I look over our shoulders as he opens the door and I nearly fall out of my fucking chair.

Golden feathers shimmer in the light. I'd know those purple eyes anywhere.

Arulius?

What the hell is he doing here?

Kastian's dark aura immediately spikes in the air around us. Shadows and dark dust dance in the small cottage with his fury.

Moro's speechless. Apparently we all are, because no one's saying a godsdamn thing.

Arulius stands formally, arms crossed behind his back like he's here on fucking business. His golden wings are radiant with the sun at his back and his gray hair, tipped in gold, is styled like he's the king of Tomorrow.

I grit my teeth as the shock starts to dull.

Kastian stands slowly, his aura becoming heavier with each tantalizing second. Moro raises a hand at Kastian and motions for him to sit back down with a hard stare. Kastian doesn't sit but his aura eases a little bit. His silver eyes are filled with rage too. He lost everything he had because of this asshole, just like we did.

"Arulius." Moro snaps his head back to the golden god, studying him carefully. I stand slowly, next to the Death God. Kastian flicks his eyes to me and I give him a supportive nod. We won't let this asshole leave here breathing.

"Moro—good to see you." Arulius smirks. His amethyst eyes rove over me and Kastian like we're just two brooms left in the kitchen.

Try us, dipshit.

Moro shifts uneasily. "Let's cut the shit. Why are you here?" he deadpans, his voice lower than I've ever heard it. I know he's got some power within him somewhere, but the bastard is good at hiding it. The blue aura that constantly lingers around his skull and by his temples makes me think he's a Gremitie—the spirits of the sea.

Arulius leans against the doorframe and crosses his arms. "I bring a message from the High Lady herself—"

Kastian barks a wicked laugh. "Our message back will be your bones." Goosebumps crawl up my spine as Kastian's death aura spills into the air with malice. I shiver the feeling away.

The golden asshole doesn't even look our way and continues on like he wasn't just interrupted. "She wants you to know that she's not entirely opposed to finding peace together. That perhaps we can make a bargain.

Though, should you intervene and try to save Elodie, Violet will order me to kill Margo first and then her."

I scoff at that and clench my fists tightly at my sides. "Peace? The only peace that will come is if you two are wiped off the face of Tomorrow," I snarl at him as I raise my own powers, itching beneath my skin. Thorns start to creep along the walls and my poisonous thorn whip hangs in my hand.

Arulius shrugs and smiles like this is funny, like we're all just a godsdamn joke.

Moro raises his hands quicker than I've seen any god move and wraps them tightly around Arulius's throat as he slams him into the doorframe. Kastian and I both lunge forward to help as a knee-jerk reaction, but he doesn't need it. Moro's a badass.

"Gods—a little sour, are we?" Arulius chuckles, though he seems to be struggling in Moro's grasp.

Moro bares his teeth and his silver eyes become wide with power. "Tell me why we shouldn't kill you right now."

Arulius considers him for a moment. "One: because you can't. Two: I think it's cute you think you can. Three: you'll kill Elodie through the bond." His smile widens and Kastian growls low beside me. Gods, that's right... fucking Eostrixes and their damn bonds. "Don't you want to know the bargain? It entails Elodie being freed and everyone living happily ever fucking after."

I glare at him but I'll bite... Anything to save Elodie. "What is it?"

Moro and Kastian give me hesitant gazes like I'm crazy for even considering this, but fuck, what else are we supposed to do? Gods know what Elodie's going through right now. I can't leave her there... I *won't*.

Moro slowly releases Arulius but keeps his fists closed tightly, like he's going to punch him. The golden god pats Moro's shoulder like he made a good choice.

"Kastian—take a walk with me. I'll give you the details as it mainly pertains to you." He jerks his head for the Death God to follow him out and Kastian clenches his jaw tightly before he reluctantly follows.

Moro and I watch them from the doorway as they chat behind a cottage down the road. What the fuck could Violet want? I'm so done with the High Lady. Why I ever served her is beyond me.

"Violet's up to something..." I mumble and flick my eyes over to Moro. He runs a hand through his silver hair and nods.

"She always is, isn't she." He looks over at me and presses his mouth in a thin line. He looks tired, like really fucking tired. His appearance is young, like all of ours here in Tomorrow, but his soul is old. "Have you ever heard of Liasium?"

My eyes widen as the name swirls within me. Elodie

is the one who told me of that place and I never expected to find what I did there. I nod.

Moro dips his chin, his eyes growing distant. "I'm going there once I can get a handle on the new Hollows. I think it's time I remember everything." He sounds like it's something he really doesn't want to do, and I don't blame him. The idea of merging with your former consciousness is horrifying to fathom.

"Do you think that will help?" I mumble as I let my eyes find the two gods again. Kastian looks pissed. He's running a hand through his hair like he's about to start yelling.

"Yes—unfortunately."

Kastian returns and Arulius takes to the sky, his golden wings shimmering in the setting sun's rays as he flies back to Nesbrim. Gods, I wanted to at least punch him...

The Death God looks perplexed, but I see a glint of relief in his eyes too.

"Well? Out with it."

Kastian shoots me a look but sighs as he walks straight to the table to sit. "We aren't to step foot in Nesbrim for seven months." He rubs the back of his head. "The bargain begins then and we're bringing her home no matter what."

Seven months?

My heart sinks.

Moro frowns. "Well, what are we doing until then?"

Kastian looks up, his elbows on his knees and his fingers interlaced in front of him. "We're going to become unstoppable."

1

Elodie

Tomorrow is as ugly as it is beautiful.

I set my palms against the crystal windows overlooking Nesbrim. The cottages below are dusted orange in the sunset's warm glow. I've grown to love the sunsets here. I let a hot breath curl up the pane as Arulius thrusts his dick roughly into me from behind. A loose smile turns my lips upwards with pleasure.

It's been six months since they took me. Six long fucking months since I last saw Margo and my friends escape safely. Six months of harrowing pain and suffering at Violet's hands.

Six months of pure hell.

I'm not sure when I broke—well, broke more than I already was—but after ten-hour days of Violet shattering my bones beneath her heels and bleeding me dry day in and day out, I stopped resisting at some point. I stopped fighting and started to accept it. Accepted my fate here... and gave in to my body's lust for the one who betrayed me.

The one I hate more than anyone else... because it's better than feeling nothing, isn't it?

Arulius lets out a roar and grabs my hips tightly as he buries himself in my pussy with one last hard thrust. He holds me against his sweaty chest as his dick throbs inside me. I press against the crystal panes and moan in sync with him, feeling every pulse of the Eostrix inside me. I enjoy it too much and it makes me hate myself. I furrow my brows and flex my jaw with annoyance.

I hate him.

I hate him for what he's made me.

He slowly pulls himself from me and I straighten, turning toward him with rage building in my chest. His amethyst eyes shimmer with what he knows comes next.

I back him onto our bed. Yes—*our* bed. We've lived together this entire time, just as he promised we would. He tilts his chin up obediently and I wrap my hands around his neck tightly. His Adam's apple bobs beneath my palm and sends a surge of heat through me. His gray hair, tipped with gold, flickers in the glow of the suns and his sharp jawline begs to be bruised.

I've become a horribly violent human—scratch that—Eostrix.

He gasps and winces as I squeeze his throat with the fire I feel burning within me. The anger that's been smoldering in the darkest parts of my soul for six fucking months.

He made me this. He made me wrathful and violent, because I can't forgive him. Not for what he did. Not for the lies he spun or for bonding with me.

I'll make him regret every decision he's ever made.

"Elodie," he rasps through what little air he can get.

I narrow my eyes at him and squeeze tighter, feeling the bones beneath his flesh snapping. I feel the pain in my own throat and relish it. "Shut up, Arulius."

His purple eyes close and he flinches under me. I loosen my grip and slide my hand over his chest. The pain isn't enough. It never is anymore. Small, scalpel-size blades of aura rise from my fingertips and cut into his skin just over his ribs. He lets out a sharp cry and grits his teeth as I take a deep breath and hum in the agony that I wring from him through the bond. His raw and deep pain is the only feeling I can wash my soul clean with at the end of the day.

If I have to suffer, so should he.

He truly is the God of Wrath, enjoying every bit of

my revenge. He smiles weakly beneath me and his beautiful features ease my hatred for a moment.

I despise him. I do... but my stupid heart still cries for him. Still longs for his touch and his blood. But most of all, for the way he looks at me and for the love I know his heart still carries. He's been enduring everything alongside with me. The torture I face, he faces without batting an eye. I'm never alone with my bonded male, and in a twisted and sad way, I've become reliant on it.

I smile back and lean forward onto his bloody chest. I press my lips against his and slip my tongue into his mouth. His hands gently glide up the smooth skin of my lower back.

Though I hurt him and abuse him for his sins against me, he's never once been cruel to me. He touches me with kindness and tenderness. In hopes, perhaps, that one day I will forgive him and return to my loving self. But the unfortunate thing is that *that* girl is dead.

She died in the forest on the other side of Bresian nearly a year ago. She turned to ashes with the lies and haunted fate she was dealt. Even if some shallow part of me wishes I could be her again, I know that I can't.

I'm ruined. Rotten. Twisted. And though I'm sure he wants that girl back as much as I do, I think Arulius likes the new me. He's loved me no matter who I am or what I do.

I let out a sigh and roll onto my back next to him.

Arulius glances nervously at me. "Are you feeling okay today, love?" He props himself up on an arm and runs his fingers through my hair gently. I stare at the painted ceilings above us. Gold leaves and vines wrap delicately across the ceilings and hold stone carvings of Eostrixes. Eostrixes are held above all other creatures, I've learned in my time here. Cypresses and Dreadiuses are allowed to participate in court as well, but Moss Sparrows and other bloodlines are not to rise above commoners and workers around the castle.

"Yes—why do you ask?" I mumble.

He raises a brow and turns my chin until my gaze is resting on his. The amethyst glimmer steals my breath every damn time. "You seem... melancholic today. You're not being as violent as you usually are," he teases and runs his fingers over the wounds I inflicted on him. The bruises and cuts heal as if they'd never existed at all, the skin melding back together like a tape in rewind.

I roll my eyes and narrow my gaze. "I was just thinking of how much I resent you. That's all." I shrug and he smiles, leaning in closer to me. I harden my expression but my heart thumps traitorously for him.

"You're an awful liar, love." His nose brushes against mine and I turn to avoid his kiss. His lips press softly on my cheek and he lets out a sigh. I'll let myself accept the pleasure he offers, his companionship, and his kindness. But I won't let him give me his love.

Never again.

He will *never* hold my heart. He ruined me so completely, undid all the fixing and gluing he'd managed before his betrayal.

"You're wrong," I murmur, sounding a lot more somber than I'd like. I glance over at him after he doesn't say anything for a few moments. His sun-kissed skin and gold-tipped hair gleam in the last beams of the sunset. The drops of light dapple his cheek brilliantly, leaving him as the last lit gem in the dimming room. I stare into his gaze and he gives nothing away, his expression steady and calm.

"Why do you fight it, love?"

"Fight what?"

He brings his hand to his chest. "I can feel your heart, your feelings... I can feel the pain and suffering that my actions caused you." He looks away as if his words are stinging his eyes. "I know you can feel my pain too. The remorse and regret, the weight of you rejecting my love... Why are you fighting?"

I glare at him. He's not wrong and I hate it. I know he can feel what I've been enduring, and his pain... it's made my own even harder to carry. I don't want to fight my heart. I *want* to give in. I *want* to indulge and let myself have this one thing.

Him.

But if I do that, if I give in... I'm a traitor to myself. To

Kastian, Margo, Wren, Moro, and Murph. To all the creatures that are relying on me to bring them back. They've been dead for such a long time and I don't plan on leaving it that way. I *can't* leave it that way.

Still—there's a small part of me that believes he will release me one day. Let my powers truly be mine and free from his grasp.

"Will you let me reincarnate the dead? Resume the Rhythm of the realms? Let me return home to all my friends?"

Arulius's lips tighten and his brow furrows. "You know I can't do that."

"*That's* why I fight."

That's right. I needed that reminder too.

My heart yearns for them. I often wonder how they're doing. Who's taking care of Margo and making sure Kastian and Wren don't fight? Did they all split up or have their friendships held without me? My heart sinks at the thought of them moving on without me, but maybe they should...

I look back toward the window and watch as the last beam of the suns' light withers beneath the mountains. Violet's balcony resides on the back side of the main castle. Unfortunately, Arulius's terrace has a direct line of sight to it. I still haven't determined if she knows it or not because the distance is at least a few hundred feet, but I watch her each evening as the suns say goodbye to another day. I watch her as she waits until the stars light the sky.

She's still waiting for Lucius.

At first I found it fitting for such a cold-hearted bitch, but the longer the days and weeks drew out and the longer I watched her religiously wait in her solemn silence... I found that it wasn't fitting. It's *this* very pain and suffering that has made her who she is. The pain that destroyed everything.

"I wish she would stop waiting for him."

"Huh?" Arulius sits up and yawns into his palm.

I tip my chin up to Violet's silhouette against the somber orange sky. Arulius follows my gaze and sighs.

"She will *never* let him go, love."

I grit my teeth. I can't understand why she would stay undyingly loyal to him. He's been gone for centuries. "Why?" I look into his amethyst eyes.

His expression softens and he presses his hand against my cheek. "Would you let me go so easily?"

"If you had never betrayed me... but things are different now. Aren't they, Arulius."

Pain spreads through the inner walls of my broken organ and I suppress the urge to clench my hand around my chest. He gives me the same sad expression that he has had day in and day out for months and nods in acceptance. I'm so sick of seeing his pitiful look.

"Let's get some sleep. Violet wants to start early with the session tomorrow."

I flinch at the word *session*. That's what she calls her torture. Maybe it makes her feel better to pretend it's not as horrible as it truly is. That's what we all do though, I suppose—isn't it? Paint something horrible and dark as something brighter. Hide the rot and blood beneath a blanket of reasons.

I nod and lie down next to him. His dark lashes are already falling heavy over his eyes and his arms wrap around me tightly like they do each night. Desperately holding onto times long-since gone. I often find myself slipping back to those days too.

But those are our ghosts.

Wishes.

Ones that we both know will never come true.

Sleep pulls me as I think of Violet's *session* tomorrow. I've made it my purpose for now to find out what she's collecting my blood for and what she's really trying to get out of all this pain she's inflicting on me.

If I can manage that, maybe I can figure out a way to break the bond with Arulius.

2

Elodie

Violet's bone heels *clack* against the white tiles. Each step sends a shiver down my spine and sweat instinctively beads down my forehead. My body knows what that sound brings; it's been ingrained in my marrow.

Panic is always the first response to her blood-red eyes and the fiery rage that she still harbors for me. I focus on the walls of the torture room. The court calls this the *peace chamber* due to the floor-to-ceiling windows that overlook the lands of Tomorrow, and apparently a God of Peace used to hold meetings here too. But I only know this place as hell. Three gigantic white walls and an entire wall of glass. It's insanely bright in here and the only color seems to be the stains of my blood.

I try to calm the trembling in my hands, though I quickly lose that fight. She's coming and bringing her arsenal of pain with her. I close my eyes and manage to at least get my breathing under control.

She's managed to completely break me. I didn't think she could do it at first, but she made me eat those words the second I stepped into this room for the first time.

Violet's a sick woman. She will inflict pain in any way, shape, or form that she can. She knows I loved Arulius, and that he still cares for me, so she makes him watch as I suffer at her hand. He is scathed by my torture too, through the bond. His wounds aren't visible, but he feels everything I do. At least that's a small form of revenge I can enjoy during this.

My first shattered hand and twisted leg... I'll never forget the unexpected pain that I passed out from, and from that day on, the floor has always been bloody by the time she's done with me. A small drain sits just beneath where she keeps her bucket of blood. *My* blood. Fucking bitch—she's been collecting it religiously since I've been here and I still can't figure out why.

My eyes shift over to her favorite guards, Kol and Willow. I already knew the horribly cruel Dreadius from my encounters with him in battle. His black horns and hair still haunt my dreams. But Willow was new to me, so I didn't have a predetermined opinion of her upon arriving, and I still don't have a solid one now.

She's a beautiful Eostrix. Standard ivory wings, clad in white bone armor much like Arulius's gold set. Her eyes are a fiery green and her hair a soft light brown. Her olive skin is perfect and so is her smile.

I frown as I watch her engage freely with a few other guards, all Eostrixes as well. The species seems to keep to themselves—that much I've noticed.

My eyes dart over to Violet, who stands close to the wall of glass, briefing Arulius as always before beginning our lovely torture session. My bones are already seizing at the thought of her heels grinding into them. Iron is an unfortunate taste I've become accustomed to.

"Willow, get the bucket." My eyes snap wide open at the sound of Violet's voice. My stomach churns uncomfortably and I can feel Arulius's heart falter as it does every day.

Willow bends over and picks up the black metallic bucket. Her brown hair falls over her shoulder and her male Eostrix peers gawk at her as she walks over to me, setting the bucket down gently.

I keep my head bowed low. I'm disgusted with how submissive I am, but what the fuck else am I supposed to do? I have no fight left. The less I interact, the better.

Willow stares at me, staying bent over longer than she needs to. I grit my teeth, snapping her a look saying *What?* But I find nothing but kindness in her eyes. She's always been kind to me, but I can't trust anymore.

I've been down that road.

Willow opens her mouth to say something, but is silenced by Violet's heels fast approaching. Her green eyes flicker at me and then she's off, standing back alongside Kol and the other guards.

I let out a sigh, steeling myself for what's coming.

"Elodie, dear," Violet chirps. "How *are* you today?"

I keep my eyes on her black bone heels. She hates when I look at her face and I disdain her blood-red eyes with all my being, so win-win.

"Very well, Lady Violet," I mumble, my hands pressed flat on the ground how I know she likes them.

She circles me like a predator and stops behind me. I gulp as sweat beads down my forehead, knowing that she's probably going to start with my wings today. I shut my eyes and try to think of anything to take me away from here.

Kastian's face surfaces in my mind and his soft ocean eyes graze me with affection. I focus on him, our promise to find one another again. My heart beats heavily with the guilt I feel. I never should have bonded with Arulius. I should have known that Kastian was fated for me, that he was always meant to be *mine*.

A horrible snap cracks right behind my left ear. I scream as hot blood pulses over the side of my face. My wing is nearly ripped entirely off its nub. I shudder as I try to lean as much as I can over the bucket.

She's made fucking sure I know how to collect my blood for her.

I whimper as my twisted wing hangs by just a few tendons. Arulius cripples by the windows, feeling the same sharp pain I do. She performs the same torture and methods so I know what to expect, but I know for certain that I will never get used to the agony of it.

Violet stalks around to my front and bends down to meet my eyes. I still. This is unusual, she never wants to look at my face... so why is she trying to get me to look at her?

I turn my head to the side to look out the windows, focusing on the mountains that peek over Nesbrim's walls. She laughs cruelly and grabs my chin between her sharp claws. Yeah, this bitch has claws.

Her red eyes are strained, tired, and dull. Still nause-ating, but I see something else in them that I haven't for... well, months. I wrinkle my nose at her silence and shift to try and pull my chin from her hand.

"Elodie."

I freeze, my chin still gripped tightly between her fingers. "Yes, Lady Violet?"

She studies me and for a second I think I see the hate she harbors for me falter. But her shields are up again before I can dig further into it.

"Tell me where Lucius is."

I let out a long breath.

She asked me this during my first month. Over and over. Relentless and desperate. I've told her time and time again that I don't know. That I'm *not* Talia. I bite my tongue. She'll hurt me more if I give her undesirable answers, so I try to just keep my silence.

"Elodie. Where. Is. He." Her tone is low as she keeps her red eyes locked with mine.

Gods help me—I shake my head. "I don't know."

Violet reaches her hand up and places her long black claw over my throat.

Fuck. Fuck. Please, not this.

Tears roll down my cheeks but I hold her gaze steady and true.

"Last time I'll ask today," she coos. "*Talia*, where is my love?"

I glare at her, knowing that this will earn me a worse punishment, but I don't fucking care. I thought I made this clear to her five months ago. The fire within me burns with the urge to find my fight again and I foolishly listen.

"I don't know where Lucius is, Violet, but I can tell you this. He's not your love. Not anymore. No one could love you, not even him... not after what you've become." I sit up more, watching my words as they uncoil her completely. Her red eyes twitch with fury.

Worth it.

She looks up at me. An unhinged light glints in her eyes as she glides her claw across my tender flesh. My throat spills and I choke with the assault. She grabs a fistful of my hair and slams my face into the half-filled bucket. Crimson meets my eyes and dips up my nose.

My senses flood with iron as I try not to inhale, but the blood is rising and I can't breathe. The pain in my throat pulses and I can feel the liquid pump steadily out of me. I thrash my arms and legs, trying anything to get leverage to lift my head or to push her, but she has a tight hold on me.

I start to panic. Undiluted fear takes over as my muscles begin to weaken. My lungs are on fire and I can feel blood soaking my hands and knees as the bucket overflows.

Fuck, I really pissed her off, didn't I?

I know she won't kill me, whatever her reasoning is. Maybe she thinks I do know where Lucius is and I'm just being a wrathful cunt? She's so desperate.

I feel a sharp tug on my hair and then my head is out of the bucket of blood. I inhale deeply, gasping and coughing as I'm thrown to the tile. I use the back of my forearm to wipe my eyes free of the crimson so I can see, fear still dancing in my veins. Arulius is crouched down next to me. His arm is freshly bitten and he presses it to my lips, urging me to heal, but I tighten my mouth.

He furrows his brows. "You need to feed. *Now*. You've lost too much blood, love." He tries again, bringing his arm to my lips, but I turn my head, the sliced skin of my neck still throbbing horribly.

Arulius winces at the pain and I can see his anger flaring up behind his amethyst eyes. He knows I don't actually want to die. I just want to hurt him in any way that I can, and if that means refusing his blood and letting his throat burn like mine does for a little longer, then so be it. He dips his head and stares at me with annoyance before he looks at the guards and snaps his fingers.

"Willow, come here."

The beautiful Eostrix paces over quickly and is on her knees at my side within seconds. She keeps her eyes on me as Arulius bites her wrist and offers it to me.

I falter.

I didn't mean for her to get dragged into this. I glance from her to Arulius and back. She keeps her green gaze locked on mine and nods, telling me that it's okay. I don't want to, like *really* don't want to. I've never tasted another Eostrix's blood except Kastian's and Arulius's.

"It's okay, Elodie." Willow's voice is steady and light. I

can't imagine what she thinks of me, having watched me be the High Lady's toy for half a year now. She's nice—not nice enough for me to trust her, but enough for me to accept help.

I take her arm into my mouth and bite down, taking in her blood in hard pulls. She shudders under my lips. Her blood is rich, thick with flavors of hearty fruits. Pomegranate maybe? I take another deep pull of her and break my contact from her skin.

My wing snaps straight, painlessly, but the sound still makes me nearly dry heave. My throat warms and the flesh molds back together. I let out a low breath, relishing in the instant relief. Willow smiles at me kindly and quickly hops up and makes her way back to the guard line.

Arulius keeps his eyes trained on me. My chest tightens with his torment. I'm no stranger to his agony, his endless torture that he faces alongside me. In truth, I think he feels everything worse than I do. His guilt is ruining him. I can see it in his gaze day in and day out. Slowly, his light is diminishing, and I'm not sure how much more he can take.

Watching me slowly wither plagues him, twists his heart, and makes him beg for my own hand to strike him.

I bite my quivering lip to keep my emotions reigned in. I never asked for any of this. I just want to... exist. Is that so much to fucking ask for? I want to be happy. With Margo, Kastian, Wren, and Moro, and... and Arulius too, but that all was fucking ruined.

We can never go back. Our fates are forever scathed and we can only move forward.

I let my eyes dull as I stare, half-lidded, up at Violet, praying to the gods that she is done for the day. She's got her fucking bucket of blood.

She holds my gaze with her dark crimson eyes. "That will be all." She flicks her wrist at Arulius and motions for Kol to collect her bucket, and then she makes her way out the small door in the far corner of the white room.

I try to follow her with my eyes. I have to figure out her plan with all of this, because none of it makes any godsdamn sense. But my eyes are blocked as the golden Eostrix moves in front of my view, brows drawn tight and worry emanating from his amethyst eyes.

"Let's get you cleaned up, love."

"Don't fucking touch me," I spit at him. His eyes widen. I don't want to even look at him. Old memories have been warring with me all morning, more than usual, and I have the urge to tear his throat out.

He tries to move to help me as I stand, but I glare at him, stopping him mid-motion. Arulius bites down on his lip to keep whatever he wants to say to himself. *Thank gods.*

I stand on shaky legs and steady myself before walking barefoot back to my prison cell. Well, not really a cell, it's Arulius's entire mansion, but it's a prison to me. Jailed. Kept from the things I love and from being free. There aren't many things I can find happiness in anymore, but one thing I've grown to love is my day pass in town. To fully explore and enjoy Nesbrim as long as I have a guard. It's the one decent thing about Violet—she may be a bitch, but at least she doesn't give a shit what I do as long as she collects the red liquid in my veins.

I keep my pace quick as my golden one follows close behind. Violet's court is beautiful, there's no denying it, though after walking these halls so many times, often leaving a trail of blood in my wake, the lure is almost completely gone. Almost.

As we pass the main doors of her palace I turn and catch a glance at them, the doors I walked through for the first time with Wren under a year ago.

Borvon and Talia. Their hands reaching for one another, never to connect, wrought in white stone and clad in permanent gold.

My heart sinks at the thought, but I smile, because for a brief time we did reach one another. I blink slowly, refocusing my attention to the cobbled streets of Nesbrim that lie ahead.

The morning air is cold, winter-heavy with its chill. I

take a long breath, letting the ice fill my lungs with their whispers of a crisp day.

I narrow my eyes against the suns' rising beams, sending out a small wordless prayer.

Please let the café owner have the yummy sausages today.

3

Elodie

Nesbrim teems with life under the array of the three suns. Creatures of all sorts are busy tending to their duties and keeping the streets bustling. Moss Sparrows hang laundry over the clotheslines on their balconies above the shops. The moss balls on their heads seem a little less green in the winter, much like normal plants. Eostrixes dressed in soldier attire walk the streets, ensuring order and helping where they're needed.

One positive side of being bonded to Arulius is that I'm a relatively free prisoner. Violet is cruelty and malice incarnate—but she's fair. She lets me enjoy what lies within Nesbrim, knowing that I can never stray too far. I always have a guard around too, but the real rope around my neck is the bond.

Invisible chains that bear the weight of our two souls.

I try not to dwell on my binds and let myself take in the energy that radiates off of the smiles and laughter as I walk down the main street. Cobblestones pave the entirety of the city and each brick that builds up the cottages on both sides of the path is worn down with age. Green vines cling to the walls; even in winter their foliage still thrives. We're lucky the snow hasn't fallen yet. I have shit for clothes and all my boots are loaded with holes.

Scents of freshly baked bread and my favorite break-fast sausages fill my nose. My mouth is immediately watering and my stomach cries with the need to be filled with more than just blood.

Thank gods, at least one good thing is happening today. The café has been out of sausages for days now.

I lift my nose to the sky to inhale the cold air of Nesbrim and let my eyes follow the Eostrixes above. They swoop through the sunrise and I can tell from their smiles that there's nowhere else they'd rather be.

My chest becomes heavy at seeing them so happy. The wing Wren damaged never truly healed right. I never got the chance to learn to fly and now I'm a prisoner, so my odds of learning are bleak.

A hum sounds from behind me, drawing my attention to the guard that accompanies me during the day.

Naminé. She's a gorgeous Cypress with gold translucent leaves that dance in her ash-blonde hair. A white Vernovian Thorn wraps around her pale neck and her eyes are an alluring amber hue. I think we could be good friends if I tried to open up more. She's the nicest creature in all of Tomorrow.

"What're you craving for breakfast today, Naminé?"

Her eyes light up, as always with the talk of food, and she shrugs. "I'm down for anything, I'm starving!"

I smile at her. Her energy is absolutely contagious but I've got her down to a T. I know her favorite food is the café's sausages, just like mine is. I hum and put my finger up to my lips as I pretend to mull over my options.

"Well, how about the pancake parlor down by the south gates?" I smirk as her face scrunches involuntarily. We went there once a few weeks ago, and when I say that their pancakes were the soggiest mess I've ever had, it's an understatement of the actual slosh it was. It blows my mind that they're even still running. It doesn't help that the owner is a rotten Moss Sparrow either.

Naminé shuts her eyes and simply nods. I can't hold back the laugh that stirs in my chest.

"And I'll order you the *biggest* plate. Then you can have some leftovers to take home."

Her eyes shoot open and she can't pretend to go along with it anymore. "Please—Elodie, no!"

I let my laughter roll into the crisp morning air and she scowls at me, realizing I'm pulling her leg.

"That wasn't funny!" she laugh-shouts and I laugh harder at her furrowed brows. She looks me over for a few moments and her expression sullens. I tilt my head at her shift.

"What's wrong?" I ask, looking around to see if something is amiss.

She pulls her white cloak off and wraps it around me, clasping the ruby brooch in the center before giving me a weak smile. "You look horrible today... and cold. I'm not sure how much more of this you can take."

Okay, ouch.

My eyes widen, and I clutch her hands over the brooch. Her amber eyes flick up to mine as I say, "You don't need to give me your things, Naminé... I'm fine." She doesn't look pleased with that so I add, "And I look horrible? Are you calling me ugly?" My sarcasm is as toxic as it is funny and she laughs and pushes me.

"You know that's not what I meant!" She walks past me and crosses her arms, her black sweater barely enough to keep warm in this weather. "And I have forty cloaks just like that, so don't even think about giving it back."

I smile to myself for a moment and place my hand over the ruby brooch, whispering my thanks quietly enough I'm sure she doesn't hear me. My chest warms with her kindness. I just hope the world doesn't steal it from her.

I walk up beside her. "Let's go to *our* café." I spin back around to trot down the cobblestones and audibly hear her release her breath in relief.

"*Sausaaaage!*" she cries and we both laugh again.

As we approach our favorite café, I see the Dreadius owner, Greysil. Her three horns are clear, translucent with an orange glow, like icicles against the winter's dawn, taking on every light source that dares to dance upon her head. There is one on each side of her head and one down the center, the length of most Dreadius horns, just a little longer than their head. They tilt up at the ends. She's bent over, tending to her signs and making sure that no ice lies on the steps to the café.

"Hi, Greysil," I chirp. She straightens and turns to greet us. We're regulars and have become quite friendly. It's the interactions like this one that make my heart warm, some semblance of normality in my existence here.

Naminé averts her eyes quickly as Greysil looks at her with interest. Her dark brown skin shimmers with the morning's orange hues and her piercing green eyes hold pools of kindness. Her sharp shoulders make her black apron look intimidating, but she wears it as well as she does her pearly smile. She's a sight to behold and I half wonder if her presence is what makes this café so alluring.

"Good morning, Elodie, Naminé." Greysil's eyes linger on Naminé, as if she's hoping she will look back at her.

Obviously I've caught on by now that these two have eyes for each other. I don't bring Naminé here nearly every damn day just to have our coffee and to get some breakfast sausage. Nooo—I want her to get a chance of a date. It's not easy to play matchmaker in a realm where we're all spirits and gods, but damn it, I have to try. There's nothing else to spend my time focusing on anyway.

I've thought about escaping, but there'd be no point. Arulius is bonded to me and I'm staying here to keep my friends safe. I think of Murph every day, the sacrifice he gave for me... No one else needs to suffer on my behalf.

So a petty matchmaker is what I've been reduced to.

"I'll grab us a table, Naminé. Can you order?" I wink at her and quickly swing the café door open before she can get herself out of it. Once inside, I snatch the booth closest to the front window so I can watch their exchange.

Naminé's shimmering, ash-blonde hair rolls beautifully over her shoulders and her cheeks are cherry red. I smirk to myself. I knew she liked Greysil.

They engage in awkward conversation as I assume the Dreadius lists out the specials for today, and Naminé nods respectfully. She reaches for the café door and Greysil does something I wasn't sure she was brave enough to do:

she grips Naminé's wrist gently and turns her to face her. The Dreadius's sage-green eyes fill with hope as she asks her something.

Fucking hell, just go on a godsdamn date already!

I try to get a better angle from my booth, so I lean as far off to the side as I can, cheek against the window in a shameless attempt to see the fruits of my matchmaking labor.

Both of their faces are red and plastered with smiles that make even my cheeks hurt. A warmth swells in my heart because I know at least *something* good has come of today.

I straighten myself in the booth before either of them can see me with my face against the glass like I'm watching two puppies meet each other. The door swings open and Naminé finds our booth immediately.

"Why are you sitting up here? We always sit in the back." She raises a brow and I don't miss the glint of worry in her eyes that I might have seen their encounter.

I place my hands on the wooden table and cross my fingers together smugly. "Oh, I just wanted to get a view of the sunrise this morning."

She narrows her eyes, not buying one bit of my bullshit. I can't help but laugh as she notices the oily circle of my cheek print on the glass. She looks from the spot, to me, and back at the mark before her eyes widen at what I've done.

I quirk a smile.

"You... you set me up! How did you know I liked her?!" Naminé runs her fingers through her hair worriedly and smiles at me. Her amber eyes painfully remind me so much of Wren. I hesitate for a second, but shake the image of him from my mind. I'm sure he's happy and finding a new fulfilling life.

"And?" I rest my chin on my palm, elbow to the table.

"And what?"

"What did you say?"

She furrows her brow and sucks in her lips—a nasty habit she has, really. "I said yes."

"What was that? I can't quite hear you when you whisper like that." I cup my ear like I'm hard of hearing.

"I said yes!" She leans forward and smacks my elbow, earning me a forehead bang to the fucking table.

I raise my head, dumbfounded, and stare at her in shock. Her eyes are equally as surprised. Did she just... did she just smack me? Naminé, the sweet and kind guard? Smacked... me?

My lips turn up and I rub my forehead. "I like you— you're quirky like me," I say between chuckles. She holds her lips tightly, probably worried that I'll report her to Kol. No one is to touch me except Arulius and Violet. But besides her, I haven't had someone treat me like an actual fucking person in all my time here. So I happily let the throb on my forehead spill its pain and embarrassment through me.

"I'm so sorry, Elodie, I shouldn't have done that." She frowns and rubs her arm. I can't help but think of Kastian and Wren when I look at her. She actually makes me happy, like my life isn't a complete shithole.

"You're welcome." I wave her off dismissively. "Just invite me to the wedding, okay?"

Her eyes widen as Greysil comes around the corner with our drinks and usual orders.

"What wedding? I swear, I never get invited to those things."

I glance at Naminé and watch her beg me with her eyes to do no more *helping*. "Oh, just someone at the High Court. No one you know." She takes my answer and smiles at Naminé before dashing back into the kitchen as more customers enter the café.

"We're going to dinner tomorrow night," Naminé mumbles as she takes a large bite of the sweet sausage. I indulge in a too-big bite myself and hum with delight at the swirl of flavors that dance on my taste buds. Savory and sweet, the food here never dulls, not like it does in the human realm.

"You're welcome," I chirp before my next bite of eggs.

She laughs. "You're absolutely not what I expected when they said I had to guard the Life Goddess."

I'll take it.

The steps to Arulius's mansion are old and worn. Moss covers each corner of every tattered stone. I always take my shoes off just before I start my ascension. The feeling of the rocks beneath my feet makes me nostalgic for my forest.

I sigh and a blissful smile grows across my lips. I think of my shed—how I'll never see it again. I miss the cozy way it suited me, Margo lying at my feet while I read a good book. But just because I can't be there doesn't mean that the image left in my mind isn't still tangible. I close my eyes as I take each step slowly, my feet stealing the coolness from the stones.

I'm there, walking along the trail, Margo by my side, on our way to my parents' house. We're going to have a nice day at the lake. The air smells crisp, but there are no ponderosa pines.

My eyes flick open and my smile instantly fades. There are no pine trees here in Nesbrim, not within the walls.

I stop on the flat stone halfway to the mansion. Each side of the stairway is normally covered with lush greenery, but in the midst of winter, nothing but brambles and frost cling to the land. Atop the hill lies Arulius's pompous manor. The stones themselves are black, onyx like the night, flaked with gold windows, doors, and pillars.

It's a view I've seen a hundred times over, yet I still pause to take it in. Not for the beauty of it—and it is beautiful—but for how starkly opposite it is from Kastian's haunted glade. From his brilliant white castle of death.

Death filled with so much life. I miss the plants that climbed the three-story-high ceilings and dappled over the glass panes.

I take a deep breath and exhale loudly.

"What's wrong?"

My shoulders tense. *Shit. Why can't I have two seconds to myself?*

I turn my head and find Arulius standing just a few steps behind me. His golden wings hang low and brush against the stones. A flash from his glimmering amethyst eyes catches mine.

He is every bit as beautiful as he's always been. My heart doesn't completely shatter every time I look at him anymore. That war ceased months ago when I gave in, but I still have the endless pain he gave me that will haunt me till the end of time.

"What do you want?" I mumble and level my gaze at him.

He kicks up a brow and one side of his lips. "Just

thought I'd walk you up today. It's cold and I knew you'd be taking your shoes off *again*."

I flinch and gaze down at my feet. They're numb already from the icy stones. I didn't know that he was aware I walked up the stairs barefoot every day.

His eyes meet mine as he takes my boots and dips his head, kneeling down to my feet. "Come on. It's too cold today, love."

I stare at him but lift my foot so he can slip my boot back on. It's hard to hate Arulius, but I won't give my heart the chance to have even a small hope with him.

"It's never too cold. Not anymore," I mumble.

4

Elodie

Violet seems off today.

More thoughtful and less violent, which is weird for her. Usually if something is bothering her she doesn't hesitate to take it out on me. Instead of trying to get a rise out of her, I watch carefully.

The High Lady is wearing her black lace dress today. The sleeves come down to her wrists and the hem falls all the way to the floor. The dress hugs every curve of her perfect body tightly and leaves nothing for the imagination. She's heartbreak on legs. Her crimson eyes watch me with her hateful glare as she paces in front of me. Her gorgeous, galaxy-black hair tinted in blues and purples sways with each turn she takes.

I study the room. *Come on, Elodie. What's different?* I sharpen my mind and look at every wall and corner with new eyes. The guards are standing in their usual places. Willow entertains her comrades and they swoon over her like they always do, except the dark-haired Dreadius who's looking at me. I glance to the windows and wait—

Why is that Dreadius watching me?

I narrow my eyes on him. Come to think of it, I don't recognize him. He must be new. I'm surprised he isn't drooling all over Willow like everyone else.

After searching the remainder of the room, I determine that the Dreadius, Arulius's absence, and Violet's strange behavior are the only differences. So it must have something to do with him. But what? Are my guards being rotated? I bite the inner wall of my cheek with anxiety as the High Lady's heel stops on the tile in front of me.

I keep my head bowed. Maybe today I'll try to not get on her bad side.

"Elodie, lift your head."

I shudder at her untamed tone. She sounds wild, which is *very* unlike her. I dip my head before sitting back on my haunches, sweat dripping on the floor, and set my hands respectfully on my lap. I hesitate but manage to bring my eyes to meet hers.

She's just staring at me. Not with her normal wrath or anger, but with something strange, a feeling I haven't seen in her gaze before. I focus on keeping my face flat and expressionless. I don't miss the shuffle of the guards on my left either.

"It's your lucky day today, Elodie." She reaches down and grips my chin gently with her long, sharp nails. I shiver under her touch but keep my face lax. She seems impressed with my handle on fear, by the glint in her eye. "Rune, dear, please come say hello."

I shift my gaze to the Dreadius as he walks over in a slow, steady stride. As he comes closer, sweat starts to bead down my forehead. He looks similar to Kol. Too similar. They have to be brothers or half-brothers. His horns are a deep maroon and his eyes... his eyes are red like Violet's. My stomach curls at his appearance. He's fucking beautiful, tatted up to his jawline, but he looks like evil incarnate. His black sweater is rolled up to his elbows, revealing more tattoos on his arms, and the V-collar shows the tip of his chest.

He stops shy of an inch from me and I've never felt so small. I nearly have to kick my head all the way back to see up to his height—granted, I'm sitting, but still. He makes even Violet in her three-inch heels look short.

Rune bows to her and returns his dead, bloody gaze to me. Goosebumps raise on my skin and I carefully look back at Violet. She has a tight smile sewn across her lips, promising well-thought-out bullshit.

"Today you receive the curse of blood repulsion."

My eyes widen but I hold my gasp. Blood repulsion, what the fuck is that? My lips are already feeling dry just from the tainted words.

"I know you and Arulius have been enjoying one another. But I'm impatient and tired with our progress. You'll be separated, and if I start to see results, we can chat about lifting the curse." I look for Arulius only to remember that I didn't see him when I scanned the room earlier.

I have to fight my better judgment before I speak; there are so many nasty things I want to say to her. "What *results* would please you, my lady?" I bow my head. If I can get on her good side today, maybe she will reconsider. Because I really don't want this blood repulsion thing she's talking about.

"Lucius."

Fucking gods be damned. How many times have I told her I don't know? Is she really that desperate? To hold onto a hope so delusional is crazy. I recall how poorly last time ended though and decide to eat my words.

I nod. I'll have to do what I can to find him, but gods know there's no hope. I'm trapped in Nesbrim and she thinks I already have the answer.

"From this day on, you will only be able to drink

Rune's blood." I lift my head and hesitantly look at him. He's hardly moved a muscle and hasn't spoken a word either. "His won't be able to heal you as well as Arulius's blood can, so I recommend you behave, dear."

I don't miss her smug smile. She's certainly pleased with herself, that's for sure.

"Yes, my lady."

She nods to Rune and he crouches in front of me. The male is enormous and towers over me even while sitting on his haunches. Gods, I'm scared to even look at him. His blood-colored gaze spears into me a mere few inches from my face and it takes everything I have to stay sitting. He smells metallic... I can't put a finger on the scent.

I want to run. There's no way I can drink blood from him.

Violet presses one hand on top of my head and her other on his center crimson horn. Purple aura shifts like a mist around her hands and enters each of us. I watch as Rune shuts his eyes with a small wince, and seconds later I feel the same sharp pain enter through my scalp.

The pain travels through my neck and down to my chest, where it whirls and settles. Then there's nothing—I feel no different.

"There, right as rain," she says proudly, stepping back and releasing our heads. "Willow, come here. Let's test this out, shall we?"

The beautiful Eostrix trots over, her dark hair waving

to each side, and kneels beside me. She wears a look of pity but doesn't dare say anything. She offers her wrist to me and I slowly grab her arm with both hands.

I look up at Violet, who's watching expectantly. "Go on," she snaps impatiently.

Pressing my lips to Willow's wrist, I bite shallowly and take a single sip of her blood. Once I release her arm I look back to Violet and wait for gods know what. I feel fine, I don't—

Blood heaves up my throat and suddenly I'm throwing up all over the imperial floors. I barely miss Rune, turning my head to the side. My guts are twisting angrily at me and I've never felt sicker in my life. Violet starts laughing and Willow takes a few steps back in shock.

I set both hands on the tile as a fresh wave of nausea flows through me and another haul of blood releases all over the floor. This is way more blood than I took from Willow.

Panic itches in my chest and I desperately look at Violet.

She covers her mouth as she continues laughing. "It worked perfectly! You'll need to drink from the Dreadius to stop the blood repulsion, dear."

I sit up enough to lean toward Rune. His eyes are unmoving and he doesn't seem one bit happy to be my designated blood bag either. Fuck this. Fuck everything.

I don't have a choice though.

Blocking out the laughs that begin to sound around us, I take his wrist and bite into him. I've never had Dreadius blood before and I'm too scared and overstimulated with the repulsion to taste or smell anything. I take a small gulp of his blood and push his hand back to him. Rune clutches his wrist and resumes his emotionless gaze.

The nausea immediately fades and my throat clears of any threatening blood. What the fuck kind of curse is this? Like, why in the gods' names would she do this, and why now of all times?

Willow wrinkles her nose at me. "An Eostrix drinking Dreadius blood." Her distaste is obvious on her sharp tongue. I'm normally not one to feel ashamed for things, but with all of them in here watching me throw up and drink forbidden blood, I feel broken, like trash that was thrown away twice. She isn't as nice as I thought. Good thing I never let her get close.

"Why was this necessary, my lady?" I ask so sincerely there's no way she can reprimand me.

She brushes my dark hair behind my ear as she passes behind me, raising my wrist to be drained for her daily collection of blood. She sets the container below my arm as she runs her blade along my flesh. I flinch but keep my lips sealed.

"Because we have a guest coming to Nesbrim in the coming weeks and I don't want you getting any ideas."

Well that doesn't tell me anything, so I press on.

"Why did you select a *Dreadius* and not an Eostrix for this curse, my lady? We're not supposed to drink from anything but our own." It's not like I personally care whose blood I drink, but the public shaming makes it hard to want to drink from a Dreadius.

She waits until she's satisfied with the amount of blood before releasing my arm. "Oh Elodie, must you honestly ask such stupid questions? It's because I hate you, and I want you to suffer."

Not surprising. "But what about Rune? He doesn't deserve this." I look at his hands. They're clenched in rage, but he remains calm.

"No? And how would you know anything about him, hmm?" She lifts the bucket and stalks to her door in the corner. "Enjoy your days of recovery, Elodie. Do try to get to know your new blood bag."

I don't bother watching her leave today. I'm feeling particularly beat and just want to go back to bed and wallow for the rest of the day. I'd planned on going to breakfast with Naminé again, but now she's no longer my guard... I side-eye Rune.

He's patiently sitting and holding his wrist, eyes never leaving me. His dark hair crests just over his forehead. I'm sure he's mentally exhausted from all of this too.

I stagger to my feet and take in how much blood I threw up. The drains are still working to clear the puddles left behind. *Gods.* Rune rises as well, and gods,

I only come up to his shoulders. He's at least six foot five.

The walk down the hall of the High Court is quiet today. I wonder where Arulius is; he always waits outside when he's not in there himself. Come to think of it, he wasn't in bed this morning either.

I'm about to turn down the hall that leads toward Arulius's manor, but Rune steps in the way to block the corridor. Pulled from my thoughts, I stare up at him.

Greeeeat. We are going to get along just great.

"What's the problem? That's the way to my *prison*. Step aside."

He keeps his even expression and shakes his head. Oh my gods, this guy is really pissing me off.

"What do you mean, *no*? Fucking move out of the way." He gives another shake of his head and this time he takes a step toward me and bumps me back with his chest. I clench my teeth. "I'll fucking tear you apart, *Dreadius*. Move."

He crosses his arms and nods in the opposite direction. Okay, I'm really losing my shit now. This guard needs a wake-up call. Who is he to try to block my way? I take a breath and try again.

"Tell me why you're blocking my way and maybe I'll listen."

He shakes his head and that's all I fucking get.

Okay, screw the nice talk. "Are you fucking serious?" I

shout up to his face. I'm up on my tiptoes now and he flashes his teeth at me in response. I roll my sleeves up. He wants to hash it out here? Fine by me.

"Elodie, for gods' sakes, he can't speak." Arulius emerges from the hallway to his manor. He looks me up and down and frowns at my rolled sleeves.

My eyes widen and I instantly feel like an asshole.

He can't talk?

My cold heart has been wearing on me more than I thought, I guess. I glance back to Rune. He's still baring his teeth in rage and his brows are furrowed. It's the first sign of emotion he's shown and it's better than his empty expression, I guess.

I sigh and let my shoulders slump, pushing back my hair and de-ruffling my feathers with a swift stroke of my hands.

"Where have you been?" I snap at the golden Eostrix. He's dressed in his Nesbrim armor, which is unusual. I haven't seen his golden bone brackets since... *that* day.

Arulius raises a brow, but his features tell me something's wrong. "Things have been... adjusted, love. You have your own room within the High Court now. You will no longer be staying with me."

My heart clenches at his words.

I'd be lying if I said the thought of not sleeping in bed with him each night didn't hurt a little. Because it fucking does. I'll never forgive him, but a part of my heart has always been his. Still is, in a sad pitiful way... He's been the constant in all my misery, always at my side. Having him taken away like this... *No.* I clear my thoughts.

I refuse the feelings that my broken organ is trying to push through me.

"That's fine. No—it's better. I prefer it this way."

Arulius's eyes betray him and the tug on the bond sears a heavy, sorrowful weight through me. I grit my teeth to keep myself steady, biting back the tears that beg to fall.

"Rune, please show her to her new room," he orders the Dreadius and he gives me one last glance before heading to the war room just down the corridor. I watch him walk away for only a few seconds before forcing myself to look away.

I'm met with Rune's red eyes watching me closely. I'm guessing he doesn't miss the tension between me and Arulius, because his eyes flick to the golden warrior before landing back on me. I'm curious whether he knows our history.

"I'm tired," I mumble, hoping he'll understand. Thank the gods, he does. He blinks as he nods once and starts walking toward the west wing.

I've only been to the west wing a few times. Once was when I tried to break out and failed miserably, and the other time was with Arulius to fetch some extra blankets. The walls and hallways change from elegant and luxurious to common. Vines have long since broken through the cracks in the walls on this side of the castle and they grow on the ceilings and surround the windows.

I take a deep breath, taking in the earthy scent of old bricks and plants. It almost feels like I'm outside on a cold spring morning. But as I pass the window I see it's snowing. I pause at the window and notice a small handprint left behind on the pane.

I'm taken back to my shed, the night my parents pressed their hands cryptically against my window and watched me sleep, waiting for me to leave the safety of the shed to murder me.

I shudder and resume following Rune, clutching my arms tightly. Ever since regaining my memories of that night, my dreams of blood and cries evolved into running through the forest while my parents hunt me down, stabbing me each night until I wake up crying. My heart always remembers *that* throb, the same throb that it elicited when mother pressed the cold blade into me.

When *Arulius* pushed it into me.

I clutch my arms tighter. I'm so fucking cold and I don't think anything can warm me ever again.

Oof. I walk headfirst into Rune's back.

"Oh, sorry." I step to the side and peer in front of him as he looks down at me from over his shoulder.

There's an old wooden door, curved at the top like Wren's cottage door back in Caziel. I smile at the memory. I step in front of Rune and open the splintery door. The room has one single window, and it's not very big. This room in general isn't very spacious, but the light that beams from the sole window enters my soul. My smile widens and I step into the room, spreading my arms out and spinning thrice before landing on my back against the soft sheets of the bed.

Rune leans against the doorway and watches me. I don't care. He's quiet and it's not like he can make fun of me or tell anyone what I do anyway, so I'll just... be myself.

Joke's on you, Violet. I love this room. I laugh and rise to look out my new window.

Setting my palms against the window frame, I eagerly search the view that waits just beyond the pane.

Vines wrap the corners of the dusty frame, but the city below is crisp with white snow. Every rooftop, road, and cart is glowing with winter life. Creatures of all sorts walk below and I can hear them talking from here. I'm only three stories up, but in Arulius's room there was always silence. Here, I can hear the life of the world around me—I can feel it. I reach my hand up to my heart and clasp it. I can't let anyone know how happy I am that she moved me here. I won't let her take this from me.

I spin to take in the rest of the room and jolt at the sight of Rune still lingering by the door. Fuck, he's too quiet.

"I no longer need you here." I give him a tight smile. It's harder than I expect to force one out.

He just stands there with his arms crossed, red eyes sending waves of fear through me. It feels like Violet herself is staring at me.

Oookay. Is he just going to watch me all day? I roll my eyes.

"Seriously, I don't need you to—"

He steps in and shuts the door. Alarms raise in my head and I back to the corner of the room as my breathing quickens. All the hairs on my arms raise.

Rune considers me as I freeze up in the corner like a rabid dog, and then he walks to the bed, sitting calmly, and taps his wrist.

"What?" I say defensively.

He taps his wrist once more. He wants me to drink more blood?

I watch him cautiously while I decide if he is safe. Violet specifically picked him for a reason. I can't trust someone who can't even speak his own truth.

After an intense stare-down for the better part of twenty minutes, I finally ease from the corner and approach him slowly.

He's either the most patient person in Tomorrow or has nothing to live for. His will is definitely greater than my own, which is saying something.

His crimson eyes and horns are the exact same shade

of red. Now that I'm calm and close enough to see him without Violet's horrid presence, I can explore his features more carefully. His dark hair looks soft and makes his skin appear incredibly pale. His shoulders are broad and the sweater he wears exposes his collarbones where they meet in the center.

I sit next to him with a good two feet between us.

"So, what got you in this mess?" I know he can't answer, but I'm sure he enjoys people talking to him nonetheless.

He shifts so he's facing me, one leg up on the bed and bent in. Obviously he doesn't answer. He just... watches me, eyes exploring my face and daring to rove to my neck before snapping back up. I notice the thick scar that runs down the length of his neck, straight through his Adam's apple and down to the tip of his chest.

"Did you kill someone?"

That gets his attention. He raises a brow incredulously. I let a small laugh out and shrug. "Is that a yes?"

He shakes his head and keeps his eyes on the floor now.

"Well, did you act treasonously?" I put my hand out for his. Another shake of his head. He sets his already bitten wrist in my palm. "Then I guess just no one likes you then, huh?"

I'm not expecting him to answer something so cruel, but my cold heart cracks a bit when he nods solemnly. I hesitate and meet his gaze. He shows no sign of hurt, but I'm sure deep down he felt that, right?

"That makes two of us," I mutter as I lean in to take his blood, but before my lips touch his skin I'm overcome with his scent. It's so overpowering I nearly gag. He smells like blood.

I know, the irony is not lost on me. I fucking drink the damn stuff. But not once has blood smelled like... blood. It usually has an essence of that person's being. Wren has his pine sap, Arulius is honey. It never has smelled like iron and the metallic sting of death...

I toss his hand back into his lap and when he looks at me, confused, I stand up and make my way to the door, opening it and motioning for him to leave.

"I'm feeling sick. Please go."

5

Elodie

It's still dark out when I hear a loud thumping against my door. I groan and pull my pillow over my head. Fuck early mornings. Violet said I had a few days to recover now that I don't have Arulius's blood to heal me, so who's trying to wake me up?

My answer is *hell no*.

The thump sounds again, and it's not a nice knocking either. I clench my teeth. *Just fucking go away, for gods' sakes.*

I get a few moments of peaceful silence and I smile to

myself, thinking that they've given up, as the door flies open and smacks the wall hard.

"What the fuck!" I sit up quickly, fisting my pillow, ready to launch it at whoever just barged in like that.

I'm met with a very annoyed-looking and might I say asshole-ish Rune. His brows pull down more as he eyes the pillow in my hands, daring me to fucking throw it at him. My fingers flinch with the idea of it.

"What the hell do you want, asshole?" I give him my best morning glare. It's way too fucking early to be barging in here like he owns the place. His hair is rumpled and he's wearing a slouchy black sweater and boxers.

What the hell, did he just wake up? I furrow my brow more with distrust as I recall his new quarters are located just next door to mine. *Ugh. LOVE neighbors.*

He starts prowling toward me and fuck it, I throw my pillow right at his face with all I've got. He smacks it down easily and his eyes narrow more with rage.

Leave it to me to poke the fucking bear.

I squeal in surprise as he reaches for me. I jump out of bed on the opposite side. What the fuck is he doing?!

"Rune, stop!" I spit at him, flexing my wings and getting ready to wield a fist of aura around my palm to fight the bastard.

He leaps over my bed easily and lands on the floor with a loud *thud.* I clench my jaw and bare my teeth at him. Is he trying to fucking scare me? Gods, I'm going to beat the shit out of him for coming in here like this.

I hold my ground in the center of my room as he stalks right up to me and tries to grab my wrist. I pull back and thrust my other arm forward with a punch made for douchebags.

His cheek is definitely not as soft as I thought it'd be and my knuckles flare with pain. The bastard doesn't even flinch with the blow and steels himself so that his face only turns slightly with my punch.

Oh. *Super*. Fuck. You.

I grimace and take a few steps back, clutching my now-throbbing hand like a wounded animal.

He just stares at me with his jaw flexing. His blood-red eyes are boring into me and I can't tell what he's going to do next, but he looks absolutely fucking feral.

We're in a standoff for the next few minutes. His cheek is red, so I know I at least did *some* damage, but the motherfucker didn't even blink at it. Doesn't help that he can't talk either. If he has an excuse for coming in here like a psychopath then he's shit out of luck, because he can't spill the beans.

He finally takes a deep breath and relaxes his shoulders, looking me up and down like he's inspecting me before he finally takes a step toward the door.

I flinch and take another step back toward the wall. As he leaves my room, he flicks me a sidelong glance that isn't completely filled with rage and I don't look too far into it.

Gods, what the hell was that about?

I manage to get a little more sleep with a chair tucked under the doorknob giving me a little peace of mind. Of course, the suns are peeking in through my window before I feel fully rested. I might as well get up to start the day.

I wash up in my bathroom and get dressed in a casual sweater and pants. My clothes, since arriving here, have consisted of bland leftover shirts and pants from the servants. Naminé was kind enough to give me an old sweater that she said she no longer needed, but I could tell it was newish and that she gave it to me purely because she was feeling bad. I eye the beautiful white cloak she gave me the other day as well.

Great—I'm just a pity party now.

I wasn't going to complain or say no though. Free is free and I have nothing to my name.

The clouds look angry today. I mull over whether or not I want to venture outside and decide against it. I've set my sights on trying to figure out Violet's long-lost-partner situation. If I put my best efforts toward it, surely I can figure *something* out. This castle is huge and I'm sure there are hints hiding somewhere.

As I'm tapping my finger along the pane of my shabby window, an idea zips through me.

A library.

There's got to be a library here somewhere, right? It's a fucking castle, for gods' sakes. I haven't done too much exploring around the castle due to my guards, but now that I have one who literally can't rat me out, there's nothing really holding me back anymore. And besides, after our run-in this morning, I'll be sure to make him chase me around the castle today as payback.

I slip my boots on and wrap my hair in a ponytail. I check the mirror to make sure I don't look too conspiring today. I usually don't have my hair up, but a smile tugs at the corner of my lips at the way my lamb ears look more noticeable and plushy this way. My horns have grown a good inch these last six months, and I can't help but wonder how long they'll grow. My cheeks look a little sunken from my time here. I'm just happy I'm still alive.

Whatever, the longer my horns get, the scarier I'll look and people will stop fucking with me. People like Rune. I narrow my eyes as I slowly open my door just enough to peek out and see if he's out there.

I let out a sigh of relief when I don't see him in the corridor. His door is still shut. Thank gods. This day might not be cursed after all.

I quickly slip from my room and shut the door silently behind me as I tiptoe across the hall. The stones emanate cold and the wind howls outside. A shiver runs up my spine. Hopefully there's a library here and fingers crossed there's a fireplace in there too.

There's so much commotion today I can hardly believe it.

I sneak to a small nook in the corner of the main foyer to watch for a few moments. I need to figure out where a library would be—if it exists, anyway—so I might as well take in the day too.

It's weird being here in the castle and not cooped up in Arulius's room. I can sit in the middle of Nesbrim's heart and just... exist. For the first time, I feel completely and utterly normal.

I take a deep breath of the cold air and the scent of burning wood crackling in the fireplaces. It feels fucking amazing.

A draft rolls in as male Eostrix warriors stride in with their white bone armor strapped on. Their black clothes underneath are tight and show off their muscles. Cocky assholes. A group of female Eostrixes follow close behind them, equally in shape and leaving absolutely nothing to the imagination with the tight black silk that hugs their bodies.

Okay, maybe I should start training in my spare time. That way I can punch Rune in the face and knock him on his ass next time. I clench my jaw as I brood on the way he just kicked my door open this morning. Kastian would be proud to know I finally just resorted to his ways of waking up and choosing violence.

I glance over to the far end of the foyer, past the dining hall and torture room. A large group of Dreadiuses and Moss Sparrows are huddled, reviewing some documents in their hands. I quirk a brow, wondering what they're looking at. It must be important to have the castle hopping like this.

Someone sits next to me and I flinch as I cast a glance over at them.

Oh gods, for all that is holy. It's fucking Kol.

Dreadiuses are called that for all the dread they seem to bring me, I muse as I give him a hard stare that says *get the fuck away from me.*

He sits tall, dressed in his black cloak with ebony leather gloves pulled up his arms. Three black horns crest his head, tipping up at the ends, and his midnight-black eyes are narrowed on me in a death gaze. "*Elodie.*"

"Kol." I return the nasty tone and fold my arms, furrowing my brow more.

He considers me for a moment before setting his hands on his knees like the good little trained soldier he is. "You will be relieved to know that Violet has canceled your sessions until further notice." He scowls. I wouldn't be surprised if he was upset they've been canceled. He's a freaking sadist.

I wouldn't be surprised if Rune was one as well—but I *am* shocked to hear that Violet has put a pause on the sessions.

My brows pull in tighter. "You're serious?"

He wipes invisible wrinkles from the black fabric of his cloak. "Yes, I wouldn't seek to talk to you otherwise." His eyes look me up and down and anger builds in my chest from his insult.

"Good thing your fucking brother can't talk—I'm worried he'd be just as big of an asshole as you are."

Kol snarls at me and it's so raw that I know instantly I've hit his soft spot. "Don't you *dare* speak about Rune. He's suffering as much if not *more* than a bitch like you." He growls low at me, loud enough to draw a few gazes from the Eostrixes standing nearby. "You're getting every-thing you deserve, *Talia.*" He hisses my name like it's poison on his lips, making me flinch back in my seat.

"Gods, what the fuck crawled in your ass today?" I snarl back at him and I swear he's about to lunge at me, but Naminé walks up to intervene. Her ash-blonde hair swirls around her back beautifully and her white Vernovian Thorn is as elegant as Nesbrim itself.

"Hey, Kol, Willow is looking for you. She said it's urgent," she says with a serious tone. The Dreadius eyes me once more like our conversation isn't finished, before standing and storming past Naminé with a shove.

We both watch him until he leaves through the enormous front doors and then I let a breath of relief out. "Gods, he's such a ray of sunshine, don't you think?" I mutter and Naminé lets a soft laugh out. Her smile seems a little more light today and I'm wondering if it has anything to do with her date. A throb flutters in my chest at the idea of being normal and going on a casual date. The memory of Wren and me at the café with Marley brushes against my heart, and I smile at the one blissful afternoon I had in Tomorrow before shit hit the fan.

I wish I could be free like her.

She catches on to my sobering mood and sits next to me. "How's the new guard? I haven't heard who it is yet." She scoots in closer with wide amber eyes begging me to tell her.

I glance away and grunt at her enthusiasm. "It's Rune —Kol's brother."

She gasps quietly and then leans in closer. She smells like peppermint. "*No.*"

"Yes."

"Well at least he's pretty quiet, I guess..." She tries to make it sound positive.

I look back at her and deadpan, "He burst into my room this morning and fucking attacked me." Okay, maybe that's a little exaggerated, but I'm still pissed.

Her eyes grow wide and she glares on my behalf. "What?!"

"That's what *I'm* saying!"

She rolls her eyes with the same ferocity I do. Fucking. Males.

"I know he can be a dick. A quiet one, but at least he shouldn't bother you too much. I hope." She tries to cheer me up nonetheless and I really appreciate the notion.

I let out a long sigh. "Yeah, well, his room is right next to mine. They really went all out on making this an actual punishment."

Naminé glances to my side to let me know someone is approaching, but I don't turn to look. "Where do they have you staying now? I noticed you weren't at Arulius's manor anymore."

I clutch the sleeve of my sweater at the thought of being apart from him. It feels good, but there's also this hole inside me now. Like it's wrong to be away from him. Even if I hate his guts, he was still always close by. Always loving me. "I'm staying on the west end of the castle, in the shabby stone area with that small room."

She frowns and shakes her head. "Gods, I'm sorry, Elodie. With all the nice rooms here I don't know why they would have you stay in that cupboard—" I shoot her a *skip the bullshit* look and she tightens her lips. "Right... Well, I need to head off with my new assigned team now, but I'm wishing you the best. I'll try to check in on you soon." She waves as she steps away.

I wave back with a half smile and let my hand drop when she's gone. I should get on with finding the library.

The first place I search is the basement. I'm shitting my pants with how dark it is down here. I keep hearing footsteps echoing around me and seeing shadows that seem to move as I pass doorways. After wandering around in the dark for half an hour, I decide it's not down there and head up to the second story.

I trail down long, extravagant hallways with white tiles and beautiful paintings on the walls. The ceilings are insanely high and the tall windows cast shadows away with the amount of light they let in. It's much warmer up here with many fireplaces in each room.

So much better than the basement.

I hear a group of people coming up behind me and decide I don't want to get questioned or eyed for being out without my guard, so I pick up my pace as I round a corner. My steps are silent and—

I grunt as I run headfirst into someone and fall back on my ass.

There's a group of young Moss Sparrows circling around and looking at everything with wide eyes. The moss balls on their heads are dark green and their messy hair reminds me so much of Marley it hurts. My heart stings at the notion that all the youth here died young on the other side, but their happy faces and laughs quickly push that somber thought away.

I glance up to the person I ran into and of course it's Rune. He eyes me carefully, but doesn't lean down to help me up. The Moss Sparrows all gaze at me from around his legs with big eyes and curious little smiles, so I keep my attitude cheerful for their sakes. They're so fucking cute.

"Oops, sorry! Please excuse me." I bow my head and then trot down the hall a bit, looking over my shoulder to see if he's in pursuit. Rune's eyes are still on me when I turn, but he quickly looks down at the smallest young Sparrow and pats her head warmly as he hands her a bandaged-up toy. Did he fix that for them?

The little Sparrow wipes her tears away and smiles up at Rune. They all say their thanks before scampering down the hall the way I came. Rune's face remains expressionless as he watches them all run off to have fun. My heart warms a bit at the interaction. I'm blaming it on the Moss Sparrows for being too damn cute though. They make my heart yearn for Marley. Wren too. I wonder what they're doing right now. Do they think of me as often as I do them? I sigh at the thought.

I continue to watch Rune. His neck is fully tatted and it lines his jaw perfectly. His black sweater and pants match his entire vibe. Dark and broody. The Dreadius's eyes flick back up to me and I flinch under his heavy red gaze, realizing that I'm staring at him.

I snap back to walking down this hall, pretending like I didn't just watch that whole interaction. My eyes catch on a large set of double doors at the end of a hallway.

That looks like *something*. I smile to myself. The doors are a matte ebony and look ancient. Trees are engraved on them. What else would a library entrance look like? I start walking toward it, but fall short as I hear steps close behind me.

I come to a stop and so does the person following me. I glance over my shoulder and see Rune pursuing me with a pissed-off look plastered on his face. He may be good at ignoring people, according to Naminé, but obviously I get under his skin. Good.

"What do you want?" I snap, furrowing my brows as his early-morning bullshit freshens in my mind.

He crosses his arms in response and that's it. I huff and roll my eyes, continuing to saunter my way toward the library. Who cares if he follows me? As long as he leaves me alone, it's fine. Who's he going to tell? His asshole brother, Kol? I scoff.

Just as I get to the library doors, he steps in front of me to block the way. I grit my teeth. "Move, asshole. I'll punch you again, if that's what you want."

His eyes darken and he gives me a haunting smirk, a fucking shit-eating grin, and shrugs at me.

I'm speechless for a moment.

I don't know what to do, what to say, or what fucking

day it is, but I'll be damned if this bottom-feeding prick thinks he can get away with that.

I roll my sleeves up to give him what he's asking for and his grin disappears as he walks into me, pushing me back with his chest until I'm backed against a wall.

Oh my gods, this man wants to die today, I swear.

My cheeks are hot with rage and I'm two seconds from going *god* mode on his ass. Our eyes clash and I see fire burning in his as well.

He presses his hands on the wall on either side of my head and I'm wrapping my fist in aura to knock a tooth out of him when a small voice raises beneath us.

His crimson eyes are still on mine as they widen and clear instantly.

We both look down and see the small Moss Sparrow girl that he helped earlier. She has the smallest flower I've ever seen in Tomorrow in her palm. It's withered from the cold weather but completely intact. My heart fills with warmth at the sight of her.

"Hi, mister. I wanted to say thank you." She smiles so wide I think it breaks my soul as she holds the flower up with both hands. Rune bends down to her level to accept the gift from her. I watch his interaction with awe.

His crimson eyes are alight with softness and a lovely small smile pulls at his lips as he takes the flower. The Sparrow giggles and throws her arms around his neck in a tight hug, and as she does her eyes land on me. She's got big green eyes and the cutest moss balls I've ever seen sprinkled throughout her auburn hair.

"*Whoa.* Miss... you're so beautiful," she mumbles as she releases Rune and sets her attention on me.

I quirk a brow and look over my shoulder to make sure there isn't another woman standing behind me. Me? Beautiful in my secondhand clothes that fit weird? I haven't been eating well these last six months either, so I know I look rather ghastly, and I definitely didn't brush my hair today... but sure as shit, her sparkling green eyes are on me.

Gods, that was the compliment I didn't know I needed.

I crouch down to her level and smile warmly. "Thank you, that was very kind." She beams at me until she's practically glowing. "But you shouldn't let Lady Violet hear you say that, okay? She wouldn't like it—I'm a prisoner."

The girl's eyes go round and she looks a bit upset at that, but my stern look drills it in and she nods. Rune watches me closely, like he doesn't trust me, but I ignore him.

"Can I touch your ears?" she mumbles and puffs out her cheeks like it would be the best thing ever if I said yes. I chuckle and nod. Her small hands grip my fluffy lamb ears and she lights up even more. "Wow. Gods, I hope I get fluffy ears like yours someday!"

Rune bends down and I try not to jolt out of my skin

as his hand reaches up and touches my ears right alongside her. There's a flash of truce in his eyes and for a moment I'm taken back to the first time Kastian and Arulius felt my ears. The memory warms my broken organ and I manage a genuine smile at him.

"I've got to get back to the game now. Thanks again, mister." The Sparrow runs off down the corridor and we both stand to watch her.

Rune holds the flower delicately as he looks down at it like it actually means something to him and I can't help but feel like maybe he and I got off on the wrong foot.

I spare a glance back to the library but decide maybe I should wait for another day. He seemed like he didn't want me going in there.

We walk silently back to our side of the castle. When we get to my room he stands there like he's trying to come up with words, but I know he can't say them.

"Are you sorry for being a dick?" I mumble and raise a brow at him.

He looks at me emptily for a few moments before nodding.

Okay, *this* I can work with. "Why did you come in like that this morning? You looked so mad at me." I furrow my brow but keep my voice light. He shakes his head at that. "You weren't mad?" I ask.

Another shake.

"Okay, well... I don't know your reasons, but knock

that shit off, otherwise that punch will be the least of your worries." I lift my chin and he gives me that shit-eating grin again. I smirk back this time. "You think I'm kidding?" I lean forward. I'm going to just push him, but my foot gets caught on one of the jagged stones and I fall into him, taking him by surprise.

We both fall to the floor and I'm on top of him like I just tackled his ass on purpose. Gods, I have to commit to it now.

"See? I'm not joking—" I get cut off and let out a shrill sound as he flips us so I'm beneath him and a surge of heat goes straight through me. His arms are taut and his shirt has lifted enough so that his stomach is bare. My eyes lag to meet his as I take him in, but when I do I'm surprised I don't find anger burning there.

There's a different kind of fire in his eyes now.

Oh. This might work out.

6

Elodie

Snow brushes the windows gently. The flakes are the size of coins and fluffy, falling slowly to the earth in a silent dance around the cottages and shops outside my window.

It's been nearly a week since Violet set the repulsion curse on me.

I haven't had a sip of blood since. Rune tries to get me to drink from him, but I just can't... His scent is so intoxicating and stirs fear deep in my chest each time I even consider it. I've been okay so far though. It's the longest

I've gone without blood and I can feel the ramifications, but it's manageable.

Feeling tired, grumpy, and weak is better than giving into Violet's bullshit. Though feeling hungover all day sucks.

I push away from my window and look over my shoulder at Rune. He's been leaning against the wall all morning, just watching me. His red eyes flicker as our gazes meet, but his expression remains unmoving.

I give him a small smile anyway—I've come to enjoy his presence.

He answers by closing his eyes and resting. I'm still trying to figure him out completely, but I've pieced together that ignoring me is a good sign. And we haven't had another episode of him intruding in my room in the dark hours of the morning.

Thank gods.

It's been a long, boring week though. My torture sessions with Violet were all canceled like Kol said they would be. I thought he was pulling my leg at first, but she hasn't called for me once all week so it must be true. I know something's going on to keep her away from her favorite pastime, aka bleeding me dry, and it has to be big for her to completely change her ritual like this. It must be her *guest* that she spoke of.

I reach into my dresser and pull out leggings and a tight, black long-sleeved shirt, tossing them on the bed as I throw open my closet doors to grab my white cloak. Today I want to visit the Hollows. The very thought pulls a smile at the corner of my lips.

They were never released. Violet and Arulius have their reasons for keeping them here, and again... I'm nowhere close to finding answers. Maybe it's to keep the Rhythm even further ruined, or because she just wants to be a bitch.

It's difficult when you're isolated and have no allies. I've thought of ways to break out all the Hollows but there are so many of them... I'd have to blow a hole into the side of the atrium. Gods know I can't manage that, at least not yet.

The thought makes all my males flash through my mind. My chest clenches at the memories of them and the short amount of time I was able to be with my gods. We forged unforgettable connections during our time together.

My broken organ twitches inside my chest, letting me know that it's still not completely ruined.

I grab the white cloak and throw it on the bed as I send a silent thanks to Naminé for giving it to me. It's beautiful, with imperial white fabric and tufts of cream fur lining the hood. The brooch is a ruby that matches my new guard. I let my hand linger over the gem as I gaze into the swirling red hues that dance in the light.

Rune raises his head to watch me and I notice. I

flatten my mouth at him. He usually takes the hint that I'm getting dressed and looks away. Don't tell me he fancies me now. I narrow my eyes but he still stares at me.

"I'm going to go see the Pine Hollows today. I can't be cooped up any longer this week," I mumble as I lift my sweater up over my head, switching it out for the black long-sleeve. His eyes explore my torso with desire and heat flares through my veins at the fire in his gaze, settling low in my abdomen and between my thighs.

His dark hair and crimson eyes send thrills through me. He's rugged and easily the most mysterious male I've ever met. Not only because he can't talk. He's so guarded in everything he does... I can never tell what's going through his mind.

Brave asshole, but I'm not some sad girl looking for love anymore. I'm a broken fool who will use anything for my gain, never to let my wicked wounded heart out of its cage ever again.

I lock eyes with him and part my lips as I slowly slip the black shirt over my head and pull it down, letting my fingers linger by my stomach as my thumbs hook into my pants.

His gaze is heavy, waiting for me to make my next move. Is he daring me? What the fuck is this—actually, I don't care, I'm quite enjoying it.

I pull my silk pants down, and once they're at my knees I let them drop to the floor. His nostrils flare but his expression remains stone. Fuck, he's the god of control, I swear.

Okay, I'll try something else.

Keeping my gaze on him, I set a knee on the bed and lean forward enough for him to get a full view of my backside, only wearing a black thong, as I reach exaggeratedly across the sheets for my leggings.

His eyes flick to my near-bare pussy and his cheeks redden. He quickly looks away with his brows furrowed.

Lightweight. I smirk to myself as I snatch the leggings.

Rune's not as hardcore as I thought, but at least I have a feel for him now. The more I know about him the better. Being manipulative isn't something I ever thought I'd be, but then again I also never thought I'd been some goddess reborn just to be traumatized and eternally fucked.

So, there's that.

I finish getting dressed and am not surprised when Rune follows me as I leave my room. He's been at my side constantly. I've thought about daring a trip to the library, but I'm still not sure how he'd react.

I miss Naminé and the occasional Willow. I don't really mind not seeing the Eostrix anymore, but I really miss my Cypress guard and wonder how her date with Greysil went. I should have asked her when I saw her last in the foyer.

As we walk down the corridors and enter the streets of

Nesbrim, I halt at the foot of snow that covers the cobblestone roads.

"Shit, I didn't think there was this much already," I mumble, looking down at my worn boots. They aren't made for winter. Prisoners don't get the luxury of clothes for every season, that's for sure.

I glance up at Rune. He's gazing up into the sky, watching the snow fall. He has an air of melancholy about him as he stares at the white winter land around us. I almost don't want to interrupt him as he takes in the crisp air with a deep breath, but I do anyway.

"You go ahead... I've changed my mind about the Hollows today. I'll see you later." I don't want to sound pathetic for not wanting to go because of my boots. The less I complain about the better. I turn to return inside the High Court castle, but stop at the sight of a figure in the doorway.

Arulius grins at me like just the sight of me makes his morning better. "Going to breakfast, love?" I shake my head and cross my arms. I'm still pissed at him for ditching me last week and he's been AWOL lately—not that I *want* to see him, but the idea of being so easy to forget sucks. "I have some free time this morning. What are your plans?"

I look behind me at Rune. He's back to focusing on me again. *Ugh.* I don't like having an audience when Arulius and I interact, but Rune can't talk, so...

"For the fucking thousandth time, I don't want to

spend time with you." My chest gets heavy as the words come out. My mind is firm on the decision that I can't forgive him, but my heart wants nothing more than to be close with him. I try to blame it on the bond, though there's not really a way for me to know if that's true or not. I despise the idea that I've become attached to him. But he's been the only person by my side constantly for months—how could I not?

Arulius frowns and dips his head. His soft amethyst eyes rove from me to Rune before he steps closer to me. "Come now, love, don't you miss me? I've missed you more than I can bear." His eyes narrow on me with sorrow as he wraps an arm around me and hugs me desperately.

I let a curt laugh slip through my exhale. "Arulius. What you did can *never* be undone. I *don't* miss you and I *don't* want you."

I'm a little shocked at my audacity today. Usually I'm not this snappy with him unless Violet has drained my blood from me. Maybe the time away from him has built up the walls around my heart—callousing against his love. Or perhaps it's the hunger that's been building inside me with this blood-repulsion curse. I've always had Arulius's blood close by, a daily hit of the golden ecstasy in his veins. I'm feeling particularly grumpy that I can't have it.

The golden Eostrix brushes my hair behind my ear with a longing look in his eyes. "It's okay... I'm a patient god, love. You'll want me again someday. Just know that I love you and I'll be here when you're ready."

He presses a kiss to my forehead and I'd be a liar if I said it didn't spark a fire in me. It's become hard to tell what the bond shares between us. My walls are up, but so are his. The assault of feelings the bond usually sends is less intoxicating than it was days ago.

"I'll see you soon then, love. We have a dinner to attend tonight, so be sure to wear the dress Willow is delivering to your room this afternoon." He turns and waves over his head as he walks back into the High Court.

Dinner to attend? What the fuck is he talking about? I look to Rune for an explanation and he just shrugs.

"Sorry you had to hear that. I'm sure you've heard what transpired between us." He shakes his head and raises a brow. I can't hold back the sarcasm in my voice when I say, "Oh good, story time later. *A God of Wrath and Lies.*" I pat his arm as I begin walking back to the castle too.

Rune steps in front of me, blocking my way, and I quirk a brow at him. "What's wrong?"

He nods toward the streets. He wants to go see the Pine Hollows still?

I shake my head reluctantly. "You go on without me. My shoes aren't ready to take a foot of snow. I can wait until the streets get shoveled." I smile warmly at him. It's getting easier to do so.

Crossing his arms, he gives me an annoyed expression and nods off toward the street again. I shake my head once more and move to pass him.

Stubborn asshole.

He grips my wrist and I flinch at his calloused hand. His skin is warm against the chill in the air. I turn to look at him, the surprise still surging through me that he actually stopped me.

His crimson eyes and three sharp horns pierce the winter sky around him as the snowflakes crash into his dark hair. He towers above me, and though he's absolutely terrifying, he looks like a fallen god. Rough and abused, staring at me in his silence and speaking with only his eyes and actions. He's like a drop of blood in the snow.

I'm speechless, and all I can do is stare at him like he does me.

He slowly reaches down, eyes never leaving mine as he lifts me into his arms, cradling me like I've been wounded. *What the hell is he doing and why am I letting him do it?* My heart threatens to war against the walls I've built but I quickly soothe the beast, reminding it of the pain we've already endured.

I choose not to say anything. I'm trying to take a page from his book.

He holds me tightly in his arms. His muscles are taut and I feel fragile in his embrace. After he's sure I won't retaliate, he begins walking down the cobblestone streets toward the Pine Hollow enclosure.

My cheek is pressed warmly against his chest, his black sweater soft and welcoming. I can hear his slow heartbeats with each step he takes. It's lulling and I never want to leave.

I watch his face as he normally watches mine, and the longer I look the more I see. His long scar stretches from under his chin to his collarbone. I wince at the brutal wound. This close I can see that it's a clean line, but thick... so someone must've inflicted it with a knife or aura blade.

I reach up and run my fingers softly down his throat on the ridge of his scar. Rune flinches at my gentle touch and glances down at me with a feral look in his eyes.

I tense and knit my brows. "Sorry..." I whisper as chills crawl up my spine. His expression dulls. He seems downhearted that I noticed his scar... and there goes my broken organ again, warring against the walls inside me. Wanting to reach out and hold him, heal him, and connect with his heart.

"I wish I could hear you."

He looks ahead as we pass some Moss Sparrows exiting a small shop. I press my face into his chest again. I can only smell his heavy scent of blood, metallic and sharp. He has no sage like Kastian, pines like Wren, or rain like Arulius. He only has the ominous and dark scent of blood.

"I wish I could hear your stories," I press on, feeling like I need to say something after touching a pain point of his. "Maybe one day you'll tell me."

He lets a deep breath escape his lips. I watch as it curls in the brisk air.

"One day... maybe when I'm listening in the way you need me to."

The glass atrium of the Pine Hollow enclosure is beautiful with the white layer of snow atop its panes.

Naminé told me the first time we came here that it's a type of magic used by creatures called *Gremitie*. It's the first I'd heard of them—spirits of the sea she said, creators of doorways to worlds. The glass serves essentially as a portal to another location, which explains why it's lush and green here, warm with the sun beaming through the glass.

I can't help but wonder what Gremitie look like as I admire the glass.

Once we enter the atrium, Rune sets me down. I tousle his hair as thanks, earning me a raised brow from him, but he quickly straightens his features back to empty nothingness. I laugh and can't help but smile at how soft his dark hair is.

The grass is green in the atrium and rich with plants, small animals for the Hollows to hunt, and of course, many, many Pine Hollows.

I grab the container filled with treats that sits just by the entrance and whistle for the beasts. They've come to know me by my weekly visit. Being around them centers me, brings me close to my gods I've left behind, and in a way I feel close to Margo and Murph this way too. Sometimes I pretend I can see her in the distant fields here, frolicking around and having fun with the other Hollows.

I let my imagination run wild and picture my afterlife if Arulius had never betrayed me. All of us laughing and smiling, riding Hollows, drinking tea at Moro's cottage. I'd spend time in Kastian's beautiful court, learn to fly with Arulius, help Wren raise Marley... there are so many things I wanted to do with them. All of them.

I frown at what could have been. Another life that seems so far away.

Rune shifts on his feet uneasily as the Hollows move toward us. I laugh and grab his hand to reassure him. He quickly looks down at me and pulls his hand back, giving me a sharp stare.

Yeah, because *holding hands* is crossing a line. Gods. I

roll my eyes and grab it again, holding it tighter this time so he can't pull away.

"Calm down—you've never visited the Pine Hollows before?"

His red eyes steady and he considers my question before shaking his head. He looks down at our joined hands with a crease in his brow. I didn't think he was afraid of anything, but I guess we all have insecurities and things that make us anxious.

I grab a handful of the meat grains, treats that a Nesbrim shopkeeper makes for the Hollows, and set them in Rune's hand. I've visited the shop a few times. The shopkeeper is a kind man. He loves the Hollows like Moro would, it makes me feel a little less guilty about them all being contained here. At least they are well cared for and loved.

Rune looks from me to the treats, expecting some sort of explanation. I tighten my lips to keep my amusement in. He's never fed an animal before?

Come on, that's sad.

"Like this." I hold my hand out, a small pile of treats in the center, as I wait for the Pine Hollows to come. He copies me and holds his hand out. His rolled-up sleeves and his tattooed arms make him look fierce and brutish, but the fear in his eyes kills me, I have to bite down on my tongue to keep the smile off my face. "Perfect, now we wait."

He nods hesitantly and keeps his eyes on the crowd of Hollows that are trotting over to us.

They're magnificent, each so beautiful and unique in their own way, representing some semblance of the dogs they were once upon a time. Black, tan, red, brown, gray, all sorts of colored beasts approach, stampeding the grass below as they come to a slow pace.

Rune sucks in a breath and his eyes widen with the sheer power and size of the Hollows. He wasn't kidding, he's never seen one before. I chuckle as I step in front of him, holding my hand out to my personal favorite Hollow. I've named him Brevik. His gray fur is long and coated with a black, tar-like speckle. His rider is out there somewhere and I hope one day he finds them.

Brevik lets a low hum rumble from deep in his throat as he greets me. I pet his muzzle and turn toward Rune, showing him it's safe.

The Dreadius looks at me with unsteadiness in his gaze, stepping next to me, so close that our thighs are touching and I have to take a deep breath to quell the heat that builds in my abdomen. He's entirely too hot to keep nudging up to me like that.

Rune offers his hand to Brevik and the Hollow considers him. A few of the other beasts are curious about the new visitor as well and begin to swarm around us to smell him.

Rune's eyes flicker with what I dare say is panic, but

he keeps perfectly still as the Hollows inspect him. A tan female sniffs his head and nudges at his sweater while a black one gives him a lick across his cheek. Rune's shoulders start to relax as the Pine Hollows show him their friendly nature and it warms my icy soul just a bit watching the emotionless male that is Rune be calmed by the beasts I love so dearly.

"See? What did I tell you, aren't they wonderful?"

I look up at Rune and he holds my gaze for a few moments, giving me a nod and the smallest curve of a smile before icing himself over once more.

But I saw it.

He's inside there somewhere and I plan on finding him.

7

Elodie

Well this dinner is going to be a shit show.

I've only just arrived, Rune beside me, and everyone I don't care to be around is here. Kol and his prick soldiers are all seated along the center of the table that can easily seat over fifty people. Willow stands by the doors on guard duty and gives me a tight smile as I pass by. I return it but I keep my wits about me. I can't trust anyone in this fucking room and it's suffocating.

Why is a *prisoner* expected to attend this stupid thing? Violet is an enigma.

The room is enormous, with gorgeous arched windows along both sides of the table. The walls are made of grayish-tan stones and the lighting is warm. The night sky twinkles with the stars painting the universe above. At least the view is decent.

I'm uncomfortable as I try to stretch the chic white dress down past the cup of my butt. Did Arulius pick this out or Violet? I can feel the stares of every creature here and my cheeks couldn't be redder if someone slapped me. This dress is beautiful but entirely too revealing. My breasts feel like they're going to jump ship and my ass is too big for this style of dress.

Gods.

Rune's wearing his usual charcoal gray sweater and black pants. I haven't uncovered why he gets away with dressing so casually compared to everyone else yet, but I'm determined to find out. The Dreadius walks over to a chair by Kol and I'm left standing awkwardly alone at the end of the long table as the seats quickly fill up.

"Over here, love." I flinch at Arulius's voice and find him sitting next to the head of the table. Violet's chair is empty for now, but the throne awaits her nonetheless.

I steady myself and sip in a tight breath before walking over to him. The golden Eostrix stands and pulls out my seat with a gentle smile playing at my heart. I try my best not to meet his amethyst eyes. Those are my real undoing.

My eyes skirt across the table. It's filled with crystal cups and plates gorged with meats, potatoes, and sides of every bready goodness. I'm drawn in by a familiar red and catch Rune's heavy gaze. He's across the table from me and down a few seats, but we might as well be sitting across from one another.

He's always watching me.

A strange throb pulses through me. One that I haven't felt in a long time. I'm not sure I even know what to call it anymore, but it feels like... a calling maybe? I felt this with Kastian too when I first saw him. I try to push away the sensation because I *can't* have any feelings for anyone here no matter how tempting it may be, *especially* Rune.

I break our connection and sit in the chair as Arulius pushes me up to the table.

I take a breath. *Clear your mind, Elodie. Stay focused.*

Arulius grasps at my wrist and I flinch under the sting. I whirl to look at him, surprised at his aggression. He's been nothing but kind and understanding this entire time no matter what I did to him, so why's he so pissed at me now?

"What was *that*, love?"

I furrow my brows, my blood thickening. "What was *what*?"

His purple eyes narrow at me. "Love, I'm a patient

god but I'm *not* sharing. What was that you just sent across the bond? Because I know it wasn't for me." His words drip with venom and I'm holding my breath unconsciously.

Gooseflesh crawls up the back of my neck and I shake my head. "I don't know what you're talking about."

His mouth remains pressed flat and he turns to look across the table, surely finding Rune and his crimson stare just as I do. *Fuck. Why can't he stop watching me for two godsdamn seconds?*

Arulius lets out a low growl and his grip tightens on my wrist. Pain surges through my forearm and I bite my lip to hold back the cry that wells in my throat.

"Stop," I hiss at him, trying to avoid any unwanted attention from the other guests, but a few of them look at us anyway.

When he turns to look back at me, I see possessiveness in his glare, mixed with jealousy. An ugly beast curls inside him and it has finally come out to play.

"Why is he looking at you like that, love? You. Are. *Mine*. If he so much as touches you I'll fucking kill him." I can feel the blood drain from my face. I've never seen Arulius so angry. Ever. "Do you understand me? I'll fucking kill him."

I nod, shaking uncontrollably beneath his bruising hand.

He notices the trembling and quickly releases me. I

grasp my wrist and hold it carefully against my chest, peeking down at it and finding it blackened and purple already.

Gods. I know I've given him worse bruises but it hurts that he'd do it to me... especially in front of all these people.

I slide my napkin over my arm to hide the damage. My heart's still racing with adrenaline and nausea. I never thought he would hurt me... not physically. My eyes water only for a brief second before I'm blinking the evidence of my feelings away. I don't want him to know how much it affects me.

The chatter around the table dies down as the main dining room doors open. Violet is probably entering. I feel so fucking broken right now though I don't want to look. My arm stings and I'm embarrassed at all the eyes I still feel on me.

If I wasn't a prisoner I would have already run to my room by now—to cry maybe, or to sulk. Stare outside my window and wait... wait for Kastian to come save me like he did once so long ago.

Every head turns toward the High Lady as she enters the dining room. I dare a small glance up and of course, *of course*, he's still looking at me.

I keep my eyes hooded, but more importantly I keep my heart caged.

Rune's red gaze falters. He saw what Arulius did to my arm and I don't want to talk about it, *ever*. Thank gods he literally can't talk, though his eyes say more than anyone else can see, and more than I want to receive.

I look back to my empty plate as I wait for Violet to take her seat at the throne. I'm seated directly to her left. She likes to keep me close, to shame me as much as she possibly can for things I never did.

Oh Talia, I wish I wasn't you.

Nails drag behind my neck, sending shivers down my spine. Violet's lavender scent fills my nose and makes my arm throb more than it already did.

She takes her seat and gives me a sinister smile. I study her appearance. Her black hair is twisted up into a tight bun that complements her crimson dress. Her boobs are pushed up higher than I've ever seen them and I'd be lying if I said it didn't make me a little jealous.

Who is she trying to impress here anyway?

I let my eyes drop to show her I'm behaving. I'm not particularly feeling like having my throat slit before dinner. This seems to pacify her as she hums with glee before taking a long sip of her wine and addressing her guests.

"I'm pleased to see all of you here tonight." Violet stands and clanks her glass, which is unnecessary because everyone's already watching her. "As you know, the winter festival is next week. We have much to do in preparation for it and I have an important guest traveling a far distance to get here. I want everything to be *perfect*."

The table murmurs in agreement, I keep my eyes on the plate in front of me, wondering when we'll get to eat. A festival sounds fun and I'm already planning what I can wear and what Rune will be interested in eating. I'm sure there will be tons of food and drinks.

I zone her out as she continues to address her commanders and advisors. She gives a few awards out, one being to Arulius for tricking me and capturing the long awaited Goddess of Life, and then we finally, *finally* get to start eating.

I grab a few slices of meat, a spoonful of potatoes, and some steaming soup that already has my mouth watering from the savory broth. I snatch a piece of bread and lather it in butter before dunking it into my soup.

At least the food here always tastes amazing. My memories of the human realm's food is trash compared to this.

After the meal everyone engages in idle chitchat. I sit awkwardly as Arulius and Violet talk over me.

"Has there been any progress on finding Lucius?"

Violet takes a long sip from her wine. "No."

Arulius glances nervously at me, eyes hovering over the bruise he left on my arm, and when the anguish reaches the press of his lips he continues with Violet. "How long must you keep her on the blood repulsion? It's already been over a week... You know its ramifications can cause withdrawals that other blood won't satisfy. At least give her an Eostrix blood bag."

She lets out a sick laugh. "A week is nothing. I've been without Lucius for hundreds of years. What kind of *withdrawals* do you think I've undergone?" Her eyes level with his, challenging him to fight her on this.

"I did everything you asked of me, my lady." Arulius's voice hitches with desperation and he looks at the table rather than her.

"And *I* gave you six months of whatever you wanted with her. I would say that's more than fair. Besides, she seems perfectly fine without you. If you want her back, you know the price."

"Lucius."

"*Lucius*," she echoes.

A few more hours and I'm nearly falling asleep in my seat by the time people start getting up from their chairs to leave. I eagerly stand—I don't want to be here for another godsforsaken second.

Arulius stands as well, sliding his hand in the small of my back. Violet snaps her fingers at him, drawing a raised brow from both of us.

She's been drinking wine all night, and by the way she leans on the table I'm going to guess she's pretty drunk. "Leave us, Arulius—I wish to speak with Elodie alone."

He hesitates and looks at me for the rebellion he's used to, but I'm tired, mentally drained, and done with this fucking night. I don't bother meeting his gaze. He dips his head in my peripheral and then is walking out with everyone else.

Well, almost everyone.

Rune stands by the doors, waiting. Violet considers him but returns her attention back to me. I shrink in my chair, uneasy being alone with her.

"Elodie, dear, tell me a story."

I furrow my brows. "My lady, I don't think I could tell you a story that you'd find interesting."

She swirls her glass of wine at me. "Tell me one anyway."

I try to think of anything, but there's only one story I know to tell. My story. So I tell her about Margo and Aunt Maggie. I tell her how I died.

"Then I wandered the forest... until I noticed Wren, and you know how that story ends," I mumble. Rune leans against the door still and I hope he can't hear us from all the way over there. He doesn't need to pity me. I like the way our relationship is.

"Hmm, that's a sad story, dear. One of loss and dreariness." She sets her cup down and rests her chin on her palm, elbow against the table. "Now I'll tell you a story."

My bones ache. I already know her story... but I guess her perspective might be different from the rumors. So I perk my ears in interest.

"I was swimming when I died."

Oh fuck.

"I drowned... then I woke, here in this wondrous place. Tomorrow. But unlike most that arrive, I was at the bottom of the sea. So far away from anything or anyone, left to cry the salt-filled tears of a dead girl never to be found. A lost treasure. I was born with water spirits in my blood. A Gremitie. I could breathe the water I was imprisoned in just as well as I can breathe the air."

A Gremitie? Like the ones Naminé told me about... She's the one who made the glass atrium. Gods, I may hate her, but her magic is beautiful.

She pauses and stares into an emptiness across the table. I'm already shivering with her words, but when I see the smile curl her lips into a genuine, somber lift of nostalgia, I want to cry.

"Funny though, isn't it? I drowned in my human life because I couldn't swim. So there I remained, alone and cold in the vast and dark waters. I can't say how long I existed in that state. Eventually I became stagnant. Neither here nor there, waiting for death so I could rest."

Violet's eyes meet mine and I shift uncomfortably in my seat.

"Then Lucius came. He found me in the depths of the darkest parts of the sea. I can still remember the light he carried with him. I thought he was a sun himself... You know what he said to me? When he brought me to the shores and we coughed up water, he said that he *heard me.*

He felt my very being calling for him. So peculiar... isn't it? An odd thing to imagine being possible, but how else would he have found me down there? In the dark. Alone."

She sits back in her throne, her smile fading. "That was it. There was no one else for me. I knew then, no matter what fate I had, everything was okay. It was all going to be okay because he was with me. So why can't I do the same now? Why can't I hear him calling for me? I don't feel his being sending me anything like mine did to him." Her voice cracks.

I'm an empath. Anyone else and my heart would be on my sleeve. But Violet is malevolent. I can't humanize her because then all she's done to me will seem... more understandable.

There's a small, tiny, insignificant piece of me that wants to comfort her.

I can't fathom her pain. When I look at her I can't help but see a little of myself. I've become a completely different person. Cold, calloused, and bruised. I'm not the same Elodie, I never will be... and that's her fault. Our pain and trauma shape us, stain our souls until we change with them.

A sad reality, but it's ours to keep.

She waits for a response that I don't give, and after a few minutes of silence she pushes from her throne and pats my head as she walks by, retiring for the evening.

"Sleep well, dear. We will continue to take time off of

our sessions until after the festival. I don't want to see you or Rune there, am I clear?" She pauses at the door, looking the Dreadius from head to toe before she shoots me a testing glance.

"Yes, Lady Violet."

8

Elodie

The walk back to my room is awkward.

I've had a few drinks and so has Rune. Though he is entirely composed, I still feel his gaze resting heavily on me. I know he heard my story because he has that gods-awful pity in his eyes that I was worried about.

I stop at my door and turn to say goodnight. It's actually pretty convenient that his room is right next to mine. We're literally neighbors in this cold, outcast part of the castle. It might as well be our own depressing little corner of the world.

"I'll see you tomorrow. Goodnight." I yawn and pat his taut chest as I slip by.

I'm about to shut my door but he stops it gently with a firm hand. I let out a weary sigh. How is he not completely drained? It has to be at least two a.m. by now. I crack the door open and glance at him. He's giving me a concerned look.

"What?" I narrow my eyes on him. I still have some fight in me in case he wants to pull another barge-into-the-room situation.

His gaze shifts to my bruised arm. My cheeks instantly heat and I move my arm behind me. *Fucking gods, I forgot all about Arulius's tantrum at dinner.* "I'm fine—just go to bed," I say with a tight smile and hope it seems genuine.

He furrows his brow and enters my room anyway.

Gods be damned.

He moves toward my bed and sits down, patting the spot next to him. I reluctantly obey. The sooner I let him inspect my arm the sooner I can sleep.

I plop down next to him, our thighs touching, and offer him my bruised forearm. He gently holds my wrist like it will break if he moves too quickly.

My skin is a dark purple with blue splotches of deeper bruising dotted in. I wince. How could Arulius do this to me in such a public display of jealousy? I clench my teeth. Another way that proves his love is vile. My broken organ tries to crack at the thought but I keep it glued shut.

Rune dips his head down to my arm and something wet and warm drips across my skin. I flinch, but my muscles relax once I see the bruising begin to fade. My eyes widen with disbelief. I didn't know Dreadiuses could heal, how is he—

He lifts his head and nausea flows through me. His tears healed me... and they're made of blood. Streaks drip down his face and his crimson eyes glow with the red stains of death. He's crying tears of blood. I feel sick and weak... dizzy. Crap, when was the last time I even drank blood? A surge of pain thrums through me, demanding I drink blood and coiling deep in my chest.

I glance down to my arm and curl my lips at the drops of blood left there. My vision starts to blur and I'm falling into darkness before my face hits the sheets.

"Elodie, love. Why are you running?"

Father chases me with the golden dagger. His hands are covered in Margo's blood and his eyes are wide with mania.

"Dad, please don't! Please don't kill us!" I scream. My lungs burn and my legs aren't carrying me fast

enough. Margo is running at my side with an injured leg from the cut she barely dodged. Fuck, he's going to catch us. He's going to catch us and push that dagger into our flesh.

I slide down a short hill and break into a run in the gulley. Just when I think I've lost him, I'm met with yellow stained teeth smiling much wider than they have the right to. Mother embeds her kitchen knife deep in my chest, the impact stopping me like I just ran into a wall.

Her fist is nearly in my chest cavity. Blood oozes down my ankles while my lungs betray me. Blood spurts from my lips and coats her face. Her brown eyes meet mine—

"I love you, Elodie," she cries as she comes out of her bewitched state.

It's warm.

My eyes are heavy but I open them anyway. My room is dark and I'm tucked in bed. Frost clings to my window and my breath swirls as I exhale.

Cold tears wet my face and my pillow is soaked. My skin is drenched with sweat and my breathing is labored.

It's just a dream. It's just a dream, I'm okay. It's already been done.

As I come out of my drowsiness I realize I'm not alone.

I'm warm—and my room is never warm.

My hand glides down to my waist where I find some-one's arm wrapped around me tightly. *Arulius?* I consider turning to find out who it is.

But I'm so warm—I was crying and whoever it is, they're here to comfort me. Bring me out of my deep-dark screaming meemies. I don't want to turn around because my heart will try to latch like it always does. It's better if I don't know.

Even though I have a good guess who it is.

I let my body relax once more and try to coax my brain into getting some rest. The person lying with me rubs their hand up along my arm and brushes my hair out of my face gently.

My eyes are closed but my lips are awake, smiling at the silent affection.

They scoot in closer and press a kiss to the back of my head as they run their hand calmly through my dark hair until I'm falling asleep, safe in their embrace.

9

Elodie

Rune leans against the wall by my door as I untangle my hair and watch as the Nesbrim citizens work on setting up the festival. I catch sight of Naminé as her ashy blonde hair waves behind her. She's with a Dreadius. I squint harder and smile when I recognize the café owner, Greysil.

"I'm guessing their date went well." I purse my lips and smile. I wonder if they left Nesbrim to go somewhere romantic or if they had a nice dinner at a fancy shop.

I toss my brush on the bed and grab my coat. Rune keeps his eyes closed. I can't tell if he's sleeping or just resting his eyes. I often wonder if he sleeps standing up like a fucking horse.

I admire his features for a peaceful moment. His eyelashes are unfairly thick and dark like his hair. His three beautiful crimson horns tilt up at the ceiling as his chin nearly rests on his collar bones. Arms crossed, his veins and muscles are protruding even at his resting state. Each twist and curl of his tattoos makes me curious about what they mean. Was he tatted here? Did he arrive in Tomorrow with them? I never got to experience tattoos in the human realm so I'll have to wring it out of him.

It hurts to think about the things I never got to do in the human realm. Like get married or egg someone's house, visit Heirah and historical sites. I never got to eat funnel cake. I let out a soft sigh and shake the depressing thoughts from my mind.

I'll let him sleep—my silent drop of blood in the snow.

The door creaks open as I step out, and when he doesn't move I'm certain he's asleep. A smile cracks across my lips. I can finally do some snooping on my own.

I shut the door quietly and tiptoe through the hall until I'm far enough away to walk normally.

I slip my shoes off and let the coolness of the castle's tiles floor seep into my bones. Setting my shoes on the windowsill, I dart through the halls and prance to a song in my head, one of freedom and hope. My mother would sing it to me a lot when I was a child. I think it was the song of Fernestia, the end of the war. It's much too pretty of a song to be linked with war though.

I stop near an intersection in the hallway and sneak around a few chatting Moss Sparrows, deep in conversation. They have plans scribbled in their binders. They argue over what would be better lighting and food options for the festival. It sounds like it will be beautiful, and I'm already pissed that Violet has forbidden me and Rune from going.

The library is just to the left of them. They're the only double doors that scream *library* in this entire castle. I casually walk in, happy that the Moss Sparrows don't seem to notice. Once I'm in, I press my back against the door with a breath of relief.

The mildewy and stale scent of books untouched for gods know how long invades my nose. It's dark in here. There are three floor-to-ceiling windows along the back wall and a gorgeous arched window that sits between the first and second floor, but heavy, thick drapes cover the light that tries to trickle in. I don't miss the layer of dust that sticks to the bottom of my feet as I step toward the glass.

Gross. Shoes next time.

I grasp the drapes and fling each one open, light immediately piercing through the stagnant air and chasing shadows to the corners of the room. The flecks of dust dance in the sunbeams, making it look like a shimmering ghost library filled with secrets and buried treasures.

I intend to find every last one.

The door creaks open behind me and my head snaps to the door. Naminé's laugh rings through the air and I'm seizing at the thought of being caught. I don't know if she would rat on me or not, but the nice thing about not trusting anyone is having zero expectations.

I slip behind a long bookshelf and peek through the gap above dusty books. She's dressed in her soldier armor and crimson cloak, moving a large box and setting it in the corner by the enormous double doors. I let out a sigh of relief as she moves to leave, but the door swings open again and a very distraught Rune enters.

Gods, why do you hate me...

Naminé quickly straightens and nods at him like she just wants to leave, but he stops her. I feel bad that he can't just say what it is he needs, but she seems to get the memo that a guard should be guarding someone.

"Are you looking for Elodie?"

He gives her a sharp nod and glances around the dusty library. His eyes flick up to the second floor, searching them for good measure.

"I haven't seen her. I'm done working today though, I can help you if you'd like?"

Naminé, no!

I smack my forehead with my palm and curse under

my breath. She's so smart, she'll find me in a heartbeat. Just as the thought crosses my mind, my gaze lowers to the floor where I see, *clear as day*, footprints leading exactly where I'm hiding.

"Hey, there's footprints... I only know one person who goes shoeless in all of Nesbrim." Naminé laughs as she approaches my hiding spot.

I tighten my lips and try not to laugh as her eyes meet mine once she rounds the corner. Rune's just a beat behind her and his brows are furrowed like I'm psychotic for going barefoot.

He lifts up the shoes I left behind and a smile pinches in the corner of his mouth. I can't hold it anymore and I burst out laughing. Naminé laughs along with me.

"Godsdamn it—please don't tell," I manage between a few chuckles.

Naminé wipes her eyes and shakes her head. "Of course not. What are you doing here anyway, you barefoot weirdo?" She looks genuinely curious and Rune does too.

What harm could telling them do? Maybe they'll help me...

"Well I won't be able to find Lucius just sitting around in my room all day, now will I?"

Naminé's eyes shimmer with excitement. "Oh my gods—you really don't know where he is, do you?" I frown and shake my head. She believed me so easily. Why didn't I ever just come out and tell her before? I can't help but feel sorry for her... She's so trusting, as I once was. A beautiful fool. Hopefully she'll never be broken. "Can I help? I've always wondered what happened to him!"

"The more the merrier." I glance at Rune. He's looking at all the books with awe before flicking his eyes back at me. "Care to join us?" Naminé looks at him and gives him a glare like he'd better not say no.

He ignores her but half smiles at me and nods.

We spend hours here... Okay, the entire day.

Naminé takes to clearing off a large table in the center of the library, cleaning it, and then begins making stacks as she sorts through the *Creatures of Tomorrow* categories.

Rune searches the bookshelves beneath the arched window and hands anything worthwhile up to me as I perch on the windowsill. I was surprised to find it wide enough to sit on. It's like a little reading nook and I fall in love with this spot instantly.

The suns' rays warm me as I flip through old pages. My fingers are numb from all the pages I've touched and my brain is feeling mushy from all the unimportant things I found today. I take a moment to look down at my friends... Wait—*friends?* The thought scares me, but I can't deny it as I look down at them.

Even in the place I'm in now, I've somehow managed to find people like them. They could never replace the ones I've left behind but... they are their own light in my world of darkness, and whether I like it or not they've carved their way into my heart.

Naminé's sitting criss-crossed on the table, thumbing through an old book, while Rune's leaning against the edge and he's... he's looking up at me.

My heart skips a beat at the sight of him in the sunset's orange glow. His eyes gazing at me with the heat of a million burning suns. A few of my feathers are drifting down through the sunbeams and as one passes he looks away.

My cheeks flush and my pulse quickens.

What was that? I shake my head and look back to my book pile, refusing to admit anything to myself about that beautiful moment I just shared with him.

The pile of books I've selected as *maybe useful* is growing taller than I am. I sorted them by age and category. Anything with history, Violet, Rhythm Gods, and creature guides, given that I don't know what each spirit, god, or being is capable of here. After Rune's bloody tear healed me, I'm too curious to not look into it more.

The suns are cresting over the west wall now and it's probably time to call it. I've narrowed down the books to three and carefully slip them into my inner pocket within my white cloak before jumping off the window ledge. I spread my wings to glide down softly.

Naminé looks up from her book and yawns, her amber eyes still holding that excitement of helping me search.

"Find anything useful?" She stretches and slides off the desk.

I hold up the three books I hope to find clues in and shrug. "I hope so. I narrowed it down the best I could. How about you two?"

She tosses me the book she's holding and grins like she has a secret. "This one is about Rhythm Gods. I found it hidden beneath a stack upstairs." My eyes widen at that and she looks pleased.

"Oh my gods, Naminé, you're amazing." I wrap my arms around her and flinch when I realize that I'm hugging her. She returns it without hesitation and squeezes me.

"I know," she mumbles with a laugh. My heart instantly sinks with her embrace. I don't know how long it's been since I've hugged someone this tightly... but I don't want to let go. Rune's eyes fill with warmth too—okay, too many emotions. I release Naminé and straighten my cloak.

"Let's meet again after the festival?" I ask and look from the Cypress to the Dreadius. They both nod and our smiles all reach our eyes. The air between us feels completely weightless, like it should between friends.

Naminé waves as she walks down the hallway in the opposite direction we do. The corridors are dark and empty. I wonder what time it is. I look over at Rune. He has a book in his hand as well.

"Find something that interests you?"

He looks down at me and shrugs. I huff. *Okay, keep your secrets.*

I peek down the hallway before tucking my wings close to my back and tiptoeing through the main corridors. Rune isn't as quiet, and when I look back at him he has a shit-eating grin as he watches me try to sneak around.

Prick.

It's eerily silent and not a soul lurks in the hallway. Perfect.

We finally make it to the final stretch and my anxiety peaks when I see Arulius waiting by the window near our rooms.

His amethyst eyes catch mine and he's instantly storming over to me. His fists are clenched, and I can't tell why he's so pissed, but his eyes dart from Rune to me like we've been out having sex all night.

The moonlight is dripping through the glass behind him and he looks iridescent, reminding me of my sweet Kastian the first time I saw him in the twilight in Caziel. Except this god is angry and the gold in his hair glints as light bounces off it.

My heart lurches.

I brace myself for him to drag me back to my room. My eyes closing as his arms reach out to take me. My forearm stings in memory of the way he grabbed me at dinner last night. I instantly drop my books and they clatter to the floor.

Rune pulls me back and steps in front of me in a heartbeat. Arulius's eyes flare at my Dreadius guard and he doesn't waste a second as he throws a punch at Rune's face.

"Get out of the way, you useless—"

"Stop!" I scream and try to get between them, but Rune has a firm arm out, blocking me. He lets out a feral growl.

Holy shit, he can make sounds?

Rune throws a heavy punch at Arulius's cheek and the Eostrix doesn't block it in time. His golden wings soften his fall but he hits the floor with a hard *crack*. My heart's pounding and adrenaline pulses through me. My aura is itching to get out. Pain sears into my cheek and up my spine as the bond sends Arulius's fresh wounds right through me. I stagger but remain standing, cupping my cheek gently and trying not to draw Rune's attention to me. I really doubt he knows about the shared-fate bullshit of the bond, so I can't really hold it against him. Plus, Arulius deserved that.

Gods, Rune can hit like a motherfucker though.

"How *dare* you touch me, you filthy Dreadius." Arulius's purple eyes are ominous and radiate a wave of dread through me as he stands and wipes the blood from his lip. His golden aura surrounds his arms and the air around us feels charged with electricity. Discharges of small thunderbolts spark between Arulius's fingers.

My jaw trembles. I've never seen him use *this* power. "Arulius, what the fuck are you doing!?"

His eyes land on me and he looks completely unhinged, more so when he realizes I felt that punch too. "Where have you two been, love? I've been looking for you... You're sending unsettling emotions through the bond. I thought I told you—"

Rune's arm flares with a crimson fire as he cracks another skull-shattering punch against Arulius's jaw. The Eostrix's head tilts, but just slightly—he was ready for it this time. *I wasn't though.* I grit my teeth, instantly dizzy, and I fall to the ground. Rune glances at me and realization flickers across his gaze as he registers that the bond shares pain.

A string of golden aura forms by Arulius's lowered arm and I recognize the shimmering arrow—it's just like the ones he rained down in the Pine Hollows' grove during the attack.

He's going to kill Rune.

"Arulius!" I shout as I stumble up and shove Rune with all my strength. Thank gods, I take him by surprise and manage to push him out of the way as Arulius brings his arrow up like a spear. The electric strings connect with my body and my skin heats.

I brace myself for the impact of it, but the golden

arrow shatters into a beautiful dust before it can pierce my chest, swirling in the air around us like glitter. My heart's beating against my ribs and my breaths are labored as our eyes meet.

Arulius looks absolutely ruined.

His expression is desolate and horrified at what he almost did. He takes a few staggering steps back before leaning forward and wrapping me in his arms, burying my face in his broad chest and embracing me desperately like he almost lost me to the shadows of this world. His hand cups the back of my head and he presses his face into my hair. What's gotten into him? I clench my teeth and try to calm my shaking limbs. My cheek and jaw are throbbing so fucking bad.

"Love... Gods, I'm so sorry."

My broken organ... It rips right through my chest and clutches onto his. Arulius's heart is beating so hard I can feel the flutters against my cheek.

But what he did... I press a hand to his chest, pushing him away and stepping back, shaking my head and looking over at Rune. He's still sitting leaned up against the wall where I pushed him, boring holes into the Eostrix with hate-filled eyes.

"You should go," I whisper and the words hang in the air around us like a fucking noose.

He lifts a hesitant hand and then clenches it before he can cup my throbbing cheek. Cursing under his breath, he stalks past me, and I don't let my breath out until his steps are fading away.

I stand in the veil between the dark walls and the moonlight, staring at the speckles of blood on the stone floors from the fight.

Rune remains leaning on the wall... I can't even bring myself to look at him. What if Arulius *had* killed him? I wouldn't have been able to save him. I bite back the tears that threaten to fall.

After a few minutes of our moonlit silence, I finally whisper, "I'm sorry."

Rune stands and walks up to me, setting his hands on my shoulders and pushing me an arm's length away so he can survey me. I can see the pain and worry in his red eyes. It crushes me. How could someone like *me* make him worry? I've been trying to be distant with him specifically to stop this, but obviously it isn't working for either of us.

"Don't look at me like that."

He presses his brows closer together with anguish. I *won't* let him care about me.

I push him and his hands slip from my arms and hang at his side wearily.

"I will only bring you *pain*, Rune." I bite out the words and they physically hurt to say out loud.

He stands there, defeated, as I bend down to collect my books and pass him to return to my room. I'm dizzy, in pain and tired—the lack of blood has been making me feel drugged and I'm not sure how much longer I can hold out.

I stumble over the threshold of my door and fall to my knees, my books sliding across the floor. My body refuses to move as my stomach curls in on itself and makes my teeth clench tightly together. *Shit.*

Rune is at my side in a second and his worried expression has my heart aching. "I'm okay, I'm—" I cough and blood spatters across the floor. Okay, I'm joining the worried train.

He lets out a soft gasp. I swear I can nearly hear his voice on his breath, but my bobbing consciousness could be fooling me.

Rune lifts me from the floor and quickly brings me to the bed, cradling me as he sits down and holds my face up to his neck, pressing my cold lips against his skin.

I know he's trying to get me to drink, but I think I've gone too long without it. I can't move my jaw and the only things that my frenzied mind can focus on right now are the slow breaths that are becoming heavier and more painful with each inhale.

He shakes my head in his hand, trying to get me to bite him, but my vision fades.

Rune lets out a small groan and pulls me down to look at me. His eyes are panicked and I feel bad that I can't tell him *It's okay, let me fucking die.*

It wouldn't be the worst thing... to go like this.

He lifts his arm and bites into his flesh. I watch wearily, hoping that he doesn't bleed out if he bites too deeply. His blood drips hot from his elbow and patters on my stomach as he sucks blood into his mouth.

Crimson streams down his chin as he cups my cheeks and presses his lips to mine.

For the briefest second it's a kiss. My eyes widen— have I *ever* kissed lips as soft as his? As crushing and warm...

His tongue slips into my mouth, coaxing it open, and then he pushes blood into me. It's hot and warms the back of my throat like liquid fire. I drink from Rune's lips and our auras seem to brush against one another. My very soul reacts to his and once the blood is down he pulls his head away and watches me like he felt the same sensation.

His blood instantly heals my ailments. Though there's a throb of hunger still deep inside me that calls for Eostrix blood, this will have to do for now. Fucking repulsion curse.

Tears wet the sides of my face. I can't really say why I'm crying. I just... I'm so fucking tired.

Of everything.

His crimson gaze softens as warmth returns to my lips and the dizzy fog clears from my mind. I try to blink away the remaining tears but they won't go. I slowly sit up, still in his lap, not quite ready to stand.

I'm not ready to be alone again.

His hand is instantly behind me, supporting me in case I need it. I look at him, our noses a mere inch apart. He's staring as intently at me as I am at him.

"*Rune.*" My voice cracks as I begin to let the tears fall.

He brings me into a tight hug and it's the start and end of every whisper from my heart that bleeds for this. Bleeds for him.

I cry in his arms as he rocks us slowly, his strong arms keeping me safe from everything horrible and dark in my reality. My mind threatens to slip into despair. I can't continue on this painful, pointless journey of—

A hum stirs out of Rune's throat.

My thoughts disappear. I'm so shocked by the hint of his voice, and honestly the fact that he is humming to me.

Goosebumps travel up my arms as he continues to rock us slowly. He's humming me a song. I listen intently to every vibration of his tune. It's quiet, but I can hear him. After the first verse, I catch on to the chorus and start to hum along with him.

His hands tighten on my skin, drawing my eyes to his. He smiles painfully at me, like seeing me in this state hurts him more than it does me. It's the first genuine smile he's given me and I'll never forget the way his beautiful lips curve so perfectly and the light that dances in his eyes.

It ruins me.

I hum a little louder, tears spilling and crashing on my

arms, and smile back at him. He leans his head against mine and we just exist like this for a while. A beautiful, dark while.

My kind, brooding, and sweet Dreadius.

Rune.

10

Arulius

The walk back to my manor is fucking desolate.

I don't know what I'm doing anymore. I can't focus on my duty and my bond with Elodie is constantly sending me gut-wrenching pain. Nights are the worst... I don't want to know what plagues her dreams and I'll never ask. I'm certain it's what I've done to her and the thought of that kills me.

I fly the rest of the way to my manor. The winter air bites me far worse when I'm in a shitty mood and fuck... the look in her eyes when I was going to just hold her. She thought I was going to hurt her again...

"Fuck!" I grit my teeth and fist my hair.

I land on the balcony of my room and don't waste a second walking in and throwing myself on my bed. I don't have the energy to even take my clothes off.

I stare at the ceiling and take in the silence.

I miss her so much. I know Violet moved her and put the blood repulsion in place for a good reason, but fuck... this feels like more a punishment for me than anything. I know it is. She has that prick Dreadius as her guard and she seems as enthralled with him as he does her. The way he looks at her... I press my hands into my hair, gripping tightly.

The way he stares at her is nothing short of Kastian all over again.

Violet's been furious with me for showing Elodie so much kindness. She's worried the past will repeat itself, but that's laughable.

I *never* make the same mistake twice.

I clench my jaw and release my hair. My face fucking hurts. That Dreadius can hit like a motherfucker. If I wasn't so tired I would have whooped his ass and thrown him in a cell... but that would break Elodie's heart, and I refuse make her feel any more of that pain and rage toward me.

Even if I hate Rune, I know he makes her feel things I've been yearning for her to have again. I let out a sigh and rub my cheek.

127

"Busy night?"

I flinch at Kol's voice and sit up to search the room. He drops his invisibility and the asshole is smiling at my bloody clothes. He's leaning in his usual spot against the glass doors leading to the balcony. His dark hair and brown eyes are hard to make out at night. Even his horns are midnight black.

I walk by him every fucking time and never notice he's there. Invisibility or not, I should sense his aura—I'm getting sloppy.

"What do you want?" I mumble and tug my shirt off, opening my dresser and finding a clean one.

He pushes off the wall and starts to mess with my medals atop the dresser. I swat his hands and growl. He's always been handsy when it comes to other people's things. I still think he's a thief.

He raises his hands. "Easy. Shit, *you're* in a mood. What happened?"

"Trust me, you don't want to know." I raise my hand to my cheek and heal it. The sting instantly fades and I take a breath to try and relax. I wanted to keep it a little longer to remind myself to stop being an overbearing dickhead, but I'd rather heal it myself than have Kol try to do it for me.

Kol crosses his arms. "Whatever. Did you find anything on Lucius in the glades?"

My wings hurt from flying to those fucking glades

every day. The search for the High Lady's long-lost love is a burden on all of Tomorrow. "No—of course not. No sign of the Death God there either. How about your search in the southlands?" I lie back down in my bed and put my arms behind my head, spreading my wings out to hopefully help them relax to prepare for tomorrow's flight.

"Nah, nothing down there either. Though I did see a fella riding on a Pine Hollow down by the coast." Kol thrums his fingers along the dresser and the sound annoys the living shit out of me, but the Hollow rider bit catches my interest.

"What did he look like?"

"Hmm? Oh, the rider... Well, he looked fit and wore civilian clothes. He rode the most beautiful Hollow I've ever seen. Looked a lot like the white one that protected the Life Goddess the night we took her."

I sit up and fist the blanket beneath me. "What was he doing?" Moro... That had to have been Moro, or Wren maybe. They've been silent for so long and I still don't really know what to expect when I face them again. Their friendships meant a lot to me and it burns a hole in my soul having to be a puppet for Violet.

It's better this way though. Let me be their villain... As long as they're all still breathing, I don't fucking care.

"He was coming out of some cave and that was it— disappeared into the forest right after."

I picture the region in my head and don't recall any

caves. Fuck—just when I thought I could rest. "Thanks, Kol. I'm going to go check it out. If Violet asks, just let her know I went back to the glades."

Kol dips his head and I don't wait for him to leave before I'm leaping off the balcony and into the cold night sky.

Whatever you guys are up to, just don't fucking come here... Not yet.

Don't make her force me to kill you.

11

Elodie

I'm busy gawking at Rune all day.

Since our moment together a few nights ago, I've been struggling to reel in the lustful thoughts I've been having for him. He protected me from Arulius's bruising grasp and fought for me.

Ten thousand points Rune—negative a million Arulius.

He leans against my wall, heartbreakingly handsome with his arms crossed over his chest.

He's not as refined and orderly as Arulius. I like that about him. His hair is always messy and he absolutely

131

refuses to wear guard attire. He is either in a slouchy sweater or hooded cloak most days. Rebellious as hell. I hope he never loses that part of him.

I didn't get to see Rune much yesterday—at first I thought he was still sleeping, but I saw red horns down in the streets beneath my window and it was him. He was with a group of other Dreadiuses, and seeing him with some of his own friends filled my heart with an ache for my own. He smiled and they shared food easily, beautiful women swooning over him the way I wish I could. They kissed his cheeks and tried to latch onto his arms.

It's easy to forget that I'm not the main character of everyone else's story, but gods, I wish I was one of his. Watching him live a normal life outside of being my guard hurt...

I've grown to really enjoy his presence. Whatever kind of relationship we've formed has surpassed what it should be—but maybe after I'm saved from this horrible place we can be *something*.

I tilt my head back and look at him from over my shoulder. He's boring holes through me again, as per usual.

"Rune, you don't have to watch me so closely, you know. I'm not going to try to sneak off to the library or anything. Don't you have anything else to do? It's your day off, right?" I stare out the window as creatures begin to gather below for the winter festival.

He doesn't reply—obviously.

"Why don't you go to the festival with your friends?" I turn to look at him. He smiled more easily with them than he does around me. It sucks because I'd like to think he enjoys my company as much as I do his, but I get it.

He's my guard—I'm his prisoner.

That's all we are, even if I get small glimpses of more...

These were the cards we'd been dealt.

He lowers his head and looks away coldly from me to stare at the corner where the floor and wall meet. I roll my eyes and think how I can get him to go have fun tonight. He deserves it.

I lean against the window, the glass cooling the skin on my back. "How about your brother then?"

He glances quickly at me and furrows his brow as an answer. Like I'm a damned fool for even thinking such absurdities. I agree, Kol is an asshole.

"Yeah, I figured as much." I chuckle softly.

I walk over to my bed, crawl to the center, and lie on my stomach. When he shifts his head to watch me, I pat the spot next to me for him to come sit. He pushes off the stone wall and sits next to me obediently.

I roll to my back and let out a sigh. He leans over a bit so that his head is in my view. Dark hair falls over his forehead. His crimson eyes remind me so much of Violet's, but his are kinder, deeper. I've learned this in our time together and I've grown really fucking attached somehow.

Our eyes lock for a silent few minutes and when he doesn't falter the least bit, I have to pull my eyes away and look at his tattooed neck instead. I study his scar again.

"Why don't you talk?"

It's something I've been wanting to ask for a while now. I think it's probably a touchy subject, because why wouldn't it be.

He just shrugs a shoulder and frowns.

"Were you born without a voice?" He shakes his head slowly, never breaking his gaze. My cold heart thumps at his admittance. "Does it have something to do with your scar?" He doesn't answer, but I can see the sorrow in his soul. Shit—I shouldn't have asked. Subject change.

"You don't deserve this, you know, being my blood bag."

His brows crease, telling me he disagrees, I think.

"No one deserves to be my guard *and* blood bag. It's degrading for you. I think you should go enjoy the festival tonight. There's got to be a girl out there you've been crushing on." I raise a brow in hope for him.

He lets out a quick breath with a tight smirk and shakes his head easily.

"Really? I mean, you're quiet, sure—but you've got a handsome face, Rune." His jaw flexes and his eyes explore down my body in return.

Oh—I like that.

I try to think of something that will get him to leave.

He really should go enjoy the festival. Gods know he would have a little fun if he did.

"If you stay... I'm going to feed on you." When his eyes flick back to mine they're nothing but sure. He gives me a curt nod.

What the hell—I was kidding!

"Rune, I—" He presses his hand over my lips roughly, silencing me. I quirk a brow at him but he keeps his palm over my mouth for a few moments longer before leaning back against the pillows, pulling his sweater over his head.

Oh fuck, oh fuck.

I tighten my lips with the view. His body is perfect. His muscles are taut and each dip in his abs has my tongue swirling hungrily in my mouth. Dark tattoos cover his entire torso and my eyes linger at his pant line. He tosses his sweater past me, and as the fabric flies by my head I catch the scent of him. His actual scent—not just the thick metallic blood.

Roses.

He smells like the crimson flowers drowned in a pool of blood. I instinctively bring my arm up to my nose to lessen his aroma.

He's fucking intoxicating and there's no way I can control myself. I want to bury my teeth deep into his neck and feed on him for eternity.

He keeps his red eyes on mine and taps his neck, leaving his hand on his throat as if he's taunting me.

I shake my head, swallowing hard. "No, Rune. I'm not going to drink your blood. I'm not going to do what Violet wants. We both know she's only doing this to hurt me, and you... you *don't* want this."

He grunts at me with furrowed brows and taps his artery once more. I scowl at him and stand at the edge of bed. The bastard won't tell me what to do.

As I'm stepping away, he grips my arm and pulls me back to him. My eyes widen and my cry gets stuck somewhere in my throat as he lifts me by my waist like I'm weightless and places me easily on his lap so I'm straddling him. Heat curls in my center.

"Rune, I won't—"

He cups the back of my neck and holds my head so my lips press against his skin. His other arm wraps gently behind my lower back, holding me securely. Roses assault my senses and I choke on the urge to bury my fucking teeth into him. Why am I so drawn to his essence? His blood calls to me unlike anything else in Tomorrow.

I won't do it. Not to Rune.

Memories of Kastian and Arulius flood me. Wren too. My males that so willingly let me have their blood.

I try pushing away, but he's too strong. My wings are trapped beneath his arm and my struggling does nothing against this brute. After a few long minutes of fighting, I tire and slump in his arms, exhausted.

"Fuck you, Rune." I clench my teeth. His artery is so

close to my lips, I can already taste everything that he has to offer and I'm salivating like a wild animal.

He coaxes me softly, making me still in his embrace.

Every time he touches me like this my heart claws through my flesh, screaming to be freed from the cage I keep it in.

My breaths are short against his neck. He moves his hand in small, languid motions on my back while the one, cupping my neck, massages my tense muscles.

My brows scrunch and lips quiver. He's a kind creature, so gentle and calming, so opposite his appearance. Listening to all my shit while never having the chance to speak what he wants.

It breaks my cold heart.

It breaks it because I would've cared more, once upon a time, when my soul wasn't completely shattered by another love. I can never trust him like I once did Arulius.

I won't let myself trust anyone *ever* again. Right? My mind says yes, but my heart begs me to give it another go.

Gods.

But with him touching me so intimately, I can feel the first cord of warmth pulse through my weary chest. I lean into him and rest my cheek on his shoulder. His breath hitches for a moment, only a moment, and then he tilts his head so it's resting against mine.

What the fuck are we doing? We can promise nothing but pain to one another.

We stay like this, in a silent treaty of hearts and comfort, for a few minutes before he's laying us down. His back presses softly into the bed and I lift myself up enough over him to meet his eyes, my thighs on each side of his hips.

His crimson gaze pierces heavily into me, taking in my expressions. I watch him just as closely, letting myself be vulnerable in this moment.

He taps his neck once more like it's an order.

I furrow my brow but can feel myself already giving into him. "I can last longer. I don't need blood tonight. Please, Rune... please just go to the festival." I push up enough to look at him. "At least *one* of us should have fun and... truly live. One of us should be happy... and I want it to be you." I try to give him my warmest smile but his gaze softens enough that I know he sees right through me.

His palm finds my cheek and I lean into the affection. It's been so long since I've received any sort of affection. Well, affection that I'm willing to accept. It's the one thing I find more painful than death—time.

The endless suffering that time places on a soul. Being immortal will prove to be painfully brutal, because all I can think about are the ones I once loved and the way they loved me. Never to relive such warm, innocent experiences again. Not with them.

I open my eyes and my heart stops.

Rune's smiling at me, actually smiling at me, and it's

crushing. It's such a rare thing. I take it in. His beautiful lips curve so somberly. But it's in his eyes that I find the true smile he *is* happy. I try to find any sort of doubt in them but come up empty.

"You don't want to go to the festival?"

He shakes his head.

"You don't want to live and be happy? Fuck the pretty Dreadiuses that I see swooning over you?"

Another shake and a small scowl.

I smirk but hesitate. "You're happy enough... spending your time here with someone like me?" I glance away, not sure I want to see his expression when he nods or shakes his head. But he guides my face back to his and I'm met with soft rose petals in his gaze.

They don't look like the blood or death I once saw in them—they don't send shivers up my spine or curl my stomach.

No, instead they cushion my fall back into my heart, sending me straight through the bars I spent so long securing up.

He nods curtly, our noses a breath apart.

He's happy here with me? I've been nothing but trouble for him.

I bite my lip to stop the squall in my mind. Tears drop from my chin and crash on his cheeks. I don't know why I'm crying. Maybe all this shit has finally caught up to me... I'm just so fucking tired and thinking too much. I can't shake the ominous feeling that doom will follow if I indulge with him.

Rune slips his hand behind my neck once more and tugs me down to his. My ebony hair falls around us and I no longer want to fight this.

I lick the skin above his artery gently, running my tongue from his collarbone to the tender place behind his ear. His breaths are getting shorter and I can hear the pounding of his heart. He's scared, and fuck, I am too.

My teeth pierce into him and I bury my fangs to the hilt in his flesh.

He flinches under me at the feral bite, but quickly relaxes once the initial pain fades. I give him a moment to adjust before pulling his ambrosial rose blood into me. The second his crimson hits my tongue I'm moaning at the flavor of him. He's absolutely inebriating.

I've only had small sips here and there and never really got to enjoy all that is *him*. Dreadiuses taste so fucking good—who would have thought? Heat spills into my core and there's so much more than just his blood that I want. I wish his blood could fill that void that has opened within me from the lack of Arulius's blood though.

I pull harder from him and he clenches his arms around my back as a tight breath slips past his lips. His pelvis juts up to dig further into mine and his cock is so fucking hard already. Gods be damned, I'm dripping wet for him too. He grinds against me as his hands push me down roughly for friction.

I release his neck as his dick strokes my clit beneath my thin leggings and cry out before biting into him once more. The pressure of the bite has him groaning loudly against my ear and I'm not sure how we'll be able to keep our hands off each other at this point. I don't want to.

I rock my hips against his attention-seeking boner and he places his hands on each cheek of my ass while he helps me along.

Fuck. Me.

Seriously.

I pull my teeth out and lick his neck clean. Sitting up, I place both of my palms on his broad, tattooed chest. Him sweaty and panting beneath me is the sexiest thing I've ever seen. His red eyes are narrowed on me with desire. My pussy is pulsing for him and I'm not going to deny it. It's been weeks since I've had any pleasure.

His eyes widen as the effects of the feeding fade. His cheeks bloom with a red blush and his eyes clear from the arousal that was burning there. Rune's hands slow their rocking and I let out a whine in protest.

"You don't want me?"

He turns his head and stares at the blank wall. It's not a no, but it isn't a fucking yes either. Wow—can't say I've ever been denied like that before.

Embarrassment fills my core and I'm ashamed that I

thought it was anything but the feeding frenzy. Of course it wouldn't be anything else. I'm an Eostrix and he's a Dreadius. I'm the fucking prisoner here and he's my guard. What the hell was I thinking? That he actually wanted me?

I press my hand to my forehead and sigh. "I'm sorry, Rune. I'm not feeling like myself... You can go now."

I roll off him and lie on my back, staring at the ceiling as the sounds of the festival come to life outside. I shut my eyes and listen to the laughter and joy of so many unspecial spirits and gods. I wish I could join them and be a normal person doing normal things.

I want to be unimportant.

The bed shifts and I don't bother looking at Rune as he stands. I can't bring myself to meet his gaze. I'd rather not make myself feel any more unwanted than I already do. Rejection sucks and I'm a poor sport.

He taps my leg, but I wave him off. "Get out, Rune. I'm tired."

Another tap.

I run my hand through my hair and fist a handful. What the fuck doesn't he understand?

I sit up and glare at him. "I said get the fuck out!"

He watches me closely with a dark scowl, his sweater flung over his shoulder and arms crossed over his sculpted chest. What the hell does he want? Another rush of laughter rings outside and music starts up. My heart aches at the thought of what the festival is like. I just want to sleep. It's better than feeling any of the things that I've felt tonight.

Rune urges me to stand by tugging on my wrist but I rip it out of his hand. He glares back at me and for a second I wonder who will win this battle of wills.

I shake my head. "*Please...* just go."

He huffs and I damn near laugh at his stubbornness tonight. What's gotten into him?

He reaches down and plucks me up from the sheets, earning him a few kicks and scratches from me. He doesn't even flinch as I struggle. Once by my dresser, he sets me down and opens the top drawer.

Oh gods. That's my underwear drawer.

The second he sees the lace and undergarments his face turns red and he shuts it quickly. I kick up the corner of my lips at what he's doing.

He opens the second one down and pulls out a fresh pair of leggings and tosses them over my head. I tug the fabric down in time to watch him open my closet and select a red dress, a flowy short one that was another hand-me-down from Naminé. It matches his eyes perfectly.

My heart throbs painfully, sending another unwanted warm pulse through its cold abandoned chambers. Why is he picking out clothes for me? He knows as well as I do that we aren't allowed to step foot in the festival.

Rune locks his gaze with mine and walks over to me, holding the dress out so I can see it. I shake my head.

"You know I can't go," I say in a painful whisper.

He shakes the dress and nods.

"*No.*" I grab it from him and throw the leggings and dress on the floor. "Violet has eyes everywhere. I won't have you reprimanded for it." I swing back toward the window and watch as people below celebrate and dance to the music. String lights connect each cottage and create the perfect ambiance for this cheerful night.

Rune's steps creak as he approaches from behind. I ignore him and continue to gaze melancholily down at the court. His front presses against my back and I let out a short breath of surprise.

Since when has he been this intimate? Whether he wants me or not, at least he's trying to show me that he cares... and I'm not sure what to do with that sentiment.

He turns me to face him and he's holding the dress and leggings once more. I let out a long, drawn-out sigh. He just won't give up. I consider my options.

I can either try to knock him out or see what his plan is.

I size him up and he seems to pick up on my plan. He smirks and grabs each of my wrists and pushes me against the wall. He's so strong I can't move either of my arms.

"What the fuck are you doing?" I snarl at him.

He responds by raising a brow and waiting for me to admit defeat.

"Okay, fine—I won't try to knock you out."

Rune nods and smirks again as he releases me. He's strong—no wonder he was able to get two hits in on Arulius. Then again, I suppose Violet wouldn't have assigned him as my guard for no reason. He has his uses, I suppose.

Two can play at this game.

I slide my drenched leggings down and step out of the soaked underwear, leaving them on the floor for him to see. His jaw drops and his eyes flick to my naked lower half. I laugh as I walk to the dresser and grab a fresh pair of panties.

"See what you did to me, Rune? Keep up the charade of being a nice and caring brute and you *just might* fuck me over like Arulius did." I can't help saying it—even though I know it's not fair to him. He hasn't done anything to me... yet.

His gaze lingers a few moments longer before he meets my eyes. I can't help but smile. He's braver than a lot of the other males, that or extra confident.

I get dressed and admire myself in the mirror. The crimson dress flows beautifully with my curves. My cream-colored wings nearly touch the floor now and my ears and horns match their hue. I don't miss the dark circles under my honey-toned eyes, but I still look presentable to some degree.

Rune steps from behind me and I catch his smile in the mirror. Our eyes connect and my broken organ thumps hard in its cage.

12

Elodie

I can't believe we're doing this. I stop at the edge of the stones as we peer out into the snowy, string-lit streets.

"You know what, I change my mind. This is stupid and I shouldn't have let you talk me into it." I'm whirling around to charge back to my room but Rune blocks me. A sly smirk crosses his lips.

Oooh, a rule-breaker we have here.

He pulls my hood up and does the same with his. I scoff at his audacity but can't help but giggle.

"Come on—this isn't going to work, Rune. We look like bandits, for gods' sakes."

His smile stretches and the amusement reaches his eyes. Bastard.

Warm light swells around us as Rune's red aura wraps around me. I almost yelp but manage to catch myself before giving our hiding spot away. "What the hell are you doing?" My eyes widen at his power. I have to admit, I've not a clue what Dreadiuses are capable of (besides the blood tears—that was fucking crazy). I still need to read those books I found, but it's been hard to focus with the festival preparations going on for days now.

His eyes close and the light consumes us completely. I shut my eyes when I'm nearly blinded and have to blink twice when I reopen them to find nothing has changed.

I quirk a brow at him, knowing he can't verbally explain but still expecting an answer regardless. Rune steps into the street, boots crunching the snow beneath his feet, and reaches a hand for me to follow.

He looks too relaxed. I know he did *something* with that light show.

"What did you do?" I cross my arms.

Rolling his eyes, Rune steps over to a group of Eostrixes and waves right in one of their faces. I almost turn and run; I'm not getting fucking caught out here. I feel like a teenager sneaking out past curfew, godsdamn it. But I think better of it and wait to see how this pans out.

Wait. Did he just roll his eyes at *me*?!

It takes a few seconds to process all that just happened. But then it registers that the Eostrix can't see him.

"Are we... invisible?" My breath curls in the brisk night air.

That damning smile returns and he reaches his hand out once more for me to come to him. The world around us seems to glow a little brighter, the snow falling a little slower. My heart pounds hard in my chest.

He wants to be here... with me.

I slowly step to meet him, my cold hand lifting to find his warm one, and when they connect my skin comes alive. He smiles and leads the way.

I'm walking down the streets of Nesbrim freely for the first time in... well, ever. I've never been the invisible girl who can stuff her face with hot rolls and just admire the world unnoticed.

"Hey, I've been meaning to ask you." Rune doesn't turn his head toward me but side-eyes me. "Where did you get your tattoos? I really want to get one, if that's a thing they do here in Tomorrow."

His eyes light up and a wicked grin crosses his lips. I furrow my brows. "What?"

He waves at me dismissively and shakes his head, the grin remaining on his lips and giving me goosebumps. All right—we'll circle back to that later, I guess.

At first I'm a little nervous that someone will see through his ability to cloak us, but my fears tamp down as we continually pass beautiful creatures in their festival wear, women in gorgeous blue winter dresses and men in brilliant silver suits.

String lights cross overhead, attaching to the sides of the second-story cottage balconies. Large snowflakes fall past them with a beautiful orange glow. If snow can be warm, this is it.

I glance at Rune. He's eyeing the food stand with hot rolls of honey bread, and for a moment—a beautiful, stupid, and unreasonable moment—the world slows.

He flicks his crimson eyes to me, excited to show me the food stand or something I couldn't give less of a shit about it right now, because there's only him.

There's only him, holding my hand and smiling at me like nothing else has ever mattered, dressed in his gray sweater and dark pants, snow melting red on his horns.

He catches my dreaming eyes, raising a brow.

I shake my head. "I would *love* to get some honey rolls."

We have to take them secretly and pay by leaving the money in the merchant's back pocket. It's hard not to laugh at our mischief and we each eat three. Okay—I have four.

Rune just looks at me with a smile that actually reaches his eyes. We find a quiet spot in the alley off of the main street and enjoy our rolls as we watch the elegantly dressed creatures dance. Beautiful music with an uplifted beat travels through the streets. A midnight lullaby with a whisper of morning. Music unlike any I've ever heard before, but it seems to reach my bones. I wonder if Talia remembers these songs.

Beautiful women take their places alongside the men. Eostrixes dance with their own, Moss Sparrows, and Dreadiuses alike. I take a sharp breath and hold it as the music quiets and the figures stop on cue.

I nearly turn my head to ask Rune what's going on as he scoots in close to me, his thighs pushed up against mine. My cheeks heat and—fuck it—I'm going to pretend like I don't notice. I don't know when I became shy around him, but I try not to think about it too much.

The music starts back up again and the string lights get a bit brighter as the snow slows and the dancers lift into a beautiful toss across the cobblestones, Eostrixes opening their wings to catch the air as they spin around their partners with grace.

My breath gets caught in my throat.

Rune stands at my side and my eyes widen as he offers me his hand. I glance up to meet his gaze and his crimson eyes are gentle. A smile pulls at the corner of his mouth and he nods his head over to the ethereal beings dancing.

My heart leaps as I take his hand. I fight the warmth that swells within me as he guides me to the dancing creatures. I know we're invisible, but my stomach still churns as we take our places in the center of the street. Swoops of royal blue and silver flicker around us like waves of magic, frolicking with the snow and lights to a melancholic tune.

A lump forms in my throat as Rune slides his hands down my wrist and threads our fingers together, a mischievous grin pulling on his lips.

"I don't know how to dance," I whisper, never letting my eyes leave his as he draws me in closer. He simply shakes his head like it doesn't matter, and the lump in my throat grows.

The song changes and at once, on cue, the Eostrixes spread their wings and cast a beautiful array of their auras. Pink, silver, blue, sage, and yellow all twirl around the air like glittering dust. The cold air tantalizes my breath, which fogs in the sky.

This is *exhilarating*. A smile beams from my face as I glance back to Rune. He's looking at me like I'm the beginning and the end, like he's never seen a sight so enthralling. With the way his red eyes shimmer in the auras and snow, the way he tilts his head just enough to tell me he's fascinated by me, he lets me know I'm looking at him the same way.

I want to say so many things to him, but I keep my lips pressed in a firm line as the pain of my last heart wrench reminds me that I can't let myself be pulled into another's arms so helplessly again.

Rune raises a brow to let me know he noticed my shift, but instead of frowning or trying to retreat he squeezes my hand a little tighter and wraps his other arm around my waist. The song picks up and all the bodies around us start moving as one.

I stare at my crimson Dreadius with awe as he moves easily to the song. He can dance? I never would've pinned him as one to move so rhythmically. My heart's racing, and though I'm no doubt the worst fucking dancer in all Tomorrow, my feet find their step with his and after a few verses of the song we're completely in sync.

I let out a breathy laugh as the excitement builds within me and Rune's smile grows larger as the song picks up into a cheery and happy beat. He releases my hands and I'm stunned for a moment before he starts twirling along with everyone else. They raise their hands and clap along with the beat and it's so enthralling and sweeping that I join in too.

By the time the last of the song fades from the sky, I'm sweating and breathing hard. My cheeks hurt from the laughs Rune pulled from me. He bows along with all the other male beings and offers me his hand once more.

As I look down on him and his heated eyes peer up at me, I see a flicker of something I really don't want to see.

For one moment, just one, he's Arulius, his eyes filled with hope and affection for all the things we *could* be.

Like we could ever be unburdened by our fate. Before the revelation, before everything.

My heart sinks in my chest as the feathers of the airborne Eostrixes flutter, whirling the snow like falling white flakes in a glass globe.

Rune furrows his brows as my expression sullens. I wish Kastian were here.

As I'm reminiscing, ebony and gold feathers flick across the crowd in the corner of my eye and my very soul stills.

Kastian?

I'm moving through the crowd before the thought even wisps across my consciousness. The stillness in the air is tangible.

It's him.

It has to be him.

Hot tears roll down my cheeks as I surge forward, desperately needing to see him. To touch him, to smell him, to feel him. Anything. I'll fucking take anything I can get, because all of my suffering has finally meant something. Goosebumps break out across my skin as I run through the street.

My Death God has come back for me. In this life.

He's here to save me.

My breath curls in the air and my fingers are numb from the rush of excitement. I stumble a few times, but quickly find my footing again.

It's him. Kastian—I've waited for you. I've dreamed of you, lives that we've lived together and spent countless days keeping the realms in tandem.

I've—

Pain pierces my heart. Unblinking, I stare at the horror before me.

The absolute shit show of a sight.

Bile reaches up my throat and a hammer smashes my broken organ—the sad excuse for a heart that I've managed to half put back together turns into dust.

Kastian's pearly smile is beautiful, so painfully and perfectly fucking beautiful. It's him—it's really him.

So why the fuck are his ocean eyes placed on Violet?

Her laugh is so loud and annoying, I swear blood could drip from my ears any second now.

How... could he?

My eyes skirt the festival in the hope Wren and Moro are here too, waiting on the sidelines to save me or something. Because this is too evil, right? Too twisted. I should've kept my broken heart the shattered mess it already was.

The soft hand landing on my shoulder makes my shoulders tense. I turn to find Rune watching me. Fucking gods, I'm not in the mood.

He quirks a brow with concern as he follows the direction I'm looking and finds Violet next to the dark-winged Eostrix. I have no doubt in my mind he knows exactly who he is, because his eyes flicker for a moment before returning to me.

"What is he doing here? And don't you fucking bull-shit me, Rune." My voice is dripping with venom, my stolen power humming in a war against Arulius's chains. I know he can feel it because he takes a step back and considers me before shaking his head.

"I'm sick of the *'I can't talk'* shit. I'm done being nice and I'm fucking done with—with everything!" I scream in his face before sprinting down the cobblestone streets.

I'm already feeling guilty for saying that to him. So fucking stupid—but honestly, I don't give a rat's ass right now. I need to get away from everyone.

From everything.

I run until the lights from the festival are fading and the snow gets thicker on the unshoveled outer streets. I can't tell if I'm still invisible or not, but I'm thankful every single person is celebrating. I'm completely alone out here and the snow falls silently, quelling my warring emotions.

At the north wall, I finally come to a stop, staring up at the closed gates and wondering if I'll ever step foot outside them again... Would it matter? My mind is whirling trying to figure out who I can trust. Kastian wouldn't pull an Arulius, would he? But he's here at the festival, cele-brating with the woman who's been draining my blood daily.

Torturing me for months...

Wait.

If everyone, including Violet, is at the festival, this might be the only chance I get to get into her blood storage room or whatever the hell is down there.

I grit my teeth. If I have to continue existing I might as well harden the fuck up and figure out a way to kill this bitch.

No more waiting.

No more mercy. No friends. I can do this myself.

I hear the crunch of snow behind me and already know who's followed me.

I breathe out a sigh. I don't know if he will help me go against his High Lady or not, but I'm not missing this chance. No fucking way.

Spinning on my heel, I nearly face-plant into the male. I severely misjudged how close he was standing.

"Shit, Rune, why are you standing right—"

"Love, is that you?"

Arulius?! Oh, gods. Can he see me? I clasp my hand over my mouth but I know he already heard me. He's looking just over my head—that means he can't see me. He followed my footprints?

Shit.

Okay, it's fine. I can still salvage this. If I can just get to the court, then he won't be able to see footprints and I can uncover what Violet is really doing down in her chamber.

Arulius's golden wings shiver, releasing the snow from atop them. His amethyst eyes search the space in front of him for me. My chest heats with our bond, warming just at the sight of him, but I push the feelings away. The bond feels weaker somehow, easier to sidestep.

"I know it's you, love. Let's get you back to your room before Violet realizes you've ventured out." His hand aims forward, trying to find me, but I leap back and sprint down the alleyway to my left. He lets out a low laugh. "As if you could hide, love. Come on, don't make me chase you."

Fuck him.

I'm sprinting through the foot-deep snow as fast as I can and thanking the gods the bottom layer hasn't iced over or I'd already be eating shit by now. Arulius is hot on my heels, but I've played chase in Nesbrim before.

My lips curve up with the memories of my Cypress chasing me. I feel so alive. The winter air stings my lungs and the scent of the mildewy stones rushes over me. This is worth it. Even if I get in trouble, this is worth it.

I take a few familiar turns before the court comes into view. A very disgruntled-looking Rune waits at the front entrance of the court.

Just my luck.

He instantly sees me and then I'm guessing sees Arulius, because his scowl disappears and is replaced with shock. I dare a look back and see the golden Eostrix pursuing me eagerly, hunger in his eyes.

I don't slow. My heart leaps as I approach Rune. I don't know if he's going to grab me or let me run by. His crimson gaze doesn't hold an inch of resentment for me as our eyes connect. I pass him easily, and the second I hit the inner walls of the court I strip my boots off before Arulius can enter.

My socks are wet and my toes instantly freeze against the cold tiles. I tiptoe as quietly as I can toward the torture chamber off to the right.

Arulius crashes in, Rune hot on his heels—apparently invisible still, since Arulius doesn't notice him. Gods, I need to apologize to him. He's the best guard ever. Even after I cussed him out like a bitch.

I clear my mind to focus on the plan. I know Rune can see me, but he lingers around Arulius—to keep an eye on him, I'm assuming.

After I'm sure Arulius went down the wrong corridor, I slip into the large, empty torture room. The tiles are still stained with my blood in the center near the drain. A shiver crawls up my spine and I try to shake it out. The moonlight and warm glow from the festival lights trickle in through the floor-to-ceiling windows along the far wall.

Ugh, I hate this place.

I don't waste any time and swiftly move to try the small door in the corner of the room where I've watched

Violet take my blood for months. I'm surprised to find it's not locked—wow, bold to believe in your guards this much. This is next-level stupid.

I find spiral stairs made of stones as I pass the door. I follow them down until I feel the walls themselves caving in on me. It's suffocating down here and the scent of blood stings my nose. The walls are wet and it smells moldy down here.

After having nearly three panic attacks in the dark, tight stairs from hell, I make it to another door at the bottom. I push it open slowly, peeking just in case I'm not the only late visitor tonight.

It's pitch black. I can't see a fucking thing.

The door creaks silently and stale air pushes past me, smelling of mildew and old stones. My nose wrinkles with the intrusion.

I hold out my hand and focus my aura into my palm. A warm glow lights the room, dim like candlelight. I don't waste another second as I search for anything that will help me figure out what the hell Violet is doing down here.

There's nothing out of the ordinary. It's a creepy, decrepit basement.

Dust is thick along the untouched tables. Items are stored underneath them and empty bottles and rags are spread across the floor. I walk further toward the back until my light touches the far walls, and then stop in front of something with a blanket over it.

My blood chills as I stare down at the small mound before me. Something in my bones is screaming at me —*this is it.*

I hesitate, but fist my hands at my sides to steady myself. I *have* to do this.

The blanket isn't dusty at all, so Violet must be moving it every time we have our sessions. I lift it slowly and clench my teeth as I turn to the side, careful to not let the blanket touch any of the dust around me.

When I glance back, my heart stops.

What the fuck.

A crimson skull and handful of horrid bones rest in a bowl of dark blood.

13

Elodie

Of all the shit I've seen, I swear to gods this is
by *far* the worst.

It's bleeding—the skull is fucking
bleeding and thick veins curl around its crimson surface. I
can see them pulsing, supplying the long-dead god with
blood... but for fuck's sake, why?

I take a step back, unable to look away, but my insides
are screaming at me to run. My throat squeezes as I try to
hold back my dinner.

Why is Violet feeding my blood to... whoever this is?

I try to study the skull for any identifying aspects, but

the only thing that is remotely unique are the sharp teeth. They're like shark teeth. I've certainly not met a creature here with those features.

All right, got what I came here for, time to get the fuck out.

I toss the blanket back on the disturbing skull-blood soup and spin to leave.

Of. Fucking. Course. Rune is leaning against the doorframe with his arms crossed. Watching me with that unreadable face he's so good at keeping. There's no way he saw the skull with me holding the blanket and my body blocking his view. He doesn't seem to acknowledge what's behind me either. His eyes are only on me.

I try to keep my shit together, but I know I can't keep the same straight face he does.

After a silent two minutes of staring at one another, waiting to see who will move first, I decide to take the lead.

Fuck this. I'm just going to go back up to my room. Obviously Rune won't tell on me, he literally helped me run from Arulius and allowed me to come down here, so I'll rat his ass out too if he so much as—

Rune steps in front of the doorway, blocking me from exiting the basement. His metallic rose scent floods my nose instantly.

"Are you kidding me right now, Rune? This basement is creepy as hell. Let me through," I snarl at him, fury in my eyes. I'm ready to hit the bastard in the chest when he moves on me.

My eyes widen as he pushes me against the cold walls, placing his arms on either side of my head. Our eyes lock and that broken organ of mine is trying so hard to reach for his.

I study his gaze, searching for anything he'll give me, and unfortunately I find what I'm searching for... A deep fire burns in his eyes.

Really? *Now* he wants to fuck?

I can do physical stuff—love it, in fact. As long as my messy, bleeding heart stays the hell away.

His eyes dip down to my lips and he lets out a low hum, slipping his bottom lip between his teeth as if he's holding himself back from devouring me.

Dreadius is on the table tonight and I'm fucking starving.

I give him a loose smile and spread my legs a bit. He immediately notices and glances down, color filling his cheeks. I slide my hands underneath his shirt and find his taut stomach.

I wrap my arms around him and bring him close, until our chests are touching and I can hear his blood pulsing under his skin. My mouth waters, but I focus on truly enjoying him this time and not feeding. I bring my lips to the shell of his ear and whisper, "It's your turn to eat me."

The feeling of a male twice the size of you shuddering

at your words is another kind of sexy. My pussy throbs the second I feel the goosebumps raise his skin and his heart losing its steady thrum.

He presses his lips against my skin and—fuck—I just want to melt at the feel of him. My skin is coming to life with his touch and all I want is more.

Rune bites into my shoulder, making me hiss out in pain, but he quickly soothes it with a caress of his tongue. *Don't tempt me, motherfucker.* I'm eyeing his artery as we speak.

I continue to explore his chest while he presses kisses down my neck. His hand slide up my bare thigh, easily pushing away my thong as he slips into my wet folds.

"Fuck," he groans quietly on an exhale as he shoves his fingers into me. My pussy is already convulsing and he hums with delight, but my mind instantly snaps to the fact that *he just spoke.*

I jolt and try to look at him, but he presses his body into me so I can't move. His fingers pump into me unforgivingly and fill my core with the pleasure I've been needing.

"Rune! Y-you can talk?!" I struggle against him again to try to look at his beautiful face, desperate to see his lips say my name, but to no avail.

He slides his fingers out of me and starts to rub my clit. My core lights up and I'm grinding against his hand for the friction while he forces the moans from me. He keeps the pressure just right on my sensitive nub until I'm on the verge of an orgasm, but he slips his fingers back into me before I hear his beautiful voice again.

"Only when we are connected, pup. When we are one."

Oh, fuck me. My pussy convulses and grips his finger, sucking it like a starved bitch. "Th-that doesn't m-make any sense."

For all that is holy. I thought the bond between Eostrixes was a kink. Being able to talk to my silent guard only when he's inside me?

Next. Level.

He pulls his fingers from me and picks me up like I don't weigh a damn thing. My red dress isn't very long and my thong isn't enough to cover me fully, so I'm spread against his stomach while he carries me up the spiral staircase. I'm entirely aware of my slick juices running down my ass.

I clutch him tightly with both arms around his neck. Our noses touch as he effortlessly carries us to the torture room. I'm anxious at first because, gods, I've had my throat slit here more times than I can count.

Rune carries me confidently into the darkness of my despair. His lips find mine and his tongue enters my mouth. He's kissing me so deeply and it's taking everything I have to keep my heart out of it.

"Elodie."

"Yeah?" I mumble against his lips. His voice is beautiful and deep in my mind. I keep my eyes closed as I crave to hear it again.

"Do you trust me?"

My soul curls at his question.

I pull my lips from his quickly. His crimson eyes are soft as they take in every expression on my face.

"No. I don't," I deadpan.

I don't hesitate. Not after last time. Elodie the stupid Goddess of Life and Dawn is *not* going to be fucked again.

He nods in understanding, kissing me once more. *"I would be disappointed if you did."*

I moan against his lips at that admittance. He understands and isn't upset that I don't trust him.

My drop of blood in the snow. What you do to me.

He sets us down on the tile floors. The four moons light the entire room magnificently. His dark hair sweeps over his forehead and his three crimson horns bow to the moonlight.

His blood eyes devour me. Though in this pale light they are more black, they still pierce through me just as easily.

He lays me on my back and I arch at the sting of the cold floor. Rune's kissing my chest before I can even look back at him. He tries pulling my dress down to expose my breasts but it doesn't give. A low growl rumbles through his chest and I almost squeal as he tears the fabric, leaving me in only my thong.

"Hey—this is the only nice dress I have!" I scowl at him but his attention is on my tits. His lips take in my plump breast, rolling his tongue across my nub. His fingers tease my folds before slipping inside me.

Okay—fuck the dress.

"You taste like dusted sunshine—dawn itself. Did you know that?"

I'm about to say *how the fuck would I know that* but he bites my tit, making me yelp before he smoothes it over with his tongue.

Gods help me.

He moves down my stomach until he's positioned between my thighs. I want him inside me so fucking bad but I'll let him really taste me first.

Dusted sunshine, my ass—sweet words can't win me like they once did. Though I am a sucker for his voice, be it telepathic or whatever his ability is to speak without his lips.

I suck in a breath as he circles my clit with his tongue. Pleasure drips from my pussy as my back arcs. It's hard to keep my thighs from crushing his head because he is fucking devouring me. He grips each of my thighs and holds me open and my eyes roll to the back of my head.

He's worshiping his goddess, and I'll make him do this every day from here on out.

"Fuck, Rune," I pant. He's teasing my entrance but not giving me what I need. I want to be filled by his dick but for gods' sakes, at least give me something.

"You want to come, pup?"

My broken organ wants to break out of my chest and embrace every part of this and his deep voice as it echoes in my mind. *Pup...*

"Yes." I try to grind my hips to get more friction from him, but he holds me down firmly.

"Then you're going to have to beg." He stops altogether, and the pain of being so close to coming but robbed from the release pisses me off. He looks up at me, crimson eyes filled with desire to hear me beg for it.

Am I really going to do this?

"Please—Rune, please."

"Please what?" His eyes don't flicker as he waits patiently, still teasing my pussy with his finger.

"Rune! Please make me come, please." I fist his hair and push his stupid, beautiful face back down to finish me off. His laugh rumbles through his chest but I can only hear the lovely sound in my mind. I shut my eyes, burying myself in the sound of it.

He does exactly what I asked, thank gods. Rune laps at my clit like a starved man and plunges his fingers back into me, groaning at the slickness. *"Fuck, Elodie. You're so tight for me."* I'm spiraling higher and higher until finally I come so hard I can feel my pussy grabbing

169

him. I wish it was his dick instead, filling me up with his seed.

Rune smiles from between my legs as he laps up every last bit of my juices. I'm fucking vibrating from what he just did to me. Where did he learn to worship a woman like that? I'm already mad at every woman he's ever touched.

I rise to my elbows, seeing my shredded red dress around us. Great. He'd better hope we're still invisible or I'll fucking thrash him. Before I can make the effort to stand, he's crawling over me, and I'd be a liar if I said my eyes didn't immediately flick to his engorged dick.

My mouth's watering at the sight, wanting to take him and make him come down my throat. The corner of his lip kicks up before he kisses me, the tip of him pressing on my entrance. I'm excited to feel a Dreadius fill me.

"On your knees, pup."

Don't have to tell me twice. I'm on my knees in a second and he stands, his dick lined up with my lips. I glance up at him and he's watching me—always watching me.

But now it's all I've ever wanted, his eyes on only me as I take his thick cock between my lips.

I'm not sure I can get him all the way in. I lick his flesh as I pump his shaft before I take him fully. He instantly throws his head back and moans, his hand gripping the back of my head as he starts to fuck my mouth.

Gods.

His dick hits the back of my throat and my eyes start watering as I take him deep and hard, choking on his thickness. I hollow my cheeks to suck him harder and glance up at him.

His crimson eyes are hooded, focused on me. *"What a good girl you are. You want my seed in your mouth, pup? Like a good girl, you'd better swallow it."*

I moan on his dick, desperate for air. I did *not* imagine him having this filthy of a mouth, but it only makes me want him more. He pumps harder and faster as he fucks my mouth and then he holds me, pressed in as far as his dick will go, as he spills down my throat.

My eyes roll to the back of my head as he fills me, his cock throbbing on my tongue. He pulls his cock out slowly, letting me taste the saltiness of his come as he exits.

"Fuck, Rune. I didn't know you wanted me that badly." I smile at him, a little disappointed that he can't talk to me unless he's in me somehow, but that just means I can do this.

I stand and bring his head down to mine, kissing him deeply.

"I've wanted you since the day we met. But you..."

I pull away. "I know... I'm broken, but I'm not weak. I'll never love anyone ever again, so we can do whatever we want, Rune, just... no hearts attached, okay?"

His eyes narrow and he kisses me deeply as our tongues dance, tasting each other's sinful flavors. *"No hearts attached. Let's get you back to your room."* His warm lips leave mine and I feel cold at our separation.

"I wish we could always talk. I like the sound of your voice more than I like your silence." He smiles at me and plucks me up from the ground, tossing the torn dress over his shoulder so there's no evidence of what we've just done. He pulls his shirt off and hands me it to cover myself with a soft raise of his brow in apology. Gods, he's too perfect. His shirt is huge on me and covers me more than that red dress ever did.

We start walking toward the doors that lead to the corridor and my chest catches fire.

I wince. Burning—it's burning hot with... rage. Oh gods, the bond.

Arulius knows.

I was so caught up with Rune that the bond must have been sending all the feelings to Arulius.

"Rune... Arulius knows," I bite out and furrow my brow. My stomach feels twisted. I can't protect anyone with my powers being chained down as much as they are. I can only manage a small blade, and I've never seen anyone able to stand against Arulius.

Rune smirks like he doesn't give a shit.

"He's going to be pissed. Are we still invisible?" I tense as we leave the torture chamber. There are people everywhere; the festival must have ended. Now creatures are getting back to their duties and others are heading to bed.

I don't have a third eye, but I know by the way Rune's hair looks that I probably look like I've just been fucked into oblivion, so I *know* that we are still invisible when people don't look our way.

"Thank gods—let's hurry up and get to bed." I laugh as we scramble toward our wing of the castle.

14

Elodie

Rune stays in my room tonight, and although I'm already missing his voice, I'm glad for the bit of silence. My mind is whirling with literally everything that happened today.

The festival, Rune's ability to be invisible and talk telepathically, Kastian here in Nesbrim, the skull in the basement, Rune's dick—no, nope, don't think of that.

But what the hell is Kastian doing here? With Violet... I clench my teeth and try not to let out too much emotion. Rune lies behind me, chest to my back, and his breaths are slow. I really don't want to wake him.

My dark-winged Eostrix wouldn't betray me—not like Arulius did. But a part of me is so torn and ruined that, no matter what explanation I conjure, there will always, *always* be doubt planted in my mind. My soul feels darkened by the trust that Arulius stole from me. I miss when I used to see the world with brighter eyes... when I believed in those who really did love me.

It's a kind of hurt that words can't explain. It's felt with the blood lost in the process.

I can't even trust my sweet Kastian. A part of me feels horrible about that, but it can't be helped.

My chest still throbs with rage. Arulius is pissed, but he must be wrapped up in whatever the fuck Violet has him doing that's keeping him from barging in here and threatening to kill my drop of blood in the snow.

Over my dead fucking body.

I slowly turn in the bed so Rune doesn't stir. I do something that is really unlike me. But gods, I'll do anything to try and calm my anxiety right now.

I watch Rune.

I watch him like he did me so many times. Silently and without any reservations. I watch as he takes deep breaths. His beautiful black lashes make his pale cheeks look soft.

I want to be *here*. Not in Nesbrim. Not as the Goddess of Life and Dawn. I want to be here in this bed with him.

With my quiet and lovely Rune.

After I get my fill of his peaceful features, I bring myself in tight to his chest. I want to be close to him, as close as I can get, because I've learned that *nothing* lasts forever.

Nothing—even in a world where eternity is possible.

I can't be sure how long this moment will last. So I hold on as tightly as I can. Desperate to never let go.

"Elodie."

My pants are covered in cold mud as I tumble through the marshy zones of my forest. I don't know why I'm running toward Old Man Bruno's house again, but I am.

I'm so fucking scared. Margo's hot breaths are puffing into the brisk air as she leads the way.

"You can't run forever. We all know how this ends," Mom's eerie voice calls from somewhere in the shadowed woods.

Panic is pumping a hundred miles a minute through my veins. My heart feels like it will give out any second, but I can see Old Man Bruno's house.

"Keep going, Margo! You can make it!"

She turns and looks at me with weary eyes, coming to a stop completely.

I stop, slipping in the mud—no, it's red. It's not mud at all.

Everything is red and muddy and cold, prickling with rot and frost. My eyes find Margo again, her body shaking from the run, and she's already bleeding where she always is. Her body falls to the side and I scream.

"Why... I just want to wake up. Please. Please make this stop," I cry and try to rub the blood and mud from my hands. Looking up, I see two dark figures slowly exiting the forest's cover, knives in each of their hands.

But pain is already throbbing in my chest. I look down. Blood pulses out of me in steady streams. I've already been stabbed and my heart pumps life from me like it's angry with the world. I'm holding a bowl... and there's a skull in the center, pulsing, absorbing what I leak.

Devouring me.

My back is covered in cold sweat and my breaths are sharp and ragged. Rune is over me, pinning me to the bed with wide eyes. I've never seen him look so scared.

What the fuck is going on?

"Rune?" My throat stings. "Rune, what's going on?" He's staring at me, hands pressing so hard on my wrists that it hurts a little. I wince and he doesn't miss it.

He blinks like he's trying to clear his mind of whatever he just saw and slowly releases me. I stay lying down and watch him as he rubs his face and slicks his dark strands of hair back.

I try again. "What's wrong? What happened?" The panic from my dream is still very much pulsing through my veins, but it's calming down.

He lets his arms find me again and he pulls me up so I'm sitting, cupping the back of my head and pulling me into a hug like I'm precious. When he pulls me away, it's only to kiss me.

"What's going on, pup? You've been having night terrors almost every night. I was waiting until you decided to tell me yourself, but I don't think I can let this go on."

He knew about my nightmares?

"You knew? Wait, so that first night that you barged in..." My eyes widen. That night finally makes sense. He gives me a sympathetic look and nods guiltily.

"I didn't know what the fuck was happening. I thought you were being attacked and then I was pissed because you looked so mad at me." Gods... Well, that puts an end to that, I guess.

"Are you okay?" I nod. *"You were malice itself, pup.*

Evil incarnate. I've only seen such horror once in my entire existence."

My eyes flick open, my horror and confusion dancing with his.

I pull back. "What do you mean *evil?* I'm the Goddess of Life, or have you missed the memo?"

He furrows his brows at me, always so fucking serious. But Rune leans into me again anyway, our tongues eagerly searching for one another. *"Stop with the sass. This isn't normal... something's wrong. Were you dreaming?"*

I try to keep the darker, scarier parts of my dream in the back of my mind, but manage to give a small nod. Rune stares at me with his crimson eyes, and as I gaze into them, I wonder how I ever found him so haunting.

"Are you going to be able to go back to sleep?" He pulls away and kisses me on the cheek before standing and pulling his sweater over his head. I shake my head and frown at him.

"Are you leaving?" I sound so desperate and I hate it, but... "I don't want to be alone."

He stops at my door and looks back at me. My broken organ throbs with the anguish in his gaze. Did I scare him that badly? I have to fist my hands in the sheets to keep from grabbing my chest.

All I get is a somber look and then he opens the door. I hear him enter his room. I sit up more in bed and listen as he rustles through his desk, grabbing something and returning to my room. He flicks the light on and I wince against the bright invasion.

He sets down a white cloth and gives me a sleep-filled smile. He looks tired, like he's had more than one sleepless night, and my stomach clenches with guilt.

"What's that for?"

He kneels on the bed and tilts my chin up to kiss me. *"You said you wanted a tattoo, right?"*

My heart leaps and my nightmares are already fading to the farthest parts of my mind. "You do them yourself?" My eyes widen and I'm looking at all his ink with new eyes. The dark swirls look like haunting shadows over his skin, like he's painted all his demons across his body like a story. "You're so amazing, you know that?"

His lips kick up in a proud grin.

"Do you do it with magic?"

He nods and brings up his hand. His index finger glows with his dark red aura, which sharpens into a thin blade. He holds up his other hand and cuts the pad of his middle finger. I stare at him like he's performing some kind of crazy ritual, because this is *not* how they do it on the human side of the realms.

He leans in to kiss me and I'm eager to feel his lips again. *"My blood will burn into your skin and remain as a tattoo. Where do you want it, pup?"*

I shudder and pull back. "Will it hurt?" My brows pinch. I know it probably won't hurt in comparison to some of the other pain I've had. Fuck, I experienced dying and Violet's torture, so it can't be that bad.

He gives me a sympathetic look and nods a little.

"Okay, I guess it's fine as long as it's you doing it." I smile at him warmly. "Can you do one down my spine?"

Rune nods thoughtfully and waits for more.

I think for a moment. "Surprise me with the art." His eyes fill with amusement and I laugh as I pull my shirt over my head and toss it to the floor. I spread my wings up by my arms so that he has full access to my back.

His fingers glide softly against my ribcage and I bite my lower lip to fight off the laugh that's trying to break free. Gods—this is not how I envisioned my night, but I wouldn't trade it for the world.

Rune presses a wet finger to my spine and it instantly heats, burning into my skin like he's managed to do to my heart. I clench my teeth as he draws on my back. I have no idea how much time has passed, but by the time he's done the sky is lightening up a little bit outside, so morning isn't too far off.

He sits back on his haunches and wipes his hands off on the white cloth. I look over my shoulder at him. "Well? Did you botch it?" I ask sarcastically and he smiles widely like he *did*.

I laugh and hop up to look in my mirror against the wall. My breath is stolen from my lungs as a wave of emotions crashes into me.

It's a long ponderosa pine the length of my spine. In the center of the tree, lying on the branches, is a Pine Hollow pup, white and curled up, sleeping. It makes me think of Margo. Of my old forest and of what he calls me... pup.

I turn and look at him with tears brimming in my eyes. "What made you think of the young Hollow?" My voice quivers as he steps up to me with hooded eyes.

He doesn't duck down to kiss me this time—instead, the tattoo heats on my back and his voice is flooding my mind. We are connected through his blood on my spine. *"When you brought me to the Pine Hollows, you were like a pup among the herd. You love them so much and yet you still have so much growing to do. You're still so new to the world, pup. That tattoo will grow as you do."*

I have no clue what he means by *it will grow as you do*, but his words drip from his consciousness to mine and it's lovely. I don't care what kind of magic this is, it's hauntingly enchanted and *mine*. "Thank you for doing this for me." He smiles and nods like it was nothing, but I don't think he'll ever know how much it truly means to me.

15

Elodie

The snow has finally let up and I'm two seconds
from having a full-blown heart attack.

Kol came to my door this morning to get
me. He was shocked to see Rune in bed with me, but
instead of having words about it he just ordered us to get
to the torture chambers and gave Rune a look, saying
they'd have words about it later.

Rune escorts me once I'm dressed and we're silent the
whole way there.

I try not to hold it against him. We're just guard and
prisoner, after all—right? But I have a horrible, rotting

183

feeling welling in my stomach today. I saw Kastian last night... and something tells me he's going to be in there waiting for me.

I cringe as I picture him watching as Violet drains me of blood in front of him. *Please—anything but that.* My fingers tingle with anxiety and I'm boring holes into my lips with my sharp canines.

Where are Wren and Moro? Are they all still trying to save me, or... or have they all moved on? I imagine it for a second. Happy and peaceful in Hollow's Grove. Away from this hell that is Nesbrim... But I suppose Moro wouldn't be happy without the Hollows.

We reach the doors and I'm too nervous to open them. I glance up at Rune, who's watching me carefully as always.

"You'll be okay. I'll be right here."

I flinch as my spine warms, still not used to this easy connection between us. I smile up at him as the heat from the tattoo fades.

"I'm ready..." I mutter, sounding completely *not* ready.

He opens the doors and fuck everything, I change my mind. Take me back to my room, because I can't do this.

Kastian stands in the center of the room, ocean eyes crashing into me until I'm sure there's nothing left for anyone else to see. My heart drops on the floor and I swear I can actually hear it. His white hair is a little longer than it was before and his skin is just as shimmery and sun-kissed as it is in my memory.

My soul cries at this union. Seeing him here, looking at me with such tangible anguish in his eyes, shatters me.

Rune tries to coax me into the room but my bones are frozen in place. The sight of my God of Death has me shaking. He's as beautiful as he was in the last moments we stared into each other's eyes, promising to find one another in another life.

And I know it's only been a little over half a year... but fuck, it feels like so much longer. I'm not the same Elodie... I'm different now, and I'm not sure he will be able to accept the new me.

A cough brings me out of my trance and all of the sudden I'm aware of everyone in the room waiting for me. Violet's crimson eyes are practically glowing at my expression of horror.

Arulius steps toward me and gives Rune a glare that promises punishment for everything I sent through the bond last night. I grit my teeth as my blood-bonded Eostrix pulls me away and into the chamber. My legs are haphazardly working. His scent of fresh rain washes over me and I bite back the urge to be close to him.

"What did I tell you, love? I'm going to fucking *kill* that Dreadius."

That snaps me right out of my daze.

I rip my hand from his and that grabs the entire room's

attention. "You won't lay a godsdamn finger on him, *Arulius*." His amethyst eyes flare with my audacity but I don't give a fucking shit. I'll fight for this last little piece of the universe that is *mine*.

Rune belongs to me. I won't let anyone take away my silent guard who's come to mean so much to me.

Arulius smiles wickedly, sending goosebumps up my spine, but I hold my ground. He may have my power to heal, but he doesn't control my combat aura or my will.

My eyes flick to Kastian. He watches with a furrow in his brow but stays steady where he is, next to Violet. Fucking Eostrixes. I don't know who I can trust right now. No one except me, that's certain.

My golden Eostrix gets so close to me that our chests are touching. He's slightly pushing me back but I bare my teeth at him in defiance.

"You prefer he dies now then? Great choice, love." His smug tone has me absolutely fucking feral. Why's he being so godsdamn crazy?

There's so much anger and hate building inside me. The heart that was once so full of love and curiosity is now so heavy and weary. Violent and hungry for retribution.

"You touch him and I'll *ruin* you."

Our eyes lock with fire—we're testing each other's will and he thinks I'm bluffing.

"Rune, get over here. On your knees, *Dreadius*."

I clench my teeth as Rune obediently follows orders and gets on his knees in front of Arulius, facing me, without hesitating. Like his life means fucking nothing.

Arulius flashes his fangs with a sinister smile and draws out his aura, glowing gold like hot metal pulled from an inferno. He holds the blade to Rune's throat as my precious guard stares up at me with his soft red eyes, letting the warmth and affection he feels for me beam through.

The tattoo on my spine warms. *"It's okay, pup."*
FUCK THAT.

I don't know who needs the godsdamn memo but I'm done being the weak Goddess of Life that has no power. Sure, Arulius may have me chained from resurrecting, but I can still take what he wants most. What they *all* seem to want most.

I let out a breathless sigh and then break out into a manic laugh as a dark sensation itches from beneath my skin. A few gasps bounce around the room and Arulius's purple eyes fill with shock. Even Rune gives me his worried silent gaze.

I feel a hand of rage reach up from within and wrap around my soul. It's sinister and dark, like a lake of curses is consuming my mind and dragging me to the depths of its hate.

Shivers run through my bones and I'm filled with a

crimson aura. My olive skin changes into an ashy soot black and my nails are long like raven claws.

I'd be shitting myself if I was remotely sane right now, but it's like I'm a passenger in myself. Much like the time Murph died, but this—this is much darker.

The room darkens and the guards against the far walls start shrieking. Violet's shouting orders but it all sounds like mumbles. I can't understand anything anyone is saying, all I can see is the God of Wrath and the blade he holds at my Rune's throat.

And I. Fucking. Hate. It.

"Elodie? What the fuck is this?" Arulius snaps at me, but the flicker of fear in his eyes gives him away.

I laugh again and raise my new sharp claws to the darkened ceiling. They're perfect for carving and ripping —twisting and killing. There's a shadow clouding my mind and it's beckoning me to let it take hold.

"*Arulius.* What was it about the blood bond that you kept from me *that* night? Do you remember? That we are now *fated* together." I narrow my eyes at him as my claws break deep into my chest cavity, straight through the ribs and deep into the cage of flesh within, clutching my broken organ that is so useless to me. So worthless I'm willing to rip it out to rid us all of the disease that is Arulius.

The Eostrix's eyes bulge and his knees hit the floor, making the grotesque sound of bone against tile as his hands fly to his heart. The room silences and Arulius's eyes widen as he stares at me in horror. Pain throbs in my chest but I grip the useless organ harder, enjoying the way his mouth clenches in unbearable pain and hot blood courses from the gaping hole in his chest.

"I'll end it all right now. Right fucking now—is that what you want?" I let loose another hysterical laugh and a few tears slip from my eyes.

I'm scared. What the hell am I doing? What's happening?

But I can't help it. Something wicked deep within has a hold on me.

The hatred is so strong, so overwhelming, that I'm powerless against it. I can feel my own claws tearing out my heart just as lips crash into mine, breaking the shadow's hold and grabbing my focus.

My drop of blood in snow—he extinguishes me like I was nothing more than a wild flame in the midst of winter.

All at once my chest seizes and the pain swallows me whole. I can feel the long, sharp claws retract within my chest and my skin returns to normal. Rune lowers me to the floor and the room lightens as the shadows retreat.

Everything is panicked and loud. People are shouting and gasping, Violet's barking orders, and as I stare at the ceiling I see my beautiful God of Death, his gorgeous white hair falling just as perfectly as it did so long ago over his ebony horns.

"Kastian," I croak. Everything's so blurry. What's happening? Why is he here?

I catch his lips mouthing a word. I don't hear it over the chaos, but I would know it anywhere, especially from his lips.

Elodie.

The scents of fresh lilacs and lavender fill my senses. Soft sheets and a bed that I know is much too comfortable to be mine stir me awake and when I look up and find a handful of faces staring back at me, I nearly scream. Violet watches me with darkness in her gaze and it makes me feel sick.

I sit up quickly, pulling the cover with me as my memory floods back. The torture room, me freaking out, and... My hands shoot up and I sigh when I see they're back to normal.

My eyes flick back up and I look at Violet. She's is in a silk dress darker than a starless night and she's sitting on the edge of the bed, looking at me like I'm a marvel. Well *she* seems to like whatever happened to me in the torture room.

"What's going on?" I glance past her and study the other faces in the room. "Where's Rune?" I'm looking at Kastian as I ask for my Dreadius and I don't miss the pain that flicks across his expression.

Violet nods off to the other side of the room. He's leaning against the wall with his arms crossed, watching me. Relief flows over me and it takes everything I have to release the ache in my chest.

Thank gods he's okay.

"Are you going to tell us what the hell happened?" Violet narrows her eyes at me, but there's something considerably more eager in her gaze than before.

I glance at everyone in the room once more. Kol is standing behind Violet. Willow, Naminé, Kastian, and a few other familiar guards are sitting in chairs that look like they've been brought in from outside. There are wet splotches on their shoulders from melted snow. How long have I been out?

I look down at my hands once more. Small traces of dried blood are beneath my nails, but otherwise I'm clean.

"I don't know." I stare at Kastian, still not sure what exactly *this* is. And although I love him, I don't trust him. "What are you doing here?"

He doesn't break our gaze but keeps his lips sealed. If

he was going to save me, wouldn't we be fighting our enemies—not having fun with her at the festival?

Violet leans forward and taps my forehead with her index finger. "We'll give you a few minutes." She winks at me. Bitch knows how to make my nerves flare. If she's really leaving him in here with me alone, then that makes one of us that trusts in him.

I watch carefully as Violet and her guards leave. Only Kastian and Rune remain. When I look at my crimson male, he just shakes his head as if he already knows I'm about to ask if he can leave.

Fine, whatever.

The room falls silent for a few minutes before Kastian makes his way over to me, sitting on the edge of the bed and resting a hand on mine, his ebony wings resting on the bed behind him. My skin instantly reacts to his touch, warming and sending a shiver down my neck.

"I've missed you so much, Elodie. No amount of time can heal the emptiness of not having you." My heart lurches, but I watch him as carefully as he does me. I'm guarded. I know that, I know I'm probably a cold and hollowed version of the Elodie he remembers, but it's who I am now. Who I have to be... and I don't mind the new me either.

"I missed you too... " I swallow the lump in my throat and meet his azure eyes, so deep and lonely, just as I left them. "But why are you here? Like this... I've been hoping and dreaming you'd come for me, but I saw you with Violet at the festival." I look back to my safety net. Rune's red gaze is steady and gives me comfort instantly.

Kastian dips his head down. White tufts of his gorgeous hair fall over his forehead as he lifts my hand to his rosy cheek, desperate for my touch. My chest aches, and when he looks back up at me I can't help it anymore. I lunge for him, hugging him so tightly and never wanting to let go.

His arms wrap around me and he rocks me in his lap as I let a few tears out. Sage fills my senses, a lovely and endless dose of him. I'm so fucking happy to see him again. To see my God of Death. He runs his hand down my spine soothingly as he presses kisses into my shoulder.

"I would do *anything* for you. I need you to know that." He pulls from our embrace and I let out a whimper, trying to grab onto him again, but he stops me. "Elodie, look at me."

I stop and look at him with blurry eyes.

"I'm here to save you, but it's going to take time. I've... I've made a deal with Violet and it's going to be really hard..." He strokes my hair and wipes my tears. "It's going to be so fucking hard, but we're going to get out of this in the end. You have to trust me, okay?"

Trust.

I fucking hate that word more than anything in this godsforsaken world.

"I can't... You can't ask that of me." Fresh tears spill down my cheeks and I shake my head. "I can't, Kastian... I just—"

He pulls me back into a tight hug and nods his head slowly against mine. "Shit—I'm so sorry, Elodie. I understand... I shouldn't have asked. I'll *prove* to you that you can though. I'll earn your trust and I'll never fucking break it. I'll pick up every last part of your heart if I have to, okay? I'm here... I'll always be right here." He runs his hands gently through my hair and I'm unraveling in his hands.

"What deal did you make with her?" I clench my fists, not sure if I really want to know.

He hesitates but finally murmurs, "I'm cursed not to say..." I tense in his arms but he quickly runs his hand down my back. "I won't hurt you, Elodie... Never. I only agreed to it in order to break this bloodthirst of hers for you. Once she has what she needs from me, we'll both be free to go."

I feel relieved by his words but not enough to not cry.

Having Kastian here has already begun to bring my cold heart out of the frozen pits of the afterlife. Maybe it's because I finally feel what I lost sight of so long ago.

Hope.

16

Elodie

Violet and the others come back in the room and stand at the edge of my bed. She leans forward on the bedframe and taps her long nails against the oak impatiently. I can't get a read on her but I know she's planning something

"No bonding, Kastian. I've placed our sweet Elodie on a blood-repulsion curse. She can only take from her Dreadius guard." The Eostrix flicks his eyes at Rune. It's the first I've seen him acknowledge my red drop in the snow.

"That must be why she so adamantly protected him

from Arulius." He warms his gaze on me. I'm surprised I don't find any jealousy stirring like before. He was so pissed about me drinking from Wren.

I wonder if they're better friends now. Did they stay together to plan this? Who's caring for Margo? My heart stings with all the questions.

My cheeks heat as he sets his hand over mine, bringing me back to the conversation. That's right... I won't let anyone hurt Rune. He's *mine*—like they all are. I don't think I'll ever be able to let any of them go. I wonder how Kastian and Arulius will take to that.

"How is Arulius?" I finally choke out after realizing I'm thinking about him too.

Violet raises a brow and smirks. "Well, dear, you almost ripped his heart out, along with your own. You should be feeling the same, no? How are *you* feeling?"

She has a point. I take a moment to focus on myself.

"I feel fine."

"There's your answer. He's fine, just shaken from... whatever you did. Which brings me back to my original question, Elodie. What did you do in the torture rooms today?"

Fuck—like I even know.

I remember claws and soot-colored skin... long, black nails and so, so much hate and anger inside the walls of my soul.

"I was really mad, and then I was just... gone.

Drowned in my anger until it was like my power had control of me, but it didn't feel like mine. It was..."

"Darkness," Kastian murmurs, worry etching his eyes, and I feel sick that he even had to see me like that.

Violet studies me for a few more moments before clicking her tongue and motioning for me to get out of the bed. I raise a brow but slip from the sheets and stand.

"Why did you bring me to this room? Where is this?" I take another long look around the white walls and inhale the lavender and lilacs that dance on my palate.

Willow scoffs beside her. "As if we would carry you all the way to your dirty side of the castle. That's for servants."

Okay—ouch.

"Says the Eostrix who's only tasted the blood of her own," I snap back.

Naminé chuckles beside the brown-haired Eostrix. Willow's green eyes narrow at me and she crosses her arms. "And what is *that* supposed to mean? I'm *pure*, you dirty little—"

"Shut the fuck up before I rip your throat out," Kastian growls at her. She instantly shakes the nasty look off her face and smoothes her features.

Violet smiles, clearly enjoying herself today. "There you have it. Kastian, I look forward to seeing you in the war room. Arulius will be meeting us there shortly. Elodie, go do whatever it is you and Rune do behind closed doors." She says it with a tone that implies we've been fucking like two newly bonded Eostrixes.

Gods. She's not too far off.

Kastian just smiles easily at me—brushing his thumb over my lips. "Remember what I told you." I dip my head in a nod, then he's leaving with the others.

Willow gives me one last sneer before she leaves, and my gods, I just want to put my foot so far up her ass.

Naminé waits for the others to file out until it's just her, me, and Rune left. She runs over to me and throws her arms over my shoulders. I'm stunned for a second before I smile and return the embrace. Her ashy blonde hair smells like lavish herbal soap.

She pulls away and levels me with her amber eyes. "What on earth are they doing to you here?"

I raise a brow. "They're in the business of misery." I smirk, even though literally none of this is funny, and she's instantly laughing.

"I'm worried about you! Stop joking around." She pushes me back playfully.

I smile and warmth fills my chest. "I'm fine, don't worry, okay? Let's meet in the library again soon." I pull her in for another hug and she squeezes me extra hard before slipping away and flashing me one last smile as she leaves.

Rune shakes his head at me and holds his hand out. I

quickly grab it and wrap myself around his arm as we leave too, heading down the corridor to our west wing.

"I'm so glad you're okay."

He grunts and looks down at me. His crimson eyes are a soft landing for my weary soul.

My spine tingles. *"Thanks to you."*

"I don't know what I would do without you, Rune..."

He frowns a little and looks ahead. *"You'd conquer the world and forget about me. Raise hell like the spunky little pup you are."*

I bite his arm and he groans as my fangs pierce his skin through his sweater. "I'll bite you twice as hard if you ever say that again!"

He glares at me with heat in his eyes. *"Which part? That you're a brat or you'd forget about me."*

I'm bending down to bite him again but he takes off running and I let out a laugh as I chase after him

His deep, beautiful laugh fills my head the entire way back to my room.

The snowball hits my face so hard I fall flat on my ass.

My wings get engulfed in the snow. Every inch of my feathers are filled with the cold fluff.

I let out a laugh as hot tears roll down my flushed cheeks. The cold stings my nose but I've got a lock on him now. I throw my snowball as hard as I can and it nails Rune right on the cheek.

"Ha!" I shout as I'm retreating behind the corner of a cottage. I have no idea who lives here, but they're probably thinking there's a war raging out here. My hands entangle in the ivy vines that climb the stones and I smile at the greeting.

Life exists even in winter, and today, Nesbrim seems especially enchanting.

Rune hardly even flinches at the assault from my snowball and smiles wickedly back at me, revenge burning in his eyes.

I let out a squeal as he drops all his premade snow ammunition and charges after me. I make it all of ten feet before he's tackling me into the snow and burying us both in the process.

I'm laughing so hard my ribs are burning and he's laughing along with me in my mind. What I wouldn't give to hear him laugh out loud.

Yesterday sucked with the shit that went down in the torture room, but today's a new day and Rune's idea of having a snowball war was genius.

I'm shivering within seconds and he rolls us so that he's on the bottom and I'm resting safely on his chest. I raise my head and look down at him.

He's so perfect... in every way. His dark hair looks like spilled ink in the snow and his crimson horns and eyes are the red that paints my soul. His smile is contagious and his black tattoos are begging to be bitten.

My drop of blood.

I lean into him and press my lips on his. We're both fucking shivering but our tongues are hot as they dance with one another.

"I fucking nailed you with that snowball to the face."

I bite down on his lower lip and his nostrils flare.

"Careful, pup, we're in public and I'm not above having an audience."

My eyes widen. I didn't think Rune was so... open to those kinds of things. I pull back and smile at him. "Oh yeah? What are you going to do, Rune? Pull my pants down and fuck me in the middle of Nesbrim?"

He wrinkles his nose and lifts his upper lip as if he's snarling at me, but he can't hold back his smile. Gods, what I wouldn't do for this man. I push his head back into the snow before springing up and running again.

I've grown to love being chased. Wren would be so proud.

I swing past the cottages and dip down into the canal that runs right through the city. The river is completely frozen and a light dusting of snow coats the top. I slip a few times, giggling the entire way as I hurry under the stone bridge, trying my hardest to contain my laughter so I don't give myself away.

Gods, he's one hundred percent going to find me down here. I crouch down and wrap my arms around my knees as a sad attempt to be small and hide.

After a few minutes of silence, I figure I've lost him. "Wren was *way* better at this game," I mumble to myself. My smile is loose and my breath curls in the crisp air.

"I know, right? Shameful."

I gasp so loud it echoes in the arches of the bridge above. I turn quickly—are my ears betraying me? Or is it...

"Wren?!" I'm already crying before my arms wrap around his shoulders. He lets out that laugh of his that always warmed my heart and I squeeze him *hard*. The scent of pines fills me and I'm back in my forest for a moment.

I keep my eyes shut—I don't want to lose this moment.

He spins us a bit, lifting my feet off the ground as I bury my face in his shoulder. I can almost see him and Murph walking on Old Man Bruno's trails again, the fireflies rising from the fields around them as they turn and look back at me.

I wish I could turn back time. Go back to the day we met and change everything, stay a little longer, and enjoy the small things.

"It's nice to see you too." His arms tighten around me and when he finally sets me down, I take him in.

He looks well—not great, but good enough that I know he's eating and at least has a sense of hope within himself. His hair is short now, the sides buzzed and top styled. I'll never get used to seeing his dark hair without the translucent leaves, but I push back the sad thoughts their absence brings me. His Vernovian Thorn is just as prickly as it's always been.

His soft amber eyes trace my face and I can tell he's missed me as much as I have him.

"I missed you so much—but what the fuck are you doing here? Violet will have you gutted if she finds you out here." I press my hand against his cheek and he leans into it, shutting his eyes. I get stuck gazing at his beautiful dark lashes.

He was always too beautiful for his own good—my eternal heartthrob.

The Cypress rolls his eyes and pulls out a joint, popping it in his mouth and bringing out my pink lighter to spark it. I can't help but smile at the reminder of the life I left behind.

"I'm just here to say *hi*." The sarcasm is dripping from his lips and I'm instantly glaring at him.

"This isn't a joke—she won't stop until she has Lucius." I look out across the frozen river and tense at the thought of her torturing my friends.

He throws his arm around my shoulder and looks out

across the river with me. "Yeah, I know... Lighten up. You're always so serious and it gives me feelings."

I quirk a brow at him. "Gives you *feelings*? *You*?" I bump him with my elbow for emphasis and he laughs. My broken organ flutters.

"You've always had that on me," he mumbles like it's a secret. I snap my eyes up to him and when his amber gaze sinks into mine, my cheeks warm. Has he always been this charming or have I just forgotten with time? Gods.

I squirm out from his hold and face him. There's something I've been wanting to say to him for a long, long time.

"I never got to thank you," I mumble, struggling to find the words. How do you thank someone for literally sacrificing *everything* for you? When they had no reason other than being your friend?

He tilts his head and his expression becomes serious. "For what? I just got here. Unless I cracked your back or something when I twirled you, then I guess—"

"*Wren.*"

He tightens his snarky lips and stares at me when he hears my serious tone.

"I want to thank you for giving me everything... *every-thing*, when you never had to. Thank you for your sacrifices... and if Murph were here, I—"

He pulls me into a hug, silencing me from saying what

we both know. Words that are too heavy to be spoken. Too somber to even think.

"I'd give anything for you, Elodie," he murmurs into my hair, wrenching tears from me.

"But why? I wish I could go back. I wish none of this ever happened and that we could all just be... I don't know, fucking happy for once. In Caziel maybe, with Marley and Margo and all of us... *all of us.*" I sob into his black cloak.

"You know that was never possible. The Rhythm is dying. You and Kastian... you're the only hope. Don't let our sacrifices be in vain."

I shake my head into his chest. "I'm useless. I don't have my powers—I don't know how to get them back."

He rests his chin on my head. "You'll take your power back, Elodie. I know you will. You just need to find the bond's weakness. Kastian is here to help too."

"I don't trust him... I don't trust anyone. No one but you. You're the only one who's proved time and time again that you're on my side no matter what."

He lets me go and nudges me toward the streets.

"That may be so... but you're going to need your friends. This fight can't be won alone."

I turn and watch him curiously. He's got a dangerous look in his eyes. "What?"

"Run," he whispers, flicking his joint into the snow, and the motion sends shivers up my spine and a thrill through my bones. "Let's see if you've gotten any better at running from me."

Something shifts in me—pain, but the nostalgic kind, like I'm living my greatest desires. The flicker of heat in Wren's eyes has me weak.

"*Run,*" he mouths again, and I don't wait another second before I'm bolting back up the streets and laughing as my shoes clack against the cobblestones. Wren's chasing me in seconds, his black hood pulled up just in case anyone is watching. Honestly, he looks so different with short hair, I wouldn't be surprised if no one recognized him.

He's so fucking fast and he's gaining on me, reaching his hand out like he's going to grab me. I let out a shrill scream before taking a tight turn down one of the alleys that leads up toward my favorite café. He's going to catch me anyway, so we might as well have some food and coffee like old times.

Wren takes the corner just as fast and he's laughing too. The sound of it fills me, and my face hurts from the smile that's been plastered on it since hugging him.

A familiar thought flutters through me—is this real? It's so beautiful and my heart's splitting just being near him. I know this is real—and if it isn't... the sun warms me anyway. Arulius smiling with the sun and rain beaming on his face flashes through my memory.

I smile. At least he gave me a few good memories.

I reach the end of the alley before Wren tackles me and I brace myself to hit the ground ruthlessly, but he turns so he lands on the ground and I land on top of him.

Our noses are pressed together and we burst into laughter. His amber eyes blaze with affection and I'm crying again just being in his arms.

"Wow, have you gotten soft? You used to damn near throw my ass against the ground and pin my arms like an asshole," I manage between giggles.

He wipes his eyes and gives me a shit-eating grin. "Yeah, I was sort of an asshole, wasn't I?" He chuckles and his smile fades as his eyes shift to my broken wing. It's impossible to not notice the difference in length compared to the other one. His expression hardens and he smooths his hand over the feathers softly.

I try to shift his focus. "Hey, you want to get some coffee? I know a shop that puts the one in Caziel to shame." I wink at him and shove his head into the snow as I start to trot off toward the café.

He lets out a short breath and laughs. "Yeah, I would love a fucking cup of coffee." He catches up to me and wraps his arm around my shoulder.

We find a booth in the far corner of Greysil's café. She gives me a curious look and raises a brow at my friend. I put a finger to my lips and she nods without any sort of explanation. I knew she was a good match for Naminé.

She sets two cups of coffee down for us and leaves to tend to the other customers.

The suns are already well below the mountain line. The stars are starting to come out. While I feel a tiny bit bad about ditching Rune, he should be better about catching me. Wren had no trouble at all.

"You should teach Rune how to pursue his victims better," I mutter as I drop two spoonfuls of sugar into my coffee. Wren scowls at me.

"Why would I teach your guard to chase you better? Don't you want to get out of here soon?" he asks carefully. My chest tightens at the thought of leaving Rune behind and I shake my head.

"Rune's not just my guard, he's..." I stop to think because I don't even know what I'm trying to say. "He's *more*."

Wren nearly chokes on his drink as I awkwardly say the latter. "Okay, Elodie, what's going on with him?"

Gods.

"Nothing."

"Mm-hmm—I don't believe that for a second," he deadpans and I smile wickedly at him. His amber eyes fill with amusement and I can't stand it.

"*Gods*—fine. I'd rather be fooling around with the Dreadius than Arulius, okay?" I whisper across the table in case any of the golden Eostrix's soldiers are in the café.

Wren laughs and nods. "Just be careful." We look at

one another for a few minutes and just share the peace of this moment while we drink our coffee.

"How is Margo? And Moro..."

His voice is light as he replies, "She misses you so fucking much. But I can see it in her eyes—she knows as well as I do that we will all be together again. Moro sees it too. We all know that we'll see you soon, Elodie. You're not alone. You've never been alone in this."

Six months.

Six long and lonely months I've waited to hear those words.

But have they come too late? Because once I hear them I realize...

I'm not alone anymore.

Even before Kastian and Wren came for me.

I've had Rune—and he put my heart back together more than I think anyone ever could.

My gaze grows distant and Wren leans forward, brushing his thumb over my bottom lip. Our eyes meet and he gives me a familiar smile. "You're still as beautiful as the day we met."

"So are you."

We share a laugh and it spills into the darkest parts of me, casting away the dread that nestled into me months ago.

Thank you, Wren, for not forgetting me.

17

Elodie

Rune was looking for me on the opposite side of the city. Gods, he's horrible at chasing.

I said goodbye to Wren by the café and he promised he'd be back soon. We talked for hours and it was really hard to say goodbye. He's laying low for now, but just knowing he's close makes my mind feel a million times lighter.

Rune gives me a puzzled look because I'm absolutely glowing from my time with Wren. My heart is buzzing with hope and a newfound motivation.

And you know what, he's right—I have to do this. Not

just for Murph and all the dead, but for the entire Rhythm.

After we get back to my chamber I strip into my undergarments and leave my wet clothes on the floor. Rune's already licked my pussy like a savage animal so I don't care if he sees me in nothing but my bra and thong. I like his eyes on me anyway.

He does the same, except his clothes get hung on the doorknob to properly dry. Bastard is always making me look bad. He's still pissed that I left him searching for me all afternoon.

"You'll have to get better at chasing me, Rune. No sense in pouting about it." I pat his shoulder playfully and he gives me a heavy frown that makes me laugh.

I pull the books we stole from the library out of the hiding spot in my closet and jump on my bed. Rune moves to lie next to me and I lean into him as I pass him a book too. It sucks that Naminé isn't here to help us search through these. I'll have to update her with what we find during our next library raid.

Rune flips through his book as heat spreads down my spine. *"I'm still pissed at you... but I have a confession to make. I can't read very well."* He gives me an apologetic grin.

I smile and lean in to kiss his lips, because he's too fucking ridiculous and he's only in his boxers. I can still taste the saltiness of him on my tongue as I pull away.

211

"Well then, what the hell were you doing that whole time in the library?" I nudge his face to the side and nuzzle into his neck to let him know that I'm hungry before burying my teeth into him.

"*I was watching you.*" His voice even sounds a little ashamed as it rolls through my mind. I take another long pull before releasing him and giving him an amused look. There's still a void in my stomach from the lack of Eostrix blood, but I try to ignore the weariness it brings me.

"I know you were."

He leans in and bites my lower lip hard to wipe the sarcastic look off my face. I wince as metallic flavors invade me, and just like that I'm ready to fuck him.

"Okay, if you're not good at reading... what *are* you good at?" I swipe my tongue over my lower lip, dragging it slowly, and I enjoy the flare that flickers across his gaze.

He kneels on the bed and I'm about to sit up too, but he presses his hand down on my back, keeping my belly pressed to the bed.

Oh fucking gods.

My thighs are burning and the ache in my core makes my pussy throb. I'm embarrassed at how wet he's going to find me, but gods, I want him so bad.

Rune nudges my legs apart and I spread them for him like a good Eostrix. I feel him shift and then his underwear is flying over my head. Heat rises to my cheeks and

I'm not sure what I should do. He's completely behind me and—

He runs a finger through my folds, feeling the slickness that has already been gathering. *Fuck.*

I'm preparing myself for his tongue or his fingers because, I don't know, foreplay? But I know a dick when I feel one. And I one hundred and ten percent feel his engorged tip teasing at my entrance.

I let out a sharp moan as he rubs his cock up and down my pussy, giving extra attention to my clit. Then he lines himself up and shoves in me all at once. He fucking almost splits me in half, but above the slight pain of him filling me is pleasure.

I curl my fists against the sheets and moan as he pounds ruthlessly into me with wet slaps of skin against skin as he burrows himself inside me deeply.

It's hot and wet and making me lose my fucking senses and—

He stops abruptly, leaving his enormous dick fully pressed inside me. I'm filled to the brim and it steals my breath but I'm pissed that he's stopped fucking me.

"Well? Get reading. I'll help from back here." His deep voice snakes around in my head and I'm fighting the urge to let my eyes roll to the back of my skull. I want to hear him every day, over and over forever.

I laugh and my pussy squeezes him, making him groan like a dying man.

"Fuuuck, keep laughing, pup. Squeeze me like you want my come inside you."

Okay—time out. I've never conversed with a male so hot and so insanely lewd, especially in my head. If I die the second death tomorrow, I'll be okay knowing it was with Rune's come warming my insides.

He pulls out almost all the way, leaving me so fucking empty, before he starts to slowly pump into me. He's grabbing my hips so hard I know I'm promised bruises in the morning.

"Get reading or I'll stop."

"Fuck you, Rune." The laugh in my voice is still vibrating as he slowly pushes in and out. Gods help me.

I grab the book about the creatures of this realm, quickly flipping to the Dreadius section, biting my lower lip to keep my moans contained. This is definitely not what I had planned when I took the books from the library.

"Trying to find my secrets?"

My eyes roll as he pushes in hard and holds himself in to the hilt. I can hardly fucking respond. "No one t-talks about your species and you're f-far too interesting. Like the mind-talking? It's murder."

He laughs in my head and I grind into his hips at the sound. He immediately responds with fucking me harder, deeper. I can barely keep my eyes on the pages.

Dreadiuses are infamous for their bleeding eyes. They

can heal any kind of wound: physical, poisoned, even wounds of the mind. Each Dreadius has their own unique ability, but many share the ability to become invisible.

Really? What the fuck have I been doing this entire time then? If he can heal my useless broken organ and all the trauma I'm carrying around, then maybe I can finally get a good night's sleep. Or maybe he's been healing me slowly. My mental state has lifted tremendously since meeting him...

But who am I without my darkness? I'm not sure I have the courage to find out.

Rune speeds up his thrusts, going so deep and hard I'm not sure I'll be able to walk for a day. He hits my sensitive flesh over and over until I'm nearing the edge. So fucking close.

"That's a good fucking girl. Now say my name and beg for my come."

This man and begging—I'm one hundred and ten percent on board with it.

"Rune, if you don't come in my pussy, I'm going to feed on you until you fucking pass out."

He groans at that and I can feel his growl vibrating down my back. He pumps into me a few more times before I'm screaming and covering my mouth in a sad attempt to keep the sound muffled that I don't think works as well as I'm hoping.

Rune thrusts once more and holds himself so hard

against me that his dick is pressing against my cervix. I can feel his swollen cock throbbing as he releases his come in me and I'm coming right along with him, our juices mixing and spilling together down my slit.

We stay like this for a few blissful moments while we both pant and catch our breath. I wish we could stay in this moment forever, where the only thing that matters is him and me. I relish in it as much as I can, remembering our scent. The feeling of his skin and his kisses that he starts to press along my spine.

"No hearts attached—right?" I whisper, sounding entirely unsure of our sworn statement.

"Can they be?"

I don't know what to say... so I don't say anything. My chest is beating a mile a minute and if I let my heart speak for me it would wrap him up in a second and say *hell yes.*

"You're mine." His deep voice echoes in me. I shiver at the thought of being exclusive, but let's be honest. I'm a prisoner and he's my guard. I'm the Goddess of Dawn and fated to the God of Death, whom I very much *do* love. But I also happen to be blood-bonded to another Eostrix and have an aching heart for my cruel Cypress.

Fuck. It's all such a godsdamn mess.

But they're *all mine.*

"Possessive much?"

"You're the one that almost ripped your heart out for

me. Doesn't that make you the possessive one?" He slowly pulls out of me and I'm already mourning our separation.

I turn to look at my beautiful male. His dark hair is wet with sweat and his crimson eyes are busy devouring me. "I saved your life, thank you very much."

He lies down next to me, our eyes dancing with one another as my tattoo warms. *"I could have taken Arulius."*

I raise an eyebrow but he's being serious. Asshole. "Then why didn't you!? I don't know what power took over me but... don't pull that shit again."

He smirks at me. *"I wanted to see how much you liked me, pup. It turns out you like me quite a lot, especially coming from someone who demands that no hearts are attached."*

He leans closer and kisses me just like I've dreamed a man always would. It's passionate and deep. My heart is fluttering like a caged wild bird. I'm not sure I can keep it in there for much longer.

He's going to completely ruin me.

"I'll take care of you, Elodie. You're mine and I'm yours. You say the word and I'll do anything for you. You want my heart? I'll cut it out for you and feed it to you myself. You want my loyalty—I'll wear a godsdamn Vernovian Thorn for you. You want other males, I'll fucking watch you take it and join in." He pulls his lips away and presses his forehead to mine, staring into my

eyes. Goosebumps ripple down my arms and I'm a fucking puddle to this god, or whatever he is.

I run my hand down his jawline, admiring his soft skin and neck tattoos. "What god are you? Why can't you talk?"

He stills at my question, not in the guilty way Arulius used to (trust me, I've figured that one out), but in a vulnerable way—like he's damaged and hurt about whatever the answer is.

"I don't know. The knowledge has been lost in time, as many of the other gods have since Violet ruined the Rhythm. One of silence maybe... I can speak. I choose not to though—it's only safe through the mind."

A gasp leaves me. He can but chooses not to?

"Why? If you can speak, then why don't you?" Pain fills his eyes and I'm already regretting asking. My eyes unconsciously drift down to his scarred throat, where it looks like someone literally ripped out his voice box. The tattoos make it difficult to see, but I've noticed it from day one.

"I'm cursed to keep silent, to keep the secrets of the world quiet and hidden away. I don't remember who placed this curse. My purpose is simply to observe and never tell... so my voice is eerie, filled with rot and horror. So dreadful that when my prior love heard me speak for the first time... she tried to kill me."

My jaw drops and tears brim in my eyes. Not my

Rune—who could ever want to hurt him? I'll kill the fucking bitch.

"I was so shocked and disoriented that she nearly succeeded... Kol cut her head off before she could finish me off. I'm left with this scar as a reminder of why I don't speak. Of why I must keep quiet. Whomever placed this curse doesn't want their secrets to get out, and I pay the price."

My heart is already being torn to ribbons over him. I reach up and hug him tightly, trying to push away the hurt with my embrace, but I doubt it even touches his pain... his trauma.

"Let me hear you."

He jolts and leans back quickly, eyes wild, and he shakes his head with fear coiling in his eyes.

I narrow my gaze and place a hand on his. "Do you trust me?"

His red eyes burn into mine for a few quiet moments before he shakes his head again. I give him a warm smile.

"Good—I'd be upset if you did." I repeat his words from the other night. His lip kicks up and I can see a flicker of hope pass over them.

We have an understanding, it seems—that our distrust in one another gives us more credibility than either of us will admit.

He sits on the bed like a wounded warrior, arms slumped forward and head down. He's completely naked and I take this moment to take every bit of him in. His pale skin makes his crimson horns so somber, along with the sadness in his eyes.

"You'll try to kill me."

I'm stunned to my core.

I've never heard a voice so whisper-like and echoey, deep but haunted. Like hearing a ghost in a dream, one that is at the other end of a dreary and dark cave. I can feel a force behind his voice, like something is trying to coerce me into evil doings, but my heart is stronger. Maybe it's because I'm life itself.

I smile.

His eyes widen and he fists the bedding like the small act alone will shatter him.

"How could your *first* words to me be so horrible?"

His eyes fill with grief and he dips his head to hide the tears that well in them. *Oh, I like vulnerable Rune.* I scoot close to him and wrap him in my arms, tipping us so that we fall into the pillows and are facing each other.

"I haven't spoken aloud to another person in over a hundred years." My spine warms and my heart breaks. What a cruel curse.

I watch him silently shed a few tears. He's so tired that he finds sleep quickly in my arms. I can't even imagine what it's like to be able to talk after gods know how long he's been mute. After his first attempt with someone he loved... I stroke the dark locks of hair from his face and press a kiss to his lips before sitting up.

He mentioned that he doesn't know what deity he is due to the Rhythm being disrupted. Kastian told me the same thing in his glades. *Everything* went to hell after the Rhythm was destroyed.

That's right—Naminé gave me a book on the Rhythm that she managed to find in the library. I grab it and start flipping through the pages. I stop the second I land on a page that has a picture of four gods.

Four. Not two.

Okay, life and death—who are the other two? I try to make out the image, but it's so smudged and old that I can't really tell what and who they are.

The Rhythm Gods: Keepers of the Realms and flow of the universe. The four must remain in a constant and steady stream. If the Rhythm is disturbed, chaos will break loose and the rules of the Realms can be altered.

What the hell... I turn the page and find a photo tucked in the crease between the pages. My heart drops as I look at the smiling and radiant Violet. Beside her is who I assume is Lucius.

The rules of the Realms can be altered.

My stomach feels twisted. I want to hate her... No—I do hate her. Yet at the same time my very bones ache for her. This must be the book she found all those centuries ago, when she discovered she could destroy everything just to get her Lucius back.

Love can turn into despair, twist into evil when it's corrupted.

I shut the book and lie down next to Rune, pulling him close and reminding myself why we can't have our hearts attached. No matter how badly I want it...

I won't let us turn into poison.

18

Elodie

I'm running.

Old Man Bruno's house has all the lights on and Margo is already through the door. I make it to the porch and turn to look back into the forest.

There's a mist shrouding the brush. It's so thick, almost like Bresian, the path between, has slipped through the entire woods. My bones are cold. The air is almost a beast itself with the frigid assault on my lungs and limbs. I turn to follow Margo into the cabin, but Old Man Bruno is standing there. He's different now—younger. I only recognize him by the oversized overalls and the light in his hazel eyes.

"Bruno? You... you're young again." I study him, feeling like we've met before. His youthful face is familiar, yet so distant in my memory.

His eyes are soft and a frown forms on his lips. "Elodie —you've been cursed."

I lift a brow. Technically it's a dream, right? It's not so far-fetched that he'd know about my blood-repulsion curse.

"It's not so bad. I have Rune."

His eyes are blank. There's only the frown and the tick in his jaw as he continues. "You. Are. Cursed." He raises a finger at me and goosebumps ripple up my arms at the act. "Run, Elodie. You must run. Run. Run. Run. Run. Run. RUN!" He screams the last part and my heart drops.

The door slams shut and I'm fucking running, because what in the gods was that? My heart is beating so fast at the cryptic message and my brain is in overdrive. I can't find a sliver of trees that isn't shrouded in the horrible mist.

Bresian is everywhere.

Where the fuck am I?

"Wren!" I call out to my Cypress, sweating horribly at the way Bruno just kept telling me to run. "Rune! Kastian!" My knees hit the forest floor and my hands are stuck in something wet and thick. It's hot and steaming against the cold air.

I lift my hands, eyes wide, and I'm shaking because I already know what it is.

But of course I look anyway.

Blood and guts are beneath my knees, the crimson seeping into my pants. My hands are covered in red, and just as I lose the hold on my sanity I catch eyes with a grungy and decrepit skull.

It's the same skull from the last dream... the one from the basement.

But it's fleshy now, with peachy-colored skin that's half torn from its face, and eyes that have no lids. They're the color of the sun, yellow. So yellow and filled with evil that my marrow freezes within me.

Bruno's voice rings in my ears until I'm nearly deaf.

"Run, Elodie. Run! You need to go home!"

I wake up standing in the frame of my window. It's still dark outside. My knees struggle not to buckle under the panic that seizes me.

"Elodie!"

My tattoo heats. I turn to look at him. He looks as fucking scared as I feel. My bones are freezing. How long have I been standing here like this?

My Dreadius approaches me slowly with both hands out, carefully easing up to me like I'm going to jump to my death.

Was I? What the fuck is happening to me? My heart lurches in my chest at the thought of seeing my parents but them not being able to see me.

My spine warms. *"Are you okay, pup?"*

I nod slowly.

Once Rune secures me from the window, he brings me to the bed and sits me down. His brows are furrowed with worry and my heart's curling in its cage.

I'm still shivering beneath his warm hands, but not from the cold. Bruno scared the shit out of me and I honestly don't know what to do. I can't trust anyone, and all I know is I need to visit the human realm... Home. I need to see what's happening there because these dreams can't be nothing.

I tell him everything. About the dreams starting small and that I thought they were just an extension from my trauma, but they're taking control now. It's something ominous and deeply rooted.

He holds my hand in both of his large ones, pressing his forehead to mine.

"Let's go."

"Go where?" I try to wiggle out of his embrace but he holds me steady.

"To your home. We need to find answers. This has

something to do with your shifting as of late too. I can feel it."

I still in his hands, hugging him tightly and burying my face into his sweater.

"Okay. Get dressed. We can take a Hollow and be back by dawn. No one will even know we're gone." He grunts at the mention of riding Pine Hollows but nods anyway.

The High Court is quiet. Everyone is still nestled into their beds and sleeping. We make it quickly through the silent streets and into the Hollow enclosure. Brevik is already awake and seems to have been waiting for us. I quirk a brow at the creature. He shakes his gray head and his fur bristles as he flexes his large paws.

"He must have sensed we were coming." I flick a look to Rune. He's tired but alert, scanning our surroundings so intently that I don't think he heard me.

A pit drops in my stomach. If my wing wasn't damaged I could have just flown to Bresian and back by myself.

I climb onto Brevik's back and stare down at Rune expectantly. He's just looking at me like I'm crazy for hopping up on the Hollow so easily.

"Come on—you can't *still* be scared of them," I tease. He narrows his eyes at me and lets out a huff, reluctantly hopping on behind me. His arms scoop around me and clutch my body tightly. His large thighs swallow mine.

Okay, I've done this plenty of times with Wren. We can do this.

"Brevik, take us to Bresian. You know the way, don't you, boy?" I pat the Hollow's head and he grunts as he pushes off the ground with the same speed I remember Murph having. My heart bleeds a little bit more at the feeling, the memory of the magical beast that introduced me to Tomorrow. I have to remind myself that I *will* bring him back.

Goodbye isn't really forever, not here. We will meet again... even if it takes a century. I'll never give up... and I'll never fucking forget.

We approach the south gate, and when Brevik doesn't slow down, I hold the scream in my throat. We're going to run straight into the gates.

But he leaps, and gods—for a second it's like we're flying. I clutch onto his scruff to keep myself from raising off his back and Rune curses silently in my ear as he joins in, grabbing a handful of fur to keep us from being airborne.

Once the paws are on the outside of the walls I let out a laugh. The air feels so much fresher out here, in the world I fell in love with. I inhale and let the cold air invade my lungs, the scent of pines and snow filling me.

Has it always been this easy to leave? I entertain the thought. It's more complicated than just leaving though.

Like Wren said, I need to find a way to break the bond. That's the true imprisonment.

The world blurs past us as Brevik wastes no time, gliding through the snow-filled valleys like it's nothing. I marvel at how different this realm looks in winter. Everything's so quiet and hushed compared to the usual loud world full of life. The colossal trees that tower into the skies have long since lost their leaves, and their black branches reach into the stars above us. If I hadn't seen them before, I would've been convinced that the stars were their natural leaves.

A few hours have passed by the time we reach a cavernous mountain of rock formations. It looks like the side of a sheer cliff with large boulders embedded in the wall, creating large crevices between them. I've never seen this area before.

"Where are we?" I mumble as my eyes search the dark spaces between the rocks. They're like voids to another dimension.

Rune leans forward and whispers, *"The Bresian gateways."*

I let out a small gasp. "What? I thought Bresian was only in one location... How do we know which one will take me home?" I slide off Brevik and Rune follows suit.

The Dreadius shrugs and I look to Brevik, feeling a little silly for putting my fate in the hands of a Pine Hollow, but hey, he might know.

Brevik sniffs me and looks to the cliff face, taking deep inhales like he's trying to scent out my home. I watch patiently, tendrils of hope filling me. I'm shaking at the thought of being in *my* forest again. Will Mom and Dad still be there? Has anyone been taking care of my shed? I look down at my worn boots, anxiety ticking away at my weary mind.

Focus on what you're looking for. I take a deep breath and wait until Brevik grunts, stepping over to a large hole in the center of the rock wall. Rune sets his hand on my shoulder with comfort and nods at me.

"Thank you, Brevik. You're a good boy. I'll be back soon, okay?" I pet his muzzle but Rune grabs my wrist before I can head to the cave.

"What?"

He furrows his brows, my tattoo warming. *"You don't want me to come with you?"* I soften my expression. I understand his concern, but this is something I need to do alone.

"I don't know how I'll be affected going back, and... I want to be alone to process it." Rune keeps his red gaze on me for a few moments and then nods, letting me go but kissing me quickly before I can turn.

"I'll be waiting here for you, pup."

I press my hand to his cheek, looking deep into the eyes I was once so wary of.

"I'll be fine, I promise." I give him my best smile but

I'm really nervous. The void grows larger with each step I take. I suppress a shudder as I cross the veil and the familiar shroud of the thick mist falls over my shoulders.

It's quiet.

I close my eyes and keep walking forward. I've never done this alone, but when I crossed with Wren we just kept walking straight. I'm taking each step slowly and waiting for the break in the mist when I catch the distinct and strong scent of my beloved ponderosa pines.

My eyes shoot open and a smile breaks over my lips. *Home.*

I'm home.

I instinctively follow the scent and burst through the edge of Bresian, eyes wide and eager to take in everything that my memories hold of my forest. But what I see stops me—sends shivers up my spine, and every hair on the back of my neck raises. The feathers of my wings bristle with shock.

My forest is... my forest is dead.

Gone.

Burned to nothing but the charred black death that fire leaves in its wake. Not a single tree is left unscathed. I can see the boulder I followed Wren to the night we met, what's left of Bruno's house in the distance, and... where's my parents' house?

I clench a hand over my broken organ, readying it for

the impact of impending doom and sorrow—but it doesn't come.

Am I truly that hollow now? Seen it all? Felt every godsdamn piece of pain the realms can manage to serve me?

I'm not convinced—not that I've seen it all.

I walk through the ashes, the embers still smoldering beneath the blanket of gray death. I take it all in with unease. It reminds me too much of Kastian's glades... filled with ashes, death, and rot. Creatures that sleep—the long dreary rest where you no longer dream.

Smoke swirls up into the sky, scarring the night with plumes of the ghosts of my forest. They dance on the bare stumps of their lost vessels, somber with the dim light coming from the single moon above.

No magic. No second chances. No hope.

My feet carry me knowingly, as if some ghostly part of me can sense the old paths I once walked. A few snaps sound from behind me but I ignore them. I keep my eyes low, not wanting to look up from the ash-covered ground, because a sick feeling is rising in the back of my throat. A knowing feeling.

I stop at the foot of my burnt shed.

Ash billows up with the cold breeze as my eyes rest heavily on the mound that once was my sanctuary. My shed is gone. I take a deep breath in and exhale slowly as my marrow churns inside my bones.

Three headstones rest at the foot of what was once my beloved shed. Three lonely carved headstones that have my family's names etched in them like it was done with a stick. I slump slowly down to my knees. The ash is still somewhat warm against the chill in the air, but my soul feels frigid.

Elodie Marrowbone

Stolen by the gods too soon. We're so sorry. We will love you for eternity. Please forgive us.

— Mom & Dad

A tear slips down my cheek and I let the curled breath inside my chest out. My insides are twisting and my hands are shaking with all of the fucking nothingness I feel.

It's fucked up, right?

So fucking sad and messed up. *They* didn't kill me, it was *Arulius*. And now...

My eyes finally find the will to flick to their headstones. The same message is written on them both. The knot in my throat chokes me as I read it.

To be with our beloved little song, our Elodie.

. . .

They killed themselves for what they did...

Because of *him*. Because of Violet.

I sit here for a long time. I'm not sure how much time has passed, but when I hear footsteps I don't bother turning to see who it is. I just continue to stare endlessly at our graves like the lost soul I've always been.

"I'm sorry," Wren whispers as he kneels down next to me.

I ignore him, not sure how he knew I was here. I continue staring at their graves, wondering who buried them next to me. Aunt Maggie is dead. I'm dead. *Everyone* is fucking dead. So who?

The Cypress lets out a soft sigh, one filled with sorrow. His hand slides over mine and he squeezes it tightly. His hands are warmer than I ever remember them being.

"The Rhythm is cruel... but I have no doubt in my mind you will meet them again. Your story didn't end here, Elodie—it's just beginning."

He leans forward and wipes the ash from the tops of each gravestone. Behind his fingers, little white plants grow from the stones. They can't be more than a few inches tall and they look like ghost flowers, white and iridescent against the death that surrounds them. Little poppies and mushrooms, dandelions waiting for impossible wishes to be made.

My eyes light up and a small warmth fills me. My

broken organ finds a large piece of itself at the sight. Maybe this is the closure I needed.

Wren glances back at me and a somber smile graces his beautiful face, his amber eyes flickering with empathy.

My oldest friend and forever heartthrob.

His thumb brushes over my cheek, swiping away tears that I wasn't aware were falling.

"Your story is a painful one... but I will *always* stand with you. We will all make it through this... even Murph. Our stories will always chase one another, around and around, until we all meet again and again, forever, in an endless cycle."

He lifts my chin to look at him and I'm sobbing now, like a child. He's always saved me from my darkest depths and I love him for it. His expression is soft and a tear escapes his eyes too.

"You are life itself, Elodie. *Dawn of the realms.*" He stands, pulling my arms so I stand with him. I stare into his eyes like I'm desperate for each word he whispers to me, because I am. "Now take back your heart. Take back all of it... and let's fix this shit."

19

Elodie

I'm staring into Wren's amber eyes as the cold, dead forest seems to swirl around us. His words penetrate deep into my heart until the key has finally turned on that cage in my chest. My broken organ steps out, scared because the world has shattered it so many times, but it's caught in Wren's embrace.

He cups my cheeks with his hands, our eyes locked. We're connected so deeply and I finally see it now.

He is the forest himself—guardian of the ponderosas. Life of the woodlands. And he was always here with me, living in my love for the woods.

He's my forest... my Cypress among the pines.

Wren smiles easily at me, that loose and gentle look he had when we first met, and I remember the kiss I never got. The one I wanted so badly from him. He lets a thrum of his power fill the ashes around us and white fireflies rise from darkness, dancing around us and orbing into the air to make this morbid place a little lighter.

He leans into me and his perfect lips press against mine. I'm flooded with his pine scent and I feel so safe in his arms.

Home.

His thumb strokes my cheek lovingly as he pulls away. I whimper as he takes a step back, wishing that he would indulge me this once.

"We can't stay long. You need to get back to Nesbrim before anyone notices you're gone," he whispers as he presses a kiss to my forehead.

A small pain spreads across my chest through the bond and I already know we're fucked.

"Too late." I wince, clenching my chest at the burn. "Arulius just found out," I bite out. Wren pushes his dark hair back with a sigh, worry flashing in his gaze.

He takes my hand and leads me back toward his Bresian gateway, the same one he originally took me through. I pull my hand from his and trot ahead in the other direction. "This way. Rune's waiting for me at the other gate." Wren trails me without hesitation.

It's easy to find our way back with the footsteps in the ash. I take one last look at my desolate forest. Nothing but burnt stumps and gray skies. Bones and graves of many creatures... and the family that perished here.

I don't know if I'll ever return again.

But I hold onto Wren's words—this is just the beginning of my story. The start of a never-ending dream. I'm going to fix everything.

"Bye, Mom... Dad. We will meet again."

Wren nods at me, smiling with those sad eyes of his. I raise a hand and caress his leafless dark hair before turning to enter the mist of Bresian.

We step through quickly. Wren takes the lead, holding my hand tightly as we pass and break through the other side.

Rune's on his feet quickly and bares his teeth at Wren. My Cypress is taken off guard by his hostility and I'm stepping between them before Rune can do anything crazy.

"Stop it! Wren's one of my closest friends. We need to get back *now*. Arulius knows," I snap at him and his brows crease with annoyance at my admittance. Crap. "Not closer than you, Rune."

Wren's jaw drops and I smack my forehead. *Fucking males.* "You're both the closest people I have, okay? End of discussion." I pace over to the Hollow and jump on its back. Rune is right behind me, scooting in close and wrapping around me possessively.

I glance at Wren. "How did you know I was here?"

"There was a strange man who told me to head to the forest. He said his name was Bruno."

My eyes widen and I clutch Brevik's scruff tightly, goosebumps spreading across my arms. *He's really here. So it wasn't just a dream... Was it a vision he sent? What do you know that you aren't telling us, Bruno?*

"I entered through the other gateway. I need to head back that way to get to Caziel. Marley's waiting for me." My heart leaps at the name of the little Moss Sparrow and Caziel. I wonder if we'll ever go to that café again and share coffee and pastries.

I nod. "We will see you soon then?" I say with too much optimism. If I say it enough times it'll come true, right?

I hold his amber gaze, his tan skin shimmering under the light of the four moons. He smiles and dips his head before he's heading back through Bresian.

"See you later, Elodie."

I watch until he's slipped back through. "Let's get back to Nesbrim, Brevik." I pat the Hollow's head and he's sprinting down the valleys of snow like a blur in the night.

Arulius is waiting at the southern gate by the time we make it back.

He has an expressionless look on his face and I'm already recoiling inward with what awaits me if Violet knows too.

We stop at the wall and I hop off. "Rune, take Brevik back to the enclosure and wait for me in my room." He gives me a hard frown and narrows his crimson eyes, flicking them over to Arulius distrustfully before eventually nodding. Brevik leaps over the wall easily and just like that, I'm alone with the asshole.

I cross my arms and look anywhere but at him. He's dressed in his beautiful gold bone armor and his gilded wings are especially glimmery in the dawn's beams as the suns crest over the mountains. My heart reaches out for him. I try to ignore it, but whether I like it or not, I can't deny that I've missed him... I want his amethyst eyes on me and for him to be begging for my attention just like he did for months.

So much has changed...

He's quiet for a few dreadful minutes and we stand

awkwardly with thick tension in air between us. I feel like I've been caught stealing, for gods' sakes.

Arulius lets out a long, deep sigh that makes me flinch, but I clench my teeth to keep my arms crossed tightly. I won't ever show this bastard my feelings again.

"You can't hide your emotions no matter how hard you grit your teeth, love."

I shoot him a glare and amusement flickers in his amethyst eyes. My hard expression falters as I take him in. He looks so fucking tired. Dark circles rest under his eyes and he carries a look of defeat that I'm a stranger to. "What were you doing out there? Tell me where you went and I'll consider not telling Violet."

I instantly let out an exhale of relief. Thank the fucking gods he cares at least a little about my wellbeing, because Violet would cut my legs off.

"I... I went to see my home."

His eyes widen but his expression remains stony. "To the human realm? Why would you want—"

"Why would I want to see my parents who murdered me? Gosh, I don't know, maybe because it wasn't their fucking fault. *Maybe* it's because I'm looking at the asshole who did it."

My chest clenches and I try to shake the hurt he's sending to me but it stays put.

"Tell me why, love."

I roll my eyes and shift on my feet. The cold is starting to numb my legs and I'm sure by now my ears have suffered frostbite. "I had to see them again... but they're dead. You probably already know that, or just don't fucking care, so... can we just go inside now? I'm freezing my wings off."

His eyes soften on me and he holds a hand out, waiting for me to take it. I study him for a moment, keeping my healing organ close to its cage, before reaching a hesitant hand to his.

Arulius pulls me into him and wraps his golden wings around us. I'm instantly encased in warmth and the strong scent of rain. I take a deep breath of him in and wait for whatever it is he has to say.

"I didn't know. I'm sorry for your loss... I know it's my fault. I know... *I know* you'll never forgive me and I'll never ask that of you. But please, Elodie, *please* let me love you." His arms tighten around me and I can feel the chaos of pain this causes him.

My refusal to love him.

"Please just let me love you. I'll do anything."

I push my hand between us and look up at him. My stunning golden Eostrix, once so beautiful and perfect. He's weary and filled with so many regrets now. Aren't we all. We're withered and weathered, a somber shadow of what we once were.

"You won't do anything though. Don't you see that? The *one* thing you could do that would be a baby step toward earning forgiveness would be to help me make this right, Arulius."

He presses his forehead against mine. "I would do that and more if I could, love... but..."

"But what? Tell me so I can at least hear your excuse." His purple eyes fill with pain and he bites his lip. My eyes stay there a moment longer than they should.

"I'll tell you... but not here or now." He lifts his head to look around us like he's worried someone's listening. "I'll come get you this afternoon. Dress warm." He leans down and kisses me quickly before unwrapping his wings from around me and turning to walk back into Nesbrim.

I follow behind with a dreadful feeling swirling in my stomach.

Rune's waiting in my room for me like I knew he would be, leaning against the wall with his head down. I'll never understand why my Dreadius likes to sleep like that, but I enjoy looking at him while he does. His tattooed arms are tightly crossed and I let my eyes linger over his sharply cut jawline, the dark lines of his neck tattoos making me hungry just looking at him—*stop.*

I shake my head.

I know he doesn't mind, even relishes in making sure I have what I need, but I hate using him like that. I *hate* thinking of him as food.

I walk in quietly and let him rest since it's my fault he's been up all night. I fight the urge to nap. There's way too much chaos in my head to sleep.

Sitting on the bed, I grab the books and spread them out over the sheets. Now that I won't be fucked into oblivion while I try to study, maybe I can learn something this time.

I open the book of creatures, skipping past all the ones I already know. I'll have to come back to them later if I ever need to know more, but for now I have to find out what Violet's powers are exactly besides creating portal-glass. I need to see if I can find anything that remotely resembles the fucked-up skull in the basement.

I have a few blissful hours of quiet. I tear out a few promising pages from each book. Of course I can't find anything that screams at me, but I do manage to find some older entries that don't have images. I toss the last book to the side and spread out the tattered pages on the bed.

I hear a floorboard creak that lets me know Rune's awake. At least he got a few hours of rest. I keep my eyes plastered to the words, looking for—there!

Gods of Ruling.

It's so old and smudged that I almost missed it. Thank gods I took a second look, this might help me get some insight on Violet. I won't have enough time before Arulius comes to get me, so I'll have to save any important pages for later. I fold the page and shove it in my pocket. Rune steps to the other side of the bed, his eyes still drunk with sleep, but he's more interested in what I'm doing than resting.

His crimson eyes meet mine and he raises a brow, glancing back down to the pages scattered across the sheets.

I raise my hand and rub the back of my head. "I'm looking for information on creatures with weird sharp teeth and bond-breaking." I try to laugh it off awkwardly but he just looks back up at me.

"Teeth? Describe them." My spine warms with his power. I wish he could be freed from the chains of his curse. He should be able to talk just like the rest of us.

"Umm... kind of like this." I raise my hands to each side of my face and make them look like fangs. *Wait—shit, I already have fangs.* I lower my hands, feeling stupid because he's already got a cocky-ass grin on his lips. "Like fangs but for every tooth." I toss a pillow at his face for being smug.

Rune swats it down and sucks his lower lip in thought. *"Where did you see a creature like that?"*

His eyes narrow like he's thought of the exact being I'm looking for.

He knows, I can feel it.

"Promise you won't tell?"

He rolls his eyes and points at his scarred and tatted throat. I wince at my slip up. "Sorry... Well, you know Violet's basement? The one where she takes all my blood?"

His eyes flicker but he remains blank. Whatever creature he's thinking of is clearly haunting his mind. He nods.

"Yeah... Well, I found a bowl with, like... bones and a skull in it. It was really fucking weird and it was filled with blood. I'm guessing mine, because that's where she always takes it. But it was like the bones were absorbing it. The skull was crimson and had veins on it." I pause and swallow the lump that's forming in my throat from the memory of the horrid thing. "It really freaked me out."

Rune's eyes widen, fear itching beneath the surface.

He knows *exactly* what I saw.

"What is it? Tell me." I lean forward on the bed and crawl over the torn pages until I'm kneeling on the edge.

His red eyes are still looking away, to some far-off place. This close I can see the sweat collecting on his forehead.

What the fuck...

"Rune!" I pound my fist on his taut chest, snapping him out of his daze. He grabs my wrists and pushes me back on the bed until he's on his knees straddling me, crumpling the pages around us and staring straight into my soul. Is it weird that I think this is hot? The tension is just making it more... intense.

"Just tell me—you're freaking me out."

I almost think he's going to kiss me because he leans down to get closer, but he stops just a breath away as his eerie voice rings through my bones.

"I don't want to jump to conclusions, but this sounds like North."

I shiver beneath him. "What the fuck is *North*?"

His jaw tightens. *"Not what—who."* He brings his hand to my throat and squeezes gently, just enough to make the air a little harder to pull in. *"North was the God of War."*

My back muscles flex because I can't tell if he's going to choke me or fuck me. I'd take either from him. "Was? Okay, so the bastard is dead. Why is Violet making nasty-ass skull soup in her basement?"

He dips down and kisses me deeply. *"I don't know. Not sure I want to find out, but this isn't something we can ignore. Is it the same skull you've been seeing in your dreams, pup?"*

I nod as I string my fingers through his dark locks of hair, digging my nails in to combat his rough grip on my airway.

He growls against my lips.

I break away and press kisses along his throat, dotting his beautiful tattoos with affection as I stroke his artery with one long brush of my tongue. I can already feel his erection through his pants. His grip tightens on my throat, making me dizzy, as he slides his pants off and nudges my panties to the side with his dick, rubbing my clit a few times before shoving into my pussy.

I jerk at the intrusion and bury my teeth into his neck as he thrusts into me. I've never been choked and fucked while I drink blood but *holy hell.*

I draw in his strong rose blood deeply, instantly moaning at the flavors of my sweet Dreadius and the orgasm that he's building by pumping his hips into me roughly. Fear dances between us but it only makes this union more intense.

"The god's been dead for centuries. But I know there's more than one way to bring back the dead."

I shift under him, pulling my teeth out too quickly and spilling blood over my cheek. "How? I thought only I could do that?"

He angles his hips and shifts my leg so he can bury himself to the hilt. He's pounding my sensitive flesh so deeply I let out a sharp cry. The asshole finally releases my throat. *"No, there're a few ways. It's not reincarnation —they're dark and twisted methods, created by the War God himself to bring back his evil loyal companions."*

I can hardly focus on his words because I'm coming so hard my eyes roll to the back of my head. He presses a final kiss to my neck before he's spilling inside me, grunting against my skin as his throbbing dick releases his pleasure.

I press my hand against his cheek. He's so fucking perfect. Rune leans his head into it and those crimson eyes of his caress my face with the same hesitation I harbor.

We're too broken for each other.

But maybe... that's why we make so much sense to one another. I trail my finger down his throat. The vertical scar from the tip of his jaw to his collarbone looks a little faded. I already know I'll never reincarnate the bitch that did this to him. Who ruined him.

I pull my hand to my chest. My healing organ wants him so badly. Wants to hear the words I so desperately want from all of my precious males, but him especially. I want him to love me—only me and forever me.

He pulls out and bends down to resituate his pants.

"Did you ever know Talia?" I readjust my pants too and shift on the bed so he can lie next to me. He rests his head on his palm and smiles at me with warmth, shaking his head.

That's a fucking relief. I think he's the only one who hasn't met her... That means he enjoys me for *me* and not the previous life I once lived.

I find solace at the thought.

"So what other ways are there to bring someone back? Do they come back complete or what? It's cheating death so it can't be normal."

He nods, looking down at the pages we're lying on. My spine warms as I hear him in my mind. *"Possession. He takes over the body of a vessel."*

What the fuck? Things in Tomorrow can do that?

"But aren't we already dead? How is that even possible?" I furrow my brows, trying to piece all this shit together.

He shrugs. *"You still have a body in Tomorrow. A vessel. Just as you can die a second death, you can lose your vessel to the darker beings. Gods of deceit and malice."*

It clicks in my head.

"Do you think that's what happened when I almost tore my heart out? My skin was ashy and I felt a sinister darkness inside me." I sit up and wrap my arms around myself. The feeling of something evil being inside me is... disturbing. The God of War? What the hell is going on with all of this?

I stand up and collect the crumpled pages, shoving them in a drawer before Arulius comes to collect me. "Well, while you're on research duty, I have to meet with Arulius, so you should probably go," I mutter as I change into thick winter leggings and grab my white coat. I've gotten used to slipping my wings through the designated holes and it takes me half the time it did a few months ago.

My Dreadius grunts angrily at me but I ignore him as I hold the door open.

"I know. Trust me, the feeling is mutual, but we're

lucky he kept his mouth shut about our adventure last night so I have to play nice." I fake smile at him to show my best acting and he smirks at me, setting his hand on my head as he walks by and ruffling my hair into a mess.

"Hey!" I bat his hand away and he turns to wink at me with a wide grin.

Arulius knocks on my door a few minutes later and I follow him down to the court's front doors. We stand outside under the terraces above that save us from the snow.

The golden Eostrix is messing with his coat, making sure it's secure and tight before turning to look at me. His amethyst eyes are holding that familiar flicker of hope within them and I don't even bother reacting to it.

"Ready?"

I cross my arms and lower my brows. "Ready for what? You haven't told me anything." I huff. My breath mists in the crisp afternoon air.

He ignores my tone and kicks up the corner of his lip. "Flying 101."

His golden wings open and the suns crest over them perfectly. They shimmer gorgeously and light the snow around us with glimmers of yellow.

I gulp. "*Flying?*" I murmur. He nods, looking amused as hell. "But I can't fly, Arulius. My wing..."

I pull my broken wing around my arm. It's a little bit

shorter than the other one—never really grew the same after Wren broke it.

Arulius pushes my hair from my face and his weak smile has my heart clenching. "You can fly. It's shorter and not as strong as your good wing, but I know you can do it." My cheeks heat with his admission.

All I can manage is a hesitant nod.

20

Elodie

Arulius lands us on a cliff face on the eastern mountains of Nesbrim.

I can see the High Court from here, but we're so high up that everything looks miniature. The clouds are fluffy around us and the thick air leaves the question of an incoming storm.

We stand close to the edge of the onyx-colored rock and my stomach is curling in on itself.

"I can't do this," I mumble as I take a few steps back.

Arulius lets out a short laugh and grabs my arm. "Yes

you can, and I'm not asking." He pulls me back to the edge and I cling to his arm like my life depends on it.

"Why are you trying to teach me to fly anyway?" I glare at him. But he just smiles wickedly at me as he pushes me off the cliff.

I let out a scream as I try to stop my body from spiraling in the air. My feathers are tight against my body.

Arulius leaps after me and is at my side in seconds, a look of mischief in his gaze. "Open your wings, love." He arcs his wings and the air catches him instantly. "Fly!"

I take a few steadying breaths and spread my wings. The shock that the air sends through me is exhilarating. I can feel the breath of this world whistling through my feathers and bones. All at once I'm suspended in the air. Arulius dips past me with pride in his eyes.

He motions his head toward the clouds and his beautiful golden wings are carrying him there before I can say anything. I flap my wings a few times to get a feel for it—it's coming a lot more naturally to me than I thought it would. My short wing feels strong and it's not throwing my balance off like I thought it might. Excitement surges through me and then I'm following Arulius higher into Tomorrow's clouds.

I'm flying.

I hold my breath for all of a handful of seconds before we are breaching the clouds, soaring high into the sky.

Arulius swoops up to me and holds my hand firmly as I steady myself in the clouds.

My wings feel so light and I instinctively know which way to angle them to shift through the sky. My mind might not remember this world, but my wings and body seem to.

The air spills into my lungs and I devour each and every delicate feeling of it.

Arulius's golden wings shimmer in the light as he twirls and shows off his wingspan. It's at least double my own. His amethyst eyes study me as if he can't get enough of my wings at work. I tense as the clouds we spotted from the cliff approach. They're angry and gray, swollen with the snow they promise. I hesitate for a second, thinking twice about what I'm doing.

"You can do this, love."

"I don't think I can." Goosebumps shiver up my skin and I give him a worried glance.

"You can," he reassures as his eyes comfort me with an invisible caress, and just like that he swoops up and the wind pulls him into the dark storm.

He's always left me to follow, and it works every damn time. He leads the way and I'm itching to chase after him.

I worry my lip and stare with fear. Doubt claws at my chest. I'm not sure why I thought I would be able to do this, or better yet, *why* I would want to do this.

I give a hesitant glance at my beige wings. The feathers lift with the urge to follow my blood-bonded Eostrix. To follow my instincts.

Fuck it all, I decide to throw away everything holding me back.

I flap my wings and fly into the storm after him.

The cloud wall breaks against my face. Fresh, cold flakes powder on my skin like dust on a chilly morning.

I open my eyes and my breath is stolen from me.

Rays of sunlight pierce through the dark winter storm, the pink and orange light at the finish line of an endless tunnel of black and gray. The warmth of the suns touches my skin and the snow dances in tandem with it.

Arulius flies ahead of me and a soft smile spreads across his lips. My heart aches and I hold my tears back as I'm flooded with memories of him.

Memories of *us*.

When he broke through to me and put in my mind a small sliver of the idea that I *am* real.

His gray and gilded hair frosts over from the chill. He's as beautiful and ruinous as he was when we met. I watch as he swoops closer to me. I sip in a breath, worried he'll see right through my walls.

"Your storms will *always* be my storms too, and if you allow it, I'll always weather them with you, love."

"But... why?" My voice quivers with the emotion I'm trying so desperately to keep from him.

His face relaxes and the rays of pink and orange hit his shimmering skin as white flakes of snow dust lovingly against his cheeks. His amethyst eyes connect to mine.

"Because that's where I found you, love." His lip slips up, I can't tell if his cheeks are reddening because of the cold or his emotions. "That's where I fucking found *you* and where you found yourself too... and I'll never forget any of it. Ever."

I can't hold my heart behind my walls anymore. A tear drops from my chin as I recite the words that have haunted my soul for the last several months.

"Even if I'm not real... the rain greets me nonetheless."

For the first time a tear breaks from his eyes too. "The sun warms me anyway." His voice trembles.

"This moment... this moment means something to me," I whisper. We're locked in a timeless world, the snow crashing through us and the sunbeams brightening at the end of the dark clouds.

"That's real enough, love. It's so much more than enough."

We collide.

I connect with him with everything I am. Our lips are cold with frost and our hands quickly wrap around one another. He hooks one around the nape of my neck and I break the kiss with a breath. Our eyes connect. Hope and affection dance in his gaze.

"I fucking hate you," I murmur against his lips.

"I love you."

"I know you do, Arulius. And it makes it hard to let you go."

"Why's that?"

"Because... because I love you too." I choke on the words and we crash into one another with the promise of rain-touched kisses and the warmth of the sun. He grasps my face and presses his forehead to mine as we twirl in the storm with wings stretched out.

"I've waited endless nights to hear you say that again." His warm breath curls against my lips.

"Yeah?" I look at him with softness in my gaze, a gentle brush of affection that I'm not sure I'll be able to live with myself for feeling for him, but I want it. Doesn't my heart get a choice? I'm beginning to think it does.

"Yeah."

I don't know if I can ever entirely forgive him, but this is a really good start. It feels like the missing piece to my healing heart. I shove him away playfully and start to fly as fast as I can toward the sunbeams that break through the clouds.

"I'm not a one-guy kind of girl anymore. So you're going to have to share. I'll never give up Kastian *or* Rune," I shout as the snow brushes my face and I feel so fucking free and clean. The pure frozen flakes wash me of all my trauma and grief. It's like I'm finally *me*.

I feel a tug of jealousy in my chest through the bond, but he's flying quickly after me with a snide grin on his lips. "Yeah, yeah, you keep your ground-dwelling pet. But your storms? They belong to me, love."

A laugh breaks from me and my healing heart spreads herself wide with the exhilaration of the skies.

I was created to fly—why the fuck did I wait so long to spread my wings? Broken or not, I'm the Goddess of Life, of Dawn.

I belong up here.

The sun's setting and we're still at least an hour's flight away from Nesbrim. Our feathers are soundless against the sky as we glide back.

"So tell me, Arulius. You promised. It's the only way I'll even consider forgiving you."

He looks at me and his expression darkens, eyes softening with pain as he nods. "It's no secret to you that I knew Talia."

I nod, keeping my eyes on the mountains ahead. Nesbrim's lights are becoming visible as the last sun rays slip into twilight, the stars mingling with the warmth on the horizon.

"She was such a beautiful goddess, but her heart was cold. The Rhythm was the only thing that mattered to her. Even the God of Death was second to it."

I furrow my brow. I'm not sure I like who Talia was.

Past life or not, she made decisions that I would *never*

make. If she'd just let Lucius and Violet be together, *none* of this would be happening, but I guess then I would never have been... me.

"Did she love Borvon?" I ask quietly.

Arulius scoffs. "She only loved the Rhythm. All the males she took meant nothing to her." There's hurt in his voice and I raise a brow at him. They obviously had... *relations*... but did he have deeper feelings for her too?

"Did *you* love her?" I turn to study him. His brows furrow and a weak smile crosses his lips.

"I did—completely, like a fool."

I let a small gasp slip out. I knew they bonded but I didn't think he loved her...

"She took everything from me. I was a fool once upon a time, and after her, I just didn't give a shit anymore. Kept my head down and followed orders. That's the way it was always meant to be for someone like me."

I bite my lip in thought. "That doesn't line up with Moro's story. He said the God of Wrath bonded with her to take her powers... so Violet could further ruin the Rhythm."

Arulius nods. His eyes look so empty as he calls on his memories. "That's true, we did bond, but it was Talia who wanted to bond with me. She wasn't aware I had the power to contain other gods' abilities. No god was as strong as her, except Borvon, but I'd already slain him."

I swallow hard at the thought of him killing Borvon. I immediately picture Kastian dying all over again and I have to shake my head to clear the image from my mind.

"Why would she want to bond with you?" It comes out a little more snarky than I was going for.

He shoots me a glare and I wince with an apologetic look.

"That's not how I meant it... but really, why?"

Arulius clenches his teeth and I can feel a swell of anger rise in my chest, though it's more distant than usual. "Because she thought *she* could control me. Her intentions were to have Violet's pet massacre her court."

My wings tilt and I immediately stop, faltering a bit with the stopping portion because it's so much easier to stay in motion. My wings bat in the air and I find my rhythm. He glides ahead a bit and turns, waiting for me.

"Talia *wouldn't* do that," I say firmly. There's no fucking way she would do something like that... right?

Arulius considers me for a moment before flying closer. "She tried, but I locked her powers up. Violet wanted her to endure the same pain she herself did. The pain of time. Though the High Lady quickly began to notice that it was the Rhythm being broken that hurt Talia more than Borvon's death."

He rolls his shoulders as if they're sore and pushes his hair from his face. My golden god looks like the sun itself in the dark. He still shimmers, as if the light can't leave him.

"So at what point did you fall in love then?" I try to swallow the lump in my throat, disgusted with my past self if what he's saying is true...

He smiles nostalgically. "I was her guard. We spent so much time together and I pitied her. She was so loyal to her beliefs. Talia was beautiful, but too lost for her own good. All she had to do was reincarnate Violet..."

My stomach fucking twists, bile rising up my throat.

"That's all she wanted... just to be with her love again. She begged, but Talia refused. After nearly a year, Talia turned her focus to me, baiting me into her love trap until I was stupid enough to fall for her. I tried to help her break the bond so that she could be free... She promised we would be together. But after the bond was broken she turned on me."

Tears are battling their way to my eyes but I hold them at bay the best I can. It's funny how different a story can sound when you hear the other side of it.

"Violet was furious that I betrayed her, rightfully so. As punishment she had me slaughter the Goddess of Life. Violet is the Goddess of Ruling. She controls all but the Rhythm Gods." He pauses and swallows like his words are choking him. "I... can still see Talia's dying smile. She was happy to press restart, because it meant the Rhythm would be cycling once more. The Goddess of

Life is always reincarnated upon dying, like a phoenix reborn in ashes. She got a new start... but I was never the same."

"Arulius..."

He reluctantly looks at me. His amethyst eyes pierce through me. "I'm sorry that I'm a monster to you, Elodie, that I fucking killed you and tricked you... ruined you. It's no excuse, but I hated you... and when Violet called for you to reenter Tomorrow, I was happy to carry out her orders. Happy, until I met you."

I have no words.

We stare at each other in silence as the twilight dips to night around us.

"You were nothing like her. You were... *you*." His purple eyes narrow as tears fill them. His jaw quivers with his attempt at holding himself together. "I'm sorry I let her make me a monster, love. But I can never go against Violet again. I *won't*. No matter how much I love you. Because... because—"

"Because she will make you kill me."

The words are like a breath of relief.

His tears stream down his cheeks and he nods silently. My heart aches at his pain—at mine too. Maybe this has been going on for long enough. I don't think I'll ever fully forgive him... but fuck, I didn't expect this.

I lift my hands to his face and wipe his tears. My golden Eostrix has been hurting for such a long time. I can feel the weight of his guilt and pain ease off through the bond and I wrap my arms around him tightly.

"Thank you for telling me. I can't say I forgive you, or that we will ever be the same as we once were, but... this is a start," I murmur into his neck. He chuckles softly and I pull away to meet his gaze.

"Thank you... for giving me a chance."

21

Elodie

The snowstorm hasn't lifted for days. I've been tempted to try flying in it alone since Arulius has been busy running Nesbrim. It's easy to forget our places here—especially now that our relationship seems so much less strained. I'm not sure everyone else will be able to see his reasons as I do... but I've been here long enough with him to know that Arulius would do anything for me, even if it means being my villain.

I smile and tap my finger on the café table as I stare outside at the snow crashing against the windows. It's already dark outside and the temperature is plummeting well below zero, I'm sure.

I hope Arulius isn't flying around in this weather.

I'm pulled from my daze by Naminé's soft laugh. My lips are perking up instantly with the sound and I look to see what's so funny.

Rune's drinking his coffee black and hardly even curls his lips against the bitter liquid. Naminé is trying to reach the last scone that was on the platter we ordered and he's holding it over his head so she can't reach it across the table. His crimson eyes catch mine over his cup and they soften on me.

A laugh tumbles from my lips. "Rune, give her the pastry." He furrows his brows and shakes his head, handing it to me instead, and Naminé's amber eyes grow big like she's about to beg me for it. I toss it to her. "You two will be the end of me."

"He ate most of them anyway!"

Rune shoots her a hard stare but then gives into a smirk. My insides warm with them around. It feels like I'm back on the human side of the realms, just catching a drink with my friend and boyfriend on a cold winter night. And in all honestly, maybe that's what this is. Why can't it be?

I take in their smiles and the warmth they give me. I won't let these rare moments slip by—I have to take them in and relish in them as much as I can. My mind feels so much more at ease now that I've mended a little with Arulius. A weight has lifted and I feel like I can finally stop warring with my heart

We finish the last of our coffee and say goodbye to Greysil. Naminé stays behind to help her girlfriend clean up the shop before closing so they can spend the rest of the evening together.

I give her a tight hug and Rune just nods in her direction as we head out into the cobblestone streets. I hook my arm through his and I lean into him as we walk back toward the High Court.

"Feels like we're on a date." I smile. The cold bites my nose and my breath curls in the air as I look up at him.

Rune smiles at me and the tattoo he gave me heats as he speaks through our connection.

"You don't want to know how long it's been since I've been on a date."

I can't say that I hate that. My smile fades at the sight of a tall Eostrix who stands in the middle of the street just ahead of us.

Rune stops and takes a step in front of me. I lean to the side to peek around him. The Eostrix's wings are huge and... black.

Kastian.

I've been yearning to see him. I move past Rune and hear him curse in my mind. Kastian's face lights up as I run to him. His arms open and I crash into them, squeezing him tightly as his arms wrap around me too.

His laugh is music to my ears and contagious. "There you are. I've been looking for you." He leans his head down on mine and nuzzles me.

"You were?" My heart flutters and I look up at him. His ocean eyes are endless and dance with the very snow that falls from the sky. His white hair is messy over his forehead and his black horns glisten as snow melts on them.

He nods with a warm smile and glances up at Rune. "Your guard is more than welcome to join us if you'd like." Kastian's voice is soft and for a second I feel bad because I actually don't want Rune to join us... I've missed my Death God.

I look over my shoulder and frown at Rune's scowl. He looks ready to fight and be an asshole. "Rune, can you head back to the High Court?"

His response is immediate. My tattoo heats.

"No."

I look back at Kastian and shrug. "He's coming too."

Kastian holds my hand as we walk into a bathhouse near the north end of Nesbrim. My eyes widen and take it all in. The front looks like most of the other shops stones and ivy with snow shoveled off the path to the front doors. A warm light glows from the lamppost right outside the entrance.

"A bathhouse?" I mumble and my brows knit together with confusion.

Kastian squeezes my hand tighter. "Not quite." A smile plays at his lips and mischief lingers in his gaze. What the heck is he up to now?

Rune looks absolutely pissed and I wish his telepathy worked both ways so I could tell him to knock it off.

"This is a hot spring," he sends to my mind and my cold bones shiver with excitement.

Oh gods, I could use a good soaking.

We enter and I'm hit with a wave of lavender aroma and steam. It's overwhelmingly amazing and I'm clenching my fists to stop myself from jumping up and down.

The ceilings are tall and arched at the top. It's like we stepped through a portal or something, because behind the cement walls and floor-to-ceiling glass ahead is an entire mountainside of steaming pools. My jaw drops and I let Kastian deal with the front desk employee as I venture over to the glass to get a better look.

It *is* a mountain! Gods, did Violet make this too? It's

wonderful... The night sky is clear above and stars shimmer welcomingly. Wherever this is, it's not in Nesbrim—the snowstorm is still raging outside here.

My tattoo warms. *"The glass is created by the Gremitie, creatures of the sea. They are versed in spatial magic that can bring large locations anywhere the glass is."* Rune stands next to me and keeps his red eyes on the stars as I do.

"Naminé told me... and Violet is one. She made this place, didn't see?" I shift my eyes to the warm pools and can already feel them warming my body.

"Yup." Rune leans against me a little more and I'm soaking it all in.

I hear Kastian thank the Moss Sparrow employee and turn to watch him walk over to us. He sets his palm on the glass and an outline of the glass door takes shape as he presses it open.

The world beyond the glass consumes me and I'm smiling from ear to ear. Kastian leans in and presses a kiss to my forehead. "Let's go have some fun." His voice sounds weary and his eyes look sunken. I think he could use this as much as I do.

I press my hand to his cheek. "Are you okay? You look really tired."

His fangs graze my palm as he presses kisses along it and heat spreads through me. He glances up at me and nods. "Couldn't be better, now that I'm with you."

He obviously doesn't want me pushing it further as he nudges me forward into the world beyond the glass. Kastian steps in behind me but Rune remains on the other side.

My heart races—at least I get to spend a little time with my sweet Kastian.

I let him take the lead and he starts on the path up the mountain. The incline is steep but I keep at his side. Our feathers touch and mingle as we silently walk.

He stops at a beautiful turquoise pool. The ground is an alluring white rock that I originally thought was snow. The plants that grow on the edges of the pool are sage-colored and iridescent in the starlight.

I look at Kastian as he sheds his coat and pulls his black shirt over his head too. My eyes immediately drink him in. His muscles are taut and the familiar tan scars still stride up his torso and arms. I let my eyes linger over him as he removes his pants next and is completely naked before me.

My perfect God of Death.

He raises a playful brow at me and nods to the pool. "Well? Are you just going to watch me enjoy this or are you getting in too?" His sun-kissed skin shimmers in the moonlight and I'm lost as I stare at his iridescent white hair. He tilts his head. "Elodie?"

I nod slowly. "I'm getting in. It's just... so crazy that we're here together, isn't it?" I mumble as I slip my white cloak off and start to pull my sweater over my head. I toss it to the ground and watch him closely. "Tell me what Violet wants from you, Kastian."

His eyes flick down to my bare breasts as I step out of my pants and underwear. He doesn't give anything away in his expression, but I can see the pain and weariness in his eyes.

"Elodie... I agreed to be cursed not to say, but I promise once it's done we will be free to leave together." He steps closer to me, his ebony wings trailing behind him. His hand cups my cheek and our eyes connect. "Now stop worrying and relax."

I give him a weak smile. I'm not entirely happy with what he said but I know he's doing all of this for me, so if soaking with him will help make him happy, then gods be damned, I'm going to do it.

I step down into the magical water and my skin instantly warms. The chill in the air instantly vanishes like a veil is sealing the heat in above us. I sink down to my shoulders and close my eyes as the water seeps into my wings.

"*Oh my gods,* this is amazing."

Kastian chuckles and submerges himself until the water covers his lips. He swims over to me on the far wall where I'm sitting on a white, carved-rock bench. Whoever discovered this place is absolutely genius for all the amenities they included.

My lips purse up as he approaches closer. His dark brows are collecting sweat and his piercing blue eyes are preying on me. I giggle and reach my hands out to stop him in case he's thinking of tickling me, because damn it, he has that look in his eyes.

"Don't even think about—"

I gasp and then my head is plunged beneath the water. I panic for a second as the heat swarms me and my eyes shoot open.

Oh my gods.

Goosebumps ripple up my arms and my marrow pacifies as I watch turquoise- and pink-hued bubbles rise around us. My nose touches Kastian's and his white hair floats above his head like a halo. His eyes are full of affection and he's looking at me like I'm the only person that's ever mattered.

If this is love, I never want to fall out of it.

My sweet Borvon. I can feel Talia brush up from within me and she's reaching for him as desperately as I am.

I smile and bubbles rise from my lips. Kastian smiles back as he leans in to kiss me. Our lips connect and I swear to gods I can feel the pulse of the realms within us, yearning for our union as much as we ourselves do.

Our love has always been fated.

At one point I was afraid of this... being destined to love someone because I felt like I *had* too. But this isn't forced, no... this is visceral. A calling from deep within my bones, like he's the half of me that I can never be without.

He deepens the kiss with his tongue and I'm not sure how much longer I can hold my breath. Kastian picks up on my worry and pulls away, smirking like he has a secret. He mouths, *"You can breathe"* then points at his lungs, showing that he's been breathing this entire time.

Ghosts of my past creep up the back of my neck. This is how I tried to kill myself in his glades when I thought he was dead. I watch him with fear ticking in my throat, but he's so calm that I quell my nerves before deciding to take a breath.

I inhale a short quick breath, just in case, and it slips through my lungs just like air. I flinch and my chest surges with overflowing excitement.

What the hell kind of water is this?!

Kastian laughs and bubbles burst from his mouth. His fangs glint with the moonlight that filters in. I grab his face and surprise takes over his features as I press into him with my entire being.

Our naked bodies crash together, our tongues exploring one another as we take each other in. I don't care about anything in the realms right now except the Eostrix before me. His white hair merges with mine in the water and his desire makes itself known beneath me.

I smile against his lips and look up at him with a fire burning in my gaze. He pulls away and presses kisses down my neck, nipping at my flesh as his fingers trail down my body and slip into my folds.

I let out a moan that gets drowned in the beautiful, magical water as he starts to circle my clit and bites into my neck. His teeth pierce deep and the pain washes away with the immense pleasure that he brings as he feasts on my blood.

The urge to drink from him is painful, but I know the repulsion won't let me, so I try my best to just enjoy him. I let my hands explore his chest and glide down his stomach to wrap my hand around his engorged dick. He grips my back tighter and pulls his fangs from me. His tongue is out like he's just tasted the best fucking thing in the world, and he runs it across his bottom lip.

I mouth, *"How do I taste?"* and he just grins as he continues to press kisses down my breasts, sucking my tit into his mouth and rolling that beautiful tongue around the sensitive nub.

He peers up from my breast and mouths, *"I don't know—but I'm going to find out."*

I bite my lip as he nudges my legs apart for him. His ocean eyes flick up to mine as he devours me. *Fuck.*

My eyes roll and I try not to crush his head with my thighs, but holy fuck, he knows how to use his tongue. Kastian holds my hips while he ravishes my pussy. I buck my hips as the pleasure grows and he doesn't let up until I'm coming undone and melting in his calloused hands.

He licks me until he's satisfied and then smirks up at me. *"Fucking amazing."*

I'm just glad he didn't say *dusted sunshine*. I nod my head up to let him know I'm heading back into the real world now, not our diluted, beautiful water-fantasy, and he follows me up.

Our heads crest the top of the water, and even though I've been breathing fine down there I take a big breath of the air. Kastian does the same before his hands are all over me again. He guides our bodies to the submerged bench and sits me on his lap so I'm straddling him. His erection is throbbing between my thighs.

"I want you, Elodie. For so many reasons, I want you." His hair is wet against his forehead and my lovely Death God has never looked so untroubled.

And the sight of it makes my heart fall apart. How much does this man deserve to smile like this? More than I could ever give him, and yet this is the first I've seen him so content and happy. My heart curls in my chest.

"I want to make you the happiest god, Kastian. You deserve everything." I try to blink away the tears that are fighting to surface, but they push through and roll down my cheeks.

He kisses them away and nuzzles his nose against mine as he grinds against me, his erection rubbing my slit and drawing breathy moans from me.

"You've brought me more happiness than any god could ever dream of. It's always been you, Elodie."

He tugs me forward and then he's entering me, spreading me, like our bodies were always carved just for one another. His dick fills me to the brim and I cry out as he thrusts into me relentlessly.

My body's on fire.

Kastian grips my shoulders desperately, like he'll fall apart if we separate, and I feel the same waves of emotions crashing into me too. Is this because we're Rhythm Gods? The feeling is so similar to what Rune draws out of me, a sensation like my veins are filling with power and a swarm of energy lives just beneath the surface of us. A calling that I will never be able to deny. I've never felt this undying connection with Arulius before.

It's consuming.

"Do you feel that?" Kastian grunts as he drives into me. I'm so close to coming again already.

"Yeah." I moan and fist his hair, pulling his head back so I can look at my ruinous god. His eyes are filled with a lust-drunk daze, but his brows furrow as his thrusts become harder and faster.

I cry out as he slams into me a final time before he's spilling his seed into me, his dick throbbing against my walls, and he's holding me down tightly so none of it spills out.

I ride out the ecstasy of it for a few moments before

slumping into his arms. "What was that?" I murmur into his neck, he leans his head against mine.

"I have no idea, but it felt like the realms and the magic in our veins were rejoicing."

He holds me against his warm skin and I shut my eyes with a blissful smile. "I've missed you."

"I've missed you too," he whispers against my shoulder and kisses my skin like the stars will never stop shining for us.

22

Elodie

Kastian's been following Violet around like her own personal Pine Hollow for days now and it pisses me off. I know he said to trust him, but I know she's doing something to make him tired and worn down. I see the dark rings under his eyes and he craves rest more and more each day.

I hate it.

At least she's been leaving our torture sessions cancelled. I can't imagine having to endure those with Kastian watching.

Since our night at the hot springs I haven't seen much

of him. There's so much I want to ask... so much time we need to catch up on. Like, what the hell was that connection we felt? It's been burning holes into my mind at night.

Wren's been heavy on my mind since our encounter in the forest as well. I let out a dreary sigh at the thought of all of us scattered across Tomorrow when all we really want is to be together.

Rune's lips press against my bare shoulder. He's already hard behind me and we've just woken up. I smile and lean into his chest to soak in all his warmth. I'm so content and safe with him. He's the closest place to *home* I've been in a long time.

I pull the sheets closer to my face and snuggle in, feeling entirely too comfortable to move.

"Good morning, beautiful."

I smile as my tattoo heats along my spine and I love the feeling of it. But it's short-lived; I hear footsteps outside my door, followed by a sharp knock.

"Ughhh."

Rune's crimson eyes flicker with amusement. He gives me one more kiss before tossing the sheets off of himself and pulling a gray sweater on. I sit up on my end and pull Rune's shirt over my head. It's huge on me and covers my ass so I'm fine with wearing this around today.

I open the door and feel heat rise to my cheeks as

Kastian's ocean eyes stare back at me. *Oh shit—what's he doing here?*

His eyes drink me in, flicking down and then back up. My eyes do the same. I'm bracing myself for him to freak out like he did when he found out about me drinking from Wren, but he's surprisingly calm.

Rune steps behind me and wraps a possessive arm around my chest.

I glance up and find him glaring daggers at Kastian. One look at my Eostrix tells me the feeling is one hundred percent mutual.

I clear my throat, hoping to end this awful tension.

"Kastian, what brings you to my room?" Rune leans his head down and rests his chin on my shoulder. Gods, I have no fucking idea how this situation is going to pan out. He didn't seem particularly pleased after Kastian and I had mind-blowing sex at the hot springs either. But I'm not sure if it's because he's jealous that someone else was getting my attention or that he didn't get to join in... Gods.

"Violet has business to see to. I have the day to do as I choose and I wanted to see you." Kastian's voice is soft as he speaks to me. I'm still unsure about all of this, but my heart takes the leap because I can't keep my feelings a secret, not with them.

"Rune's coming too then." I don't ask—I make sure it's perfectly clear.

His blue eyes flash at me with jealousy but he quickly straightens himself, nodding. "Okay... Why?"

I bite my lower lip. This was a lot easier to say to Arulius.

"I just... I'm not choosing." He raises his brow and flicks a glance to Rune, then back to me. Fuck, how do I say this... "I want... all of you."

His eyes widen, I wouldn't say with judgment, but maybe surprise?

"*All?*"

I swallow, looking down at my feet and grabbing the edge of my wing to fiddle with anxiously. "Well... You, Rune..." I look at Kastian and he does *not* look impressed, but doesn't look like he's shocked, given that I'm in the Dreadius's shirt. "Wren..."

A small gasp leaves his lips. "I'm sorry, did you say *Wren?* Since when did you two—"

"And Arulius." I spit it out because I know this one will take the cake.

Kastian's ebony wings flex at the golden Eostrix's name and he clenches his fists tightly at his sides. I hold my ground and stare at him with everything I have.

"Elodie—you are an *Eostrix*. I understand your blood-aversion curse, but Wren and Arulius? One broke your wing and the other... We don't need to talk about what *he* did."

I cross my arms and look up at Rune for support. He

doesn't owe me a godsdamn thing but he always has my back—even with this.

My Dreadius nods at me and smiles. He's always on my side.

"Wren has always been there for me. Sure, he's violent and has major issues, but there's good in him. You know it too. We aren't the same wounded people we were over half a year ago." I hesitate for a moment, thinking of how I could possibly defend Arulius. I know Arulius is a stretch, I get it. He's caused so much pain and suffering... but I long for him nonetheless. It hurts more to not love him than it does to give into it. I'm still not sure I'll ever forgive him, but I know that my heart is working overtime to patch those parts of my soul.

"You're seriously going to forgive him for murdering you and Margo?"

Margo... I'll never forgive him for that. But he thought I was Talia. His wrath wasn't for me.

It was for another love.

"He told me his side of the story. I don't know if I'll ever fully forgive him, but I still love him, Kastian."

He lets out a long, weary sigh and drags his hand over his face, like I've ruined all his plans. "Elodie. He and Violet are the *villains*, remember? They're the bad guys who kidnapped you, who killed everyone we've lost, who are trying to stop the Rhythm."

I open my mouth to argue, but he shouts as he throws

his fist against the doorframe, making me flinch. I tighten my hands at my side.

"*Everyone,* Elodie! They're *all dead.* Borvon died, Talia died, you died, I fucking died as a child in the human realm and suffered alone here for most of my life. Does that mean anything to you? How could you fall for their shit again so easily?"

I grit my teeth as tears fill my eyes and Rune steps in front of me, baring his teeth at my dark-winged Eostrix.

Kastian clenches his jaw and tries to compose himself, running a hand through his white hair.

"Was Talia the hero then?"

Rune and Kastian both snap their eyes at me. The tension is thick, but I press on.

"Was she the saint in this? I'm not believing blindly anymore, I'm listening to both sides of this story. Because to me... it really fucking sounds like Talia was the dark and corrupt one. I don't know how to cope with the fact that my past life fucked *everything up.*"

Kastian scoffs and his brows pull tightly together. "No... no, Talia was—"

"I heard she chose the Rhythm over you—that she loved her purpose to the realms more than her partners. All she had to fucking do was give Violet her love back and all this shit would've been done! Did she *ever* love you, Borvon?!"

Kastian's eyes grow wide with pain, like his past life is

speaking to him in his mind, but he stammers, "I—I... Yes... Yes, of course she did."

I'm already feeling bad for everything I've said but I can't stop.

I reach a hand to his beautiful face and cup his flushed cheek. "Then why would she refuse to reincarnate just *one* goddess? Talia let you die, Borvon. She let you die and everyone else who ever fucking mattered."

Kastian stumbles backwards and grips his head as if it's ringing. I reach after him, steadying him so he doesn't fall.

"Are you okay?" I brush his white hair from his face and he looks wild—like the core of him is shattering. His eyes are still blue, but there is a ring of pure white circling his pupil. Panic rushes me and I shake him. What the fuck is that? "Kastian... Kastian!"

Rune kneels next to me and nudges me back a bit. I furrow my brows at him, but he focuses on my Eostrix, and when his lips part I already feel the shudder of his eerie voice climbing my spine.

"Don't fight your memories, let them flow through you."

Kastian freezes, as if Rune's voice is poison, creeping into his head and whispering forbidden things.

For a second I think he's going to lunge at my Dreadius and try to kill him, but instead he takes a deep breath and lets his ebony wings slump down onto the tiles. I approach and kneel next to Rune, setting a hand on Kastian's shoulder. So it's true then... Rune's curse can't affect Rhythm Gods. If his cursed voice didn't affect me, it makes sense that Kastian would be impervious to it as well.

He's shaking.

"Kastian... please say something." I lean into him and hug him tightly. "Please, I'm so tired of fighting. I'm sorry... I just want us all to be happy and safe." His arms tense beneath me and I release him.

His ocean eyes look through me. The white circles are gone from around his pupils but he looks defeated, wounded by the cruel things I said, and my heart breaks at the sight of it.

"Elodie... I'm getting you out of here, and we both know Arulius will never let you have your powers back. So in the end you'll have to choose. You know that—you will *have* to choose. To save Tomorrow and all those in the realms or to stay here and pretend everything is fine. Pretend that you're happy with your blood bag and golden piece of shit."

I bite my tongue to hold in the things I want to say to him, the ugly and nasty things that would absolutely tear him apart. I keep it to myself. I watch as he stands and leaves without another word, his wings dragging on the tiles behind him.

Rune and I sneak into the library for the day.

Even with my wings, I'm way quieter than he is. He's so big and clunky—every time he tries to make himself small he just crouches over like he's trying to hide and it takes everything in me not to laugh at him.

Once we slip past the doors to the library, we wait for Naminé to join us. As soon as she steps through the doors, our little band of Nesbrim misfits is complete.

She stretches and yawns as she walks over to me. "What are we on the hunt for today?"

"We still need to figure out how to break the bond with Arulius." My chest tightens at the thought of letting go of our bond, because it was once a beautiful connection I loved. But if I'm ever to resurrect anything again, it has to be broken.

Rune searches the first floor while Naminé and I head up the spiral staircase to the second. She takes the far end and I thumb through the window-wall shelves.

There's a peculiar black book that I come across after a few painstaking hours. I pull out a book that's labeled *The Gods of Ruling* and find that there's another name for them. The correct name is scribbled down below on the cover: *Gods of Judgement.* Okay—why the hell would everyone call them Ruling Gods? No wonder I couldn't find a damn thing about them before.

Everything is so backwards and I'm guessing it has to do with Violet destroying most of the records of this world. I almost feel bad for tearing the page out of what might be the last physical record.

I find an entire section on gods of judgment now that I know the right name and am perfectly fucking floored by what I learn.

Apparently they're able to control most lower-tier gods and spirits. Their judgment is divine and to be honored above all else. To disobey them is like spitting in the face of... well, Violet. It works like a type of coercion. Only the Rhythm Gods have the distinct freedom of their judgment. I clench my fist tightly with rage circling in my veins. Drops of blood drip on my leg.

Why would Talia not resurrect her? Why was... why was I so evil...

I push the thought from my head and go to the first floor to tell Rune what I've found. Naminé senses my emotions and follows me down.

"That's the first I've heard of it too. Look what I found." The tattoo warms on my back as his voice flows through me.

He holds out a black book. The leather is worn and hardly holding together. I carefully take it from him and look it over. The inner page says: *North, God of War.* My heart skips a beat when I turn a few pages in and find the scariest creature I've ever fucking seen. It has rows of sharp teeth, just like the skull had, except the picture is of a male with flesh. He's demonic-looking, with soot-colored skin, and his eyes are dark like midnight blue. Black wings stretch from his back, but they aren't beautiful and angelic like Kastian's. North's wings are like those of a bat, with claws at the ends. He's handsome in a bone-chilling type of way and my stomach drops at actually seeing him.

"Holy shit. This is it—those are the same teeth as the skull." I glance up at Rune. He's frowning and his red eyes look at me with worry. Naminé peers over my shoulder and scowls at the image. I still need to catch her up on the nightmares...

"Don't tell me. We're totally fucked with this, aren't we? The God of War is going to do something that will ruin everything because Violet is bringing him back to life somehow, right?" I say it sarcastically but I'm being serious.

He narrows his eyes at me and my tattoo warms. *"Basically, yes."*

I worry my lip and he catches my trembling jaw with his palm, bringing his lips in for a kiss, and I hear his beautiful deep voice echo through my mind. *"It's going to be okay, pup. I'm going to talk to Kol and see what he knows. Maybe he can help."*

I push him back. "No. Kol isn't someone we can trust. He's her puppet! Just like Arulius is. *We* have to do this, us three. That's it." Naminé furrows her brow and looks at Rune with concern flashing through her eyes. I told her that he can talk to me through telepathy, but I'm sure it's weird as hell watching us communicate like this.

His gaze softens on me and he nods. *"Just remember that you have allies. Many of us here in Tomorrow wish to have the Rhythm restored too. We want to know that the cycle will continue, that* no *death will be permanent."* He brushes my dark hair behind my ear and I take a deep breath.

"I know... I know you're trying to help. I'm sure many of them would too... but not Kol. I watched him kill Kastian right before my eyes. I have beef with him and I'm not accepting anything from him until I can slap that motherfucker."

He smirks at me and shrugs. *"I can try to figure out what the High Lady is trying to get out of this, but the more ears the better."* He leaves it at that. I rub my arms from the goosebumps that North's image gives me. I don't want such evil to exist in the realms... not like North.

"Let's go grab some rolls from that shop on the main street."

Naminé stands quickly and passes me a book. "Perfect, I'm starving—and here, I didn't want to interrupt your weird mind conversation with the brute." I look down at the book she's shoving in my hands. It's labeled *Curses and Bonds*.

I smile up at her. "Have I ever told you how amazing you are?"

She flips her ash-blonde hair over her shoulder and crosses her arms. "Not nearly enough." I break out into laughter and she's quick to join me. I even hear Rune make a small grunt.

We all leave the library half combed-through, with the two books tucked safely in my arms.

23

Elodie

The nightmares are an every-night occurrence now. It's been an entire week since we found the War God and the *Curses and Bonds* books. We've learned both enough to take over the world and jack-shit at the same time.

They were worth the time we spent looking for them though. Apparently bonds can be broken by sheer willpower, and if you're not as versed in that, as I am, sharing your heart with other people also wears away at the bond.

My feelings for Rune must be more potent than I

thought. I knew the bond has felt weaker lately, but this proves why. All this time I've been fighting against the one thing that can save the entire realm... love.

Kastian has been avoiding me since our argument in the hallway. It's not like I've had a chance to try and talk to him since then either, with all the shit Violet has him doing for her.

I've been flying daily with Arulius. I'm shocked that Violet is allowing this, but when I asked him he just said that it's because she doesn't know. It makes sense, since she's never particularly cared what I do, more so now that our torture sessions are done. She's been preoccupied with Kastian and whatever their agreement entails. I don't like that one bit... but what can I do except wait like my Death God asked me to.

Arulius makes time for me and I find it oddly comforting. It's a time for just us. Every day I can feel my wings getting stronger and the weight in my chest easing. We especially love it when there are storms. Chasing one another to see who can reach the clouds first and getting caught in the snow and wind is something else with him.

This storm is especially torrential though.

We haven't flown this high before—I can nearly see the curve of the realm from these heights. The towering trees of the world don't look so godly with this view. I take a deep breath as I open my wings as wide as they'll go, letting the air take me where it will.

Arulius swoops beneath me, creating a gust that makes me spin and lose the nice air pocket I'd found.

"Hey! That's not funny!" I shout at him while laughing my ass off. I guess it's kind of funny.

He turns his head and shoots me the smile that used to have a chokehold on me. I falter for a second before returning it with a warm upturn of my lips.

"Come on, love, you have to be ready for *anything*." He hums as his golden wings cut through the sky like a blade of light. His black winter attire makes him seem almost like a normal civilian. It's easy to forget our roles from this high in the sky.

I look down at my hands, wondering when these happy days will pass. Because nothing lasts forever and I'm too gloom and doom to enjoy it while it lasts.

"Do you ever wish we could just go back to Moro's cottage?"

I don't know why I ask, but it's been bothering me. I have no idea how he actually feels about the past.

He considers me, his amethyst eyes taking in every inch of my face. "Yeah, I do. I miss training with you, and as much as I hate to admit it, Kastian too." I smile at him, nostalgia getting the better of me and twisting my aching heart.

"Was I *ever* the sun to you?" he asks. I quirk a brow at him because I'm not sure what he's asking. "Was I ever able to warm your soul… like you did mine?"

I'm stunned. For a second I just stare at him.

"Yeah. You were." I gaze at the winter lands before us and manage a bittersweet smile as I take in the orange-lit snowbanks. The three suns wave farewell as the moons crest over the mountaintops. "But I have new ones now."

Our flight back is quiet. I try to focus on anything except our silence. I've really improved my flight speed tremendously and my gimp wing doesn't hold me back at all anymore.

Nothing will.

Violet planned another one of her dinners for this evening and I'm dreading that I have to attend, but at least I'll hopefully be able to see Kastian. It's the first one since she told me her story...

I strip and put on my evening dress, tight black silk that hugs all my curves perfectly. Rune pulls on his black sweater and leans against the wall, watching me as I slip on my black heels.

Thank gods Arulius at least gives me the proper clothing for these dinners or I'd die of embarrassment. I wonder what Kastian is wearing to it.

Maybe I can meet him beforehand and talk to him.

I side-eye Rune. He's probably going to follow me no matter what I say, so I don't bother even trying to talk him out of it.

"Do you know where Kastian's room is?" I comb my dark hair out and smile with how healthy it looks. Even my face has regained a lot of its shimmer back.

Rune nods and cocks his head to the side.

"I just want to talk to him before dinner... Last time we spoke he was pretty upset with me."

He smirks and leads the way into the hall.

Of course Violet has Kastian staying in the most extravagant part of the castle.

I eye the walls. They're impeccably clean and the marbled ceilings are etched with gorgeous drawings of creatures and gods. As beautiful as it is, I still love my end of the castle better. Worn-down stones and vines are my thing—they remind me of Caziel and Moro's cute cottage.

We get to an enormous black door. Rune leans against the wall and nods his head to it.

"Can you stay out here? I want to talk to him alone." I brush his cheek with my hand as I open the door and slip inside.

It's warm in here, and the drapes are all pulled. I smile. It reminds me a lot of the first time I realized what I was. When I drank Kastian's beautiful blood.

The floors are heated and it takes me a second to let

my eyes adjust to the dark before I make out the shape of a bed in the far corner of his huge room.

My lips open to call out for him, but I freeze once I hear the sound of metal cutting skin. Goosebumps cover my skin and my voice gets caught in my throat.

What the fuck?

I pause and hold my breath so I can hear better, but my heart pounds so loudly I feel like I'm going to pass out.

Someone is being badly hurt... tortured... cut and suffering like I did for all those months. Then I hear the blood spilling into a bucket.

I let out a strangled gasp, one that is entirely impossible to hold in because I'm so fucking horrified. Sickened to my core. I instantly feel all the pain that Violet put me through. Kastian's head perks up from where he leans over a black pail. Violet stands above him, a curved knife in hand. His neck bleeds profusely.

I make eye contact with him, his ocean eyes flickering with shock and pain, but I don't stay long enough to let it all sink in. I can't stand to see him willingly suffer on my behalf. She's taking his blood too, but for what? For the skull?

Panic rushes me.

I've stayed here all this time to protect them...

I burst through the door and sprint as fast as I can down the hallway. Rune's head snaps my direction as I run by him and he's quick to follow.

I keep running, hopeless, scared, confused... hurt.

"Elodie!" Kastian shouts from the end of the hall but I'm already leaping from the window. We're three stories up and for a split second I wonder what it would be like to let this all end—but I'm not that girl anymore, now am I?

My wings open and I silently thank Arulius for teaching me to fly. I know Violet will send him after me for running, but I'm fucking done playing by their rules. This is what she's been doing to Kastian for the last few weeks? I know he wants to free me, but why this? I would never have let him go through with this if I knew she was torturing him.

Have I just been wasting my time here all along?

Rune stops at the window and I halt mid-flight—I can't be without him.

"Meet me in Caziel. Wren's cottage. Don't say a fucking word to anyone—" I stop because he literally can only speak to me and Kastian. The scowl on his face tells me he's thinking the exact same thing, but a smile cracks across his lips and the wind lifts his dark hair a bit.

There's no hiding the light in his eyes and the excitement that dances through them.

He's a fucking masterpiece and he's rooting for my freedom as much as I am. I love him. As I look down on him with the sunset warming my back and the sunlight dappling his face, I let my heart win.

I love him.

After he nods, I don't waste another second.

I fly as fast as I can. Nesbrim has never looked so small behind me. It feels too easy that I'm flying out of here, as if I could have the entire time. I know Arulius will use the bond to bring me back, but I'm going to fight it as long as I can. I'm not sure if he can feel it dwindling, but soon there will be nothing left of it.

The black dress makes flying a little uncomfortable and ridiculously cold, but I keep the fast pace. Caziel's dim lights orb against the darkness of night and I'm shaking with adrenaline at what I'm doing.

But nothing has *ever* felt so right in my entire life.

As the cobblestone streets and cottages come into view, my heart fills with the warmth of this cute little town. I land in front of the breakfast café I visited with Wren and Marley. Everything is closed at this hour and the streets are empty, but the string lights that hang from the balconies above are lit.

I smile and take my time walking down the streets. The snow isn't as heavy here, but every rooftop is covered with a white blanket and steam curls into the air from each chimney.

I stop in front of Wren's lot. It looks exactly the same as it did my first day here. I walk up to his door, taking a deep breath before I knock three times and wait for Wren.

I hear a few locks switch and then the door opens. Warm air pushes against my face and tears instantly fill my eyes as I'm met with Marley's wide ones. His sweater is a size too big for him and he's at least a few inches taller than he was the last time I saw him.

"Elodie?" His eyes light up and get all watery.

My own are blurry and I dip down to scoop him up into a tight hug. "Oh Marley! How have you been?" He giggles and wraps his small arms around my neck as I step in and kick the door shut behind me.

"I've been asking about you every day! Wren's missed you more than I have though."

I smile as I set the boy down and tap his nose. "Oh, is that right?"

I hear the floorboards creak in the kitchen and Wren's standing there looking at me like he's never seen anything so perfect in his entire life.

I could die right now.

He smiles and it reaches his amber eyes. His dark hair is messy on the top and faded on the sides. He's got an unlit joint settled behind his ear as he twirls my pink lighter between his fingers.

"He's not lying—little fucker has been begging for us to go tear down Nesbrim to get you." He crosses the living room and takes my face in his strong hands.

He dips down and crushes his lips against mine. I'm stunned for all of a second and then I'm gripping his face just as desperately.

"Eww, Mr. Bartholomew, don't kiss her in front of me!"

We both snap our attention to the forgotten Moss Sparrow. He's got his hands covering his eyes and we both laugh.

My heart fills and my blood pulses dreams and memories through me. I'd be lying if I said I've never pictured a life here with Wren and little Marley. Like a family. We'd go to the café every week at least three times, and—

A sharp *thump* rattles the door.

We all jerk our heads to look but no one moves to open it. Wren raises a brow at me. "Expecting company?"

I nod. "Rune!" My chest fills with warmth as I turn the knob but it completely extinguishes when I see Kastian standing there like a stone wall. His piercing blue eyes regard me with anger.

The air around us is instantly thick and Wren picks up on it before I have the chance to start punching and screaming at my dark-winged Eostrix.

"Let's talk upstairs. Marley, can you stoke the fire?" Wren tousles the Moss Sparrow's hair and gives him a nudge toward the fireplace.

Kastian looks absolutely perplexed that he's had to chase me here. His hair is wild and there's snow covering his wings and horns. We stare at one another for two seconds before Wren shoots us both a look, jerking his head at the stairs.

We reluctantly follow the Cypress. I note that all the books are still lining his stairs and I'm sad about all the stories he's read without me.

Once we're in his room, he sits on the bed and crosses his arms at both of us. His room fills me with so many memories, even though it's just as empty as it was before. Not a single picture up or anything personal to set on his dresser.

"Okay, what's going on?" he asks as he lights a joint and shoves the pink lighter back in his pocket.

"Well, we were about to complete the deal, but *this* one decided to run away."

Anger flashes through me and I clench my fists tightly at my sides. "Um, *excuse me?* She was draining you of your blood to feed to that fucked-up skull! I didn't stay in Nesbrim all this time just to have her torture you!"

Wren coughs and his joint flies across the floor. He whirls his attention back at Kastian. "The fucked-up *skull?*"

"I'm doing what it takes to free *you.* This is all for *you.*" Kastian walks toward me until our chests are touching. I won't back down. No fucking way. His sage scent consumes me and I can feel his aura brush beneath his skin, reaching for mine.

"I never asked you to!" I throw back at him.

He curls his lip in a snarl until his fangs are showing. "No, I guess you didn't. But while you've been busy collecting your jar of hearts, I've been selling my soul to the witch."

"Jar of hearts?" Wren echoes.

I shove Kastian back. "I'm *so sorry* that I was able to find a small bit of happiness while being tortured and ruined for *you*."

He growls and grabs both of my arms as he pins me against the wall roughly. "I would do *anything* for you, Elodie. Give everything I have just so I can have you safe again, so that you can breathe free air again and enjoy the life you deserve." His eyes are blazing like winter fire but his voice is cracking.

My heart wrenches against my chest so hard I feel like I'm going to collapse. He's right... We've all given more than we should. We've all been ruined and changed by this. Not just me.

"I—I'm... I don't want you to suffer for me, Kastian." The tears roll down my cheeks as I stare into his eyes. Pain flickers through them and he's giving me an agonizing frown as he holds back his own tears. "I wanted to... keep you all safe. I—I'm so sorry."

I let out the cry that's been building in my throat and press my face into his chest.

Kastian wraps his arms around me and I'm engulfed by his sage scent. It fills me and I feel so vulnerable in his arms. He lowers his nose into my hair and whispers, "I'm sorry I couldn't keep you safe in the first place, Elodie."

I let out a sigh of relief. We stay locked in our embrace for a long few moments.

Wren stands and moves toward his door. "I'll give you two a minute. Dinner's on in thirty."

Kastian squeezes me tighter before murmuring, "So you decided to finally just leave, huh?" He lets a laugh slip. "You made it look so fucking easy."

"Yeah... Well, it wasn't planned. Plus I'm sure Arulius will be coming to get me, but they'll have to find us first. Rune's on his way too." Kastian wraps his arms completely around me and I can't help but notice how broad his shoulders are. I'm so small in his embrace. He holds me like I'm about to disappear.

He lifts me and takes us to the bed, sitting me on his lap. "We can take him."

I lean into him and smile.

Rune and Kastian will get along well. They're similar with their cold, broody mannerisms and painful pasts. All they seem to care about is whatever keeps me happy and safe.

Do I deserve such love?

Yes, I *fucking* do.

"We should head to Moro's place tomorrow," Kastian says. "I'm sure Violet is already figuring out where you are so we shouldn't stay."

I nod slowly.

"I... I'm not the same Elodie I was eight months ago." I

hesitate and glance up to meet his gaze. There's no judgment in them so I continue. "I've been through so much. I'm just... different now."

He brushes my hair back and presses a kiss to the soft skin of my neck. "I'm different too and I'll never be the same. Not after you—not after everything."

I dip my head down to his so our noses are a breath apart. "I missed you so much," I whisper against his lips. "I never want to fight again."

"You're all I've ever wanted, Elodie. My soulmate—my rhythm." He threads his fingers in my hair and pulls my head back, exposing my neck to him.

I let out a soft moan as he runs his tongue over my artery.

"We've bled for each other long enough—don't you think?"

My eyes roll to the back of my head as his teeth bury into me. Chills run down my spine and heat pools between my thighs. He groans with each pull and I'm already grinding on him. His erection demands my attention.

He takes a few long pulls before retracting and his perfect azure eyes fall on mine. I wish I could drink from him too—the blood repulsion is more painful now than it's ever been.

That was her goal though, wasn't it? Because she knew we would have a moment like this one. How couldn't we?

We are fated to circle each other for eternity. Life and death, push and pull. There's nothing more that I want than to bond with Kastian. I want to feel everything he does.

Kastian leans back and my lips meet his as we fall to the sheets in a slow plunge. Our souls dance together as our tongues explore one another.

He moans into me as his hands glide down my back, the black dress letting him know exactly what's beneath. He grabs my ass and squeezes it hard enough to make me gasp.

I work to get his shirt off, pulling it over his head and wings, eager to explore everything beneath. His chest is covered in faded scars that run up his neck and down his arms. I kiss the branch-like scars, following them up to his neck as I wrestle to get his pants off.

Kastian smirks at me. "That asshole had better not walk in on us again, because I'm not stopping."

I let a laugh slip, remembering how pissed off Wren was when he interrupted us the first time Kastian and I fooled around.

"Seriously? Not even if he watched?"

His lip kicks up and he shakes his head. Holy shit, that turns me on way more than it should. A few strands of his white hair slip over his forehead.

He leans back up, kissing me and helping pull his pants down, freeing his hard dick. My eyes instinctively look down at him and gods, I don't remember him being this hung in the hot springs.

He rolls me over so I'm on my back and he's straddling me. He pulls the dress over my hips so my pussy is bare to him.

Oh, fuck me.

Kastian slips his finger through my slit and finds me already dripping wet for him. His brow raises and I don't fucking care, it's his fault for being so tempting.

Our lips connect again and he edges the head of his dick at my entrance, letting it slip up to coax my clit. I'm already moaning into his mouth as our tongues fight for this moment as much as our hearts are.

He pulls his face back and presses his forehead to mine, our eyes locked in this moment. His oceans glint with a fire that consumes me. I'm not sure I'll survive the embers.

"This isn't just sex for me, Elodie, I need you to know that. I... I love you, and I don't need to hear you say it back and I won't ever ask you to. But I want you to know. I need to say it and for you to hear it. *I love you*. I always have. You'll forever be my other half. You'll always be mine."

Tears spill from my eyes. It's been a really hard journey with Kastian, so much death and pain. But in the end he was always there for me. *Always*.

"I love you too. Forever, till the end of time, I'll love you."

I look up at him and my shaky smile must tell him everything he needs because a tear falls from his face too, and we're crashing into one another again. His dick presses in to the hilt and he fucks me so slow but ruthlessly hard, pulling out almost to the tip and then slowly pushing in until there's no more room for him and he's pressing hard against my cervix. His breaths are shortening and he watches me through hooded eyes.

Fuuuck.

He's right, this isn't just sex. We are literally connecting our souls together—dancing with the sorrows and pain that we share. It's so close to the sensation of bonding. I'm falling into oblivion with each thrust and kiss, further and further until I'm coming. He pushes in one last time and holds his pelvic bone against me as he spills inside me. Our auras merge and I can feel the same sensation I did in the hot spring. Like our beings are calling for one another, begging to join and become one.

We continue kissing and sharing this moment. When I open my eyes, his blue gaze is taking in each expression I make. I've wanted this—needed this.

Kastian.

"Forever mine," I murmur as I press kisses on his cheek and neck. He laughs and slowly pulls out, leaving me empty, and it feels so wrong. I want to go again.

"Always," he whispers as he presses a kiss to my forehead.

Kastian takes a deep breath and then leans up, staring down at me.

"I think your friend is here."

What?

I peek around Kastian's shoulders and Rune's standing there with his arms crossed and heat in his eyes.

24

Elodie

Rune's horns are dripping with melting snow. His eyes flick to mine as I quickly pull my dress down.

Heat fills my cheeks—how much did he see? Did Kastian know he was here while we were... Oh, gods.

"Rune," I whisper. Kastian pulls his pants on and presses a kiss on my lips as he helps me off the bed. I run over to my Dreadius and crash into his open arms. "I'm so happy you're here." His musky, metallic scent fills me and I feel so content with both of my males here.

Kastian clears his throat. "Well, you've officially been

welcomed into the group, I guess." He smirks and Rune just nods in return. Their exchange is curt, but I have a feeling they got off on the wrong foot. Their expressions seem much less heavy now.

My stomach growls and they each raise a brow at me. I can smell the stew Wren's making downstairs and I'm absolutely starving.

"Dinner's on! Hurry up, you noisy assholes!"

I laugh, embarrassed that we just got called out like that. "Let's go eat before Wren has an aneurysm."

Marley hands Rune a steaming cup of tea as we take our seats. I smile when Rune takes it graciously from him and rubs the Moss Sparrow's head in thanks. I think back on the sweet little girl that handed him the flower and how he kept it.

"You're welcome!" the boy chirps and then turns to me. "Would you like a cup, Elodie?" I nod my head and sit next to Rune, Wren on my other side and Kastian across from us.

It's a quiet meal. We all just sort of take everything in. How weird this is that we're sitting at Wren's table in Caziel, together again, like a family. My heart wrenches at the thought of losing this ever again, but we're not entirely whole... Arulius isn't here. Moro and Margo too. I want to cry just thinking about seeing her tomorrow. I won't ever let her go again.

Once we finish up and get the dishes put away,

Marley gives Wren a hug and it's the softest I've ever seen the Cypress with another person. He returns the affection like a father and it melts my heart. "Thanks for all your help today, bud. Why don't you go rest."

"Okay, I'm heading to bed then. It's waaaay past my bedtime." He lets out a long yawn and then hugs me too. I want to scoop him up and never let anything bad ever happen to him. He trots out of the kitchen and to the bedroom on the other side of it.

Rune leans back in his chair and sips his tea as he side-eyes me. Obviously he wants an explanation about what the hell happened back in Nesbrim. I don't blame him. I'd want one too, and I sure as hell wouldn't be as patient as he's being.

I suck in my lower lip and look at the tattoos on his arms as I take a deep breath to explain.

"I walked in on Kastian being bled dry and tortured... and at that point I snapped. It was all for nothing. All my pain and suffering to keep you all safe... it was for nothing." I look across all their faces slowly.

Rune is mid-sip and sets his cup down with a *clunk*. His eyes narrow and they burn, seeming to say *It wasn't for nothing*. He shoots Kastian a pained look and my Eostrix chooses to keep his somber gaze on the table. Wren lets out a long sigh before setting his hand on Kastian's shoulder.

"He'd do anything for you, Elodie. We all would."

I shake my head and hold back my tears. "I never want anything bad to happen to any of you because of me. Let me finish what I started... I'll take care of Violet once and for all." I've always sort of felt bad for Violet, but I think it's clear now that she will have to die. She's suffered too, I know... I know that *I* was her villain. But she has become a horrible torturer and morbid bitch that tries to resurrect dead gods, for gods know what reasons.

Whatever good was in her before is long gone.

Rune wipes his lips with his sleeve and scrunches his brows at me, and the tattoo on my spine warms. "*Are you okay, pup?*"

I shrug.

"I don't know. I just... don't know." I wrap my arms around my knees and lean my head on my arm. "Everything's so fucked up. It's just us against the realms." I shoot them all a weary smile.

Rune holds his frown, knowing I'm trying to avoid the problem like I always do. I've got issues, I know.

"What?" I narrow my eyes on him.

Rune leans in and kisses me. Heat flares through my cheeks and I worry for a second at Wren's gasp. What, I didn't tell him what Rune was to me?

His deep voice courses through me. "*Our allies are everywhere. Remember—many of us desire the Rhythm to return.*"

"You're right... It's not just us anymore, is it?" I

mumble against his lips.

He lets his expression turn sullen, distant, as he watches me in silence. Picking apart every piece of me that he can. He's so good at it and I worry that he'll know me better than I know myself soon.

Wren leans forward and sets his hand on mine. "We were never alone." Kastian stretches his wings and nods at me too, fire burning in his blue eyes. Relief floods me at the thought of us being able to take back the Rhythm. To save all those who've died the second death. To fix all this senseless pain.

But what if we can't fix it—what if I lose them all in the process?

Rune stands and offers me a hand. I ignore his gesture, standing up and going straight in for a hug. He grunts as I squeeze him and tightens his arms around me.

Wren chuckles at my side. "It's good to see you again, Rune. Does this mean you've officially joined the resistance then? We've got a Hollowless Cypress, a child Moss Sparrow, a depressed Death God, and the Goddess of Life who doesn't have her powers. You're on the winning team, my friend." His sarcasm is dripping from his lips and his smirk is just as *Wren* as it gets.

I've missed the bastard.

I pull away enough to see Rune give him a genuine smile and nod curtly. I wonder if they know one another from their days working together in the High Court.

Wren cackles. "Oh shit, I forgot you're mute. So we also have a silent Dreadius." He pats Rune on the shoulder in passing as he leaves the kitchen and settles on his couch. I don't miss the flicker of amusement in Rune's eyes and I already know I'm right that our band of misfits is going to be complete... Well, almost complete.

The Eostrix follows behind us as we make our way through the living room. "Thanks, Wren. We really appreciate—"

"Oh spare, me the dramatics, Kastian. Let's just roll with this while it lasts. I'm burnt out from the *drama* and *planning* and *doom*," he says exasperatedly as he fluffs up his pillow and leans back. "I'm sleeping out here, so you guys figure out bed arrangements." He smiles easily at me and I don't miss the amusement that lingers there.

"What are you trying to imply?" I glare at him and he's laughing again.

Kastian roars with laughter as well. "I don't think we need to guess." Embarrassment fills me but I'm too caught up in the happiness that consumes my heart at the sound of their laughs. When have we all been this happy?

It's too contagious and I end up hugging my ribs from giggling. Rune's eyes are filled with relief as he watches me laugh. A small part of me sinks knowing that he can't join in, but I hold onto the hope that we will find his voice through this. We have to.

The three of us get situated in the bedroom.

It's a little awkward at first, but the males don't make a big deal about it so I find myself relaxing as we nestle into the not-so-small bed that *is* now with a taut male on each side of me.

Words can't even begin to describe how happy I am to have them both here with me. I'm not alone.

They each cuddle up to me. I give Kastian my back. Rune's eyes are locked onto mine. His tattooed torso begs me to touch every line of ink he has and I indulge in running my fingers up and down his chest. He tucks my head into the nook of his neck and strokes my hair slowly.

"I'm sorry you walked into that today." My spine warms and his deep voice coils through my mind.

I relax my muscles and nuzzle my face into his shoulder, trying to get as much of his blood and rose scent off him as I can and into my senses.

"It's fine... Kastian, are you okay?"

Rune continues to stroke my hair calmly as my Eostrix behind me considers my words.

"Don't worry about me. It's nothing compared to the months you endured..."

"I... I think we're going to have to kill her."

Both of my males twitch but remain silent.

My heart is torn. I know she's got the monopoly on pain... Talia was so cruel to her and that sucks, but it doesn't mean she has to fuck my life and the Rhythm in every way she can.

Kastian presses his face to the back of my neck. "I'll kill her. You don't need to endure any more trauma."

I shake my head slowly. "It has to be me. I can feel it in my bones. You keep Arulius busy."

Rune frowns but Kastian replies, "Do you think he's trying to help us? I thought you were fucking crazy for wanting him a week ago... and I'm sorry for blowing up on you, but now I'm not so sure. I mean... he taught you to *fly* —why would he do that?"

"He had to have known I'd escape, right? Maybe Arulius taught me for this reason alone. His way of *freeing* me." My heart sinks. Was this his roundabout way of setting me free? So that Violet couldn't blame him directly? I wish I could have all the answers.

Rune's voice curls through my mind. *"He'll come for you. I've seen the way he looks at you. He'll never let you go, pup, whether he wanted you free or not."*

I frown and clutch onto Rune a little tighter. "He doesn't have a choice. We'll find a way to break the bond and then I'll resurrect *everything*."

Rune pulls the blanket over our heads and I look up at him with surprise. His red eyes practically glow in the gloom. I feel like a child again, hiding under the sheets from the monsters that I always thought were out to get me. Is this his way to get privacy with Kastian so close?

I bite my lips to hold back my smile.

"You're the Goddess of Dawn and Life. For whatever

reason, the God of Wrath is hell-bent on having you. I'm not sure he can exist in peace... You might have to let him go, pup." My eyes widen and I push away, our heads resurfacing. Kastian gives me a worried look.

I stare into Rune's eyes. I want everything he's saying to be wrong because I'm not sure I can *ever* let him go. I can't control the Rhythm alone... I need all of them to be by my side. Even Talia failed to keep the worlds together without help.

I sigh.

"What will you do? When everything is fixed and the realms are right." I try to change the subject to something else. The thought of Arulius dying... No.

His eyes soften, a look so melancholic and painful runs through them. I'm already bracing myself for his words. *"I'll be with you. You're the only one, Elodie. The light that takes me from the darkness. You're the sun of worlds—all of them, but especially mine."*

My heart warms and I gaze into his crimson eyes.

"You're my drop of blood in snow."

His lip kicks up and he nuzzles his nose against mine.

"And me?" Kastian teases as he licks my neck.

"You're my moonlit lullaby." I reminisce on the first moment I laid eyes on my Death God.

His lips turn up against my skin and we fall silent until we're drifting into the banks of sleep. I'm safe and sound here in their arms. No nightmares can scare me when they're here with me.

25

Elodie

We're barely awake enough to even enjoy our coffee.

Kastian is still bathing upstairs and Rune looks like he's about to fall out of his chair, his head resting on his arm as he stares at me with those crimson eyes I've come to love so much. I've never felt more beautiful in my entire life than I do when he looks at me.

Wren has an unlit joint in his mouth as he pours himself a cup of the bitter liquid. He drinks it black. I'll never understand how anyone can go without cream. His dark hair is tousled and messy—from a rough night's sleep on the couch, I'm guessing. If the bed was just a little bit bigger, we could all fit. I let my eyes glide down his body and he catches me looking.

I smile instead of looking away and he holds the joint to his lips as he sparks it with my pink lighter. "Don't I get a morning hug? I took a bullet and slept on the couch, for gods' sakes."

Rune smirks as I stand and walk over to Wren. I wrap my arms around him, pushing his shirt up and letting my bare palms feel his warm, tight muscles.

"It's your turn tonight then." I rub my cheek against the soft fabric of his black shirt. He leans into me and exhales smoke from his joint. It smells like bark and surprisingly doesn't sting my nose.

"I'll have to catch you first then. I'm addicted to the way it feels to catch you when you're running from me." His breath warms my cheek and shivers shoot up my spine as excitement coils within me.

"Lucky for you, I happen to enjoy being caught." I press a kiss against his lips and steal the joint from his hand as I retreat back to the table with a playful grin.

I take a puff of the joint and my eyes widen with the flavor and the way it immediately sparks energy into me. It's like the forest and life all crammed into smoke.

"What the hell is this stuff?"

Wren smiles at my awe. "It's just Cypress crack."

I throw the joint and take a huge drink of coffee to clear the forbidden taste from my mouth.

Wren laughs and clutches his side. "I'm fucking with you, Elodie. It's just the tobacco here in Tomorrow."

I scowl at him and look at the joint I threw on the floor, wasted at the expense of his joke. Rune pats my thigh, giving me a small grin and I smile at him.

My spine warms with our connection. *"There will be more. Don't fret about it."*

I laugh and let my hand slip onto his where it rests on my leg.

"So, why don't you talk? I've always been curious but too proud to ask. And what's up with the chemistry I'm vibing on with you two? I know you said you were sucking his dick, but I didn't think you'd be all mooshy-gooshy." Wren takes a seat across from us and sets down his mug. It feels like we're being fucking interviewed.

I furrow my brows. "Well, that was rude. You were too proud? What does that make you now?"

Wren kicks up one side of his mouth. "An asshole. You going to answer my other question? All he does is look at you like a love-drunk puppy."

That gets Rune's attention and he snaps his head at the Cypress, glaring at him. I can't help but laugh at the two of them.

Marley finally emerges from his room and is the only

one who seems awake as he hums and chews his eggs with a blissful smile on his face.

"Rune and I are two peas in a pod, okay? It's not our fault we're made for one another." I shoot the Dreadius a knowing look.

My spine heats. *"We still playing at no hearts attached, pup?"*

I can't even look at him without the emotions I feel for him spilling out. "Can they be?" I repeat his words from our night together and his brows knit like me finally admitting it hits him right in the chest.

I take another sip of my coffee, enjoying this small moment as much as I can.

"I thought Kastian was *made for you,*" Wren snarks back.

"I think you all were... In a way you're all mine. It's weird, but I can feel it. Though, Arulius kind of burned his bridge... but he did teach me to fly." I cross my arms and lean back in my seat. Wren softens his gaze and leans forward, setting both forearms on the table and lacing his fingers together.

"You know, Kastian's doing everything he can to save you. To save *everything*... and part of it might include getting *rid* of Arulius."

I flinch. A ball forms in my throat and my hands become clammy. "What makes you think that?" I ask defensively.

Wren stares at me empathetically, his amber eyes flickering with knowing pain. "How will we kill Violet? You *know* he's going to protect her with his entire being. This only ends one way, Elodie."

I clench my teeth. "Yeah? Then tell me, Wren, what's this big plan of yours? Why don't you share, since you know who *has* to fucking die."

Marley drops his fork and covers his mouth with a sharp gasp. We all three snap our attention to the small Moss Sparrow, sitting there with food dropping from his mouth.

"*Shit*—sorry, Marley. Why don't you head out to the market for a bit and get some vegetables for tonight?" Wren pats the Moss Sparrow's head and sends him out the front door quickly. I feel like such an asshole for saying that in front of him, but I didn't start it.

Wren waits until the door clicks shut and then gives me a horrified look. "Really? In front of the kid?"

Rune smiles and Kastian catches the end of our conversation as he arrives, drying his hair with a small towel. "Who said what in front of Marley?"

Wren rubs his face, looking tired, but I know he's just trying to make me feel bad. "Who else can talk besides you and me?"

Kastian narrows his eyes at him and throws the towel at the Cypress. "Fuck you." The Eostrix pushes past him and wraps an arm around me, his ebony wings tightly tucked to his body to keep from knocking things over.

"He was saying how you're going to kill Arulius…" I deadpan. Wren covers his face and groans like it was a secret and I wasn't supposed to tell. Has he lost brain cells this last year? *Gods*.

"Well… We aren't sure yet, but if he tries to stop us…" Kastian squeezes me tighter but I throw his arm off me and defensively move to stand by Rune. "Elodie, we can't let this continue. You know that," he finally grits out.

I laugh. "I don't care. I'm out, aren't I? Look." I spread my arms open. "I'm out of Nesbrim, and you know who it's thanks to? *Arulius*. I got myself out and it was fucking easy because he taught me to fly." I glare down at the table. "So why are we discussing killing him?"

Wren lets out a sigh, as if I'm soooo difficult to deal with. "It's not as simple as that and you know it. You're still bonded and Arulius isn't going to let you go. You'll never be able to save the Realms as you are. They know this—you know this. Why don't you start thinking with your head and not your emotions, Elodie," he scolds me like I'm a freshly-born Eostrix and it pisses me off.

"I know!" I snap at him. "We've been figuring out how to break the blood bond. It's been getting weaker every time I…" I pause, because I don't want to say it out loud in front of the three of them.

Wren narrows his eyes on me. "Every time you what?"

I glance nervously at Rune and he gives me a curt nod. I'll never forget the warmth in his eyes the night we learned that love is the undoing of the bond.

I swallow and close my eyes. "When I have feelings for males who aren't Arulius." Wren's eyes widen but he doesn't say anything, so I go on. "I can feel the bond weakening. It's barely there anymore. I can't even tell what he's feeling anymore. Since being here it's been silent." I clutch my chest. The thought of losing my close connection with Arulius hurts... but I'll survive.

"When you have *feelings*?" Wren pushes me to say it.

I look at Rune as I mumble, "Love."

Wren and Kastian both glance at Rune with surprise. The Dreadius gives me the biggest smile I've ever seen from him, all his fucking perfect white teeth shining, the smug asshole. My heart bursts with the glorious sight of him.

Kastian smirks at him and flicks his eyes back to me. "Love, huh? Of course it's love." His blue eyes settle on me and I sip in a breath as he pulls me in for a tight hug.

We wrap up our discussion. I can't stand a single second more of talk of Arulius's death and love. We plan on heading out to Moro's at sundown. It's safer to travel at night since Violet no doubt has Eostrixes in the sky searching for me. I know they're probably already heading my way because I think Wren's cottage is an obvious location I'd run to.

Moro's place probably isn't much safer, but we need to all reunite and figure out where we go from here. My heart beats faster at the thought of us all being together again. Maybe I can convince Arulius that he can come back with us... that he doesn't have to follow Violet's orders anymore.

Together we can find a way to break this vicious cycle. We can all be together again.

Even Violet. I want peace for her too—for everyone.

Marley returns with a bundle of veggies and meats. He's overly excited to see Brevik lying on the front lawn. For a moment I see the flash of pain in his eyes when he realizes it isn't Murph, but he gives love to the Hollow all the same.

We eat a hearty meal that will hopefully keep us full until we reach the Pine Hollow Keeper, but it's at least a day's worth of travel from here, which makes me wonder what the arrangement will be. I look at Wren and Rune—they seem to be thinking the same thing.

One Pine Hollow. Four of us.

Marley walks out with a backpack slung over his shoulder, looking proud that he is apparently coming along.

Scratch that—five of us. At least two of us can fly.

I quirk a brow and smile. "Sooo. I guess I can carry

Marley and you two can ride together?" Wren narrows his eyes at my snide grin and Rune scowls at me.

"Sounds great to me!" Marley chirps as he locks the cottage door. His shirt is buttoned up right for once and it's hard to not notice how much he's grown since I saw him last. He'll be a great warrior someday.

Rune groans but follows Wren's lead, mounting Brevik. I send out a silent thanks that he picked the largest Hollow that can actually carry two full-grown males.

Traveling at night isn't ideal, but I'm definitely taken with how beautiful the world is at night. The snow lights the realm from below rather than the sky. The four moons reflect magically off the gems of frozen water, and from up here, it's like flying through an ocean of stars.

"Wow."

I smile at Marley's amazement with flying. His eyes are taking everything in and his smile is entirely contagious.

"It's amazing, isn't it?" I murmur as I gaze down, finding Brevik charging full-speed ahead, casting plumes of snow crystals in his wake.

Moro's cottage is as wonderful as it was in the summer.

The ivy vines that cling to his exterior walls still have their greenery and there's not a step of snow that hasn't been trampled here. My heart warms at that, it means he hasn't been alone and has been busy with new Hollows as Wren mentioned.

Rune and the Cypress scowl at one another once they jump off Brevik. I entertain the thought of how on earth those two could manage to argue since one of them can't even speak. But if anyone could figure out how to start shit, it would be Wren.

Kastian lands next to me with grace. "You fly beautifully—even with the broken wing." His eyes dance like he's feeling as alive as I do. I smile with pride. Wren looks over his shoulder at me and there's so much relief in his eyes it nearly brings tears to mine.

Marley yawns and just walks straight into Moro's cottage without knocking. I hear a cheerful greeting inside and a smile breaks over my lips at the sound of Moro's voice. Wren slips past me while I wait for Rune. His crimson horns are covered in frost and his cheeks are rosy.

"Can't you two just get along?" I walk over to him and grab his hand tightly. He instantly intertwines his fingers with mine and my heart leaps as he dips down and kisses me.

"That asshole talked shit the whole time... so I smacked him. He's being a little bitch about it."

I break the kiss and laugh until tears are brimming

from my eyes. "Oh gods, you hit him?! How are you two not best friends by now?" His lips turn up and he brushes my hair from my face and lets his arm hang over my shoulder.

We walk in and Moro already has five cups of tea on his table. His smile is as warm and wide as it is in my memory. His dark skin is smooth and he's wearing thick winter gear. Looks like he just finished tending to the Hollows. I run up and hug him tightly. "It's so good to see you, Moro!"

He hugs me back. "Good to see you are well, Elodie, and I see we have a new friend?" I turn back toward Rune and motion for him to come closer.

The Dreadius looks away as if he's shy to see Moro, and I look back at the wise, silver-eyed male. His eyes are filled with his usual all-knowing look.

"You two know each other?" I'm not surprised. Moro has been here for lifetimes and I wouldn't be surprised if he literally knew every breathing creature in this realm.

Moro smiles and nods slowly. Rune finally meets his gaze and there's a somber light that fills his crimson eyes.

The Hollow Keeper walks up to Rune and holds out a hand. "I didn't know you survived that night... Gods, it was so long ago now, wasn't it?"

Rune dips his head and takes Moro's hand respect-fully. I don't think I've seen him show anyone this much respect except me.

"What night?" I ask breathlessly, even though I have a pretty good idea of what he's talking about. *That night— his scarred throat.* Goosebumps ripple over my skin and I suppress the urge to reach out and comfort Rune.

Rune keeps his head dipped and I don't miss the tear that hits the floor beneath him.

"I'm certain he's already spoken to you, hasn't he, Elodie?" Moro shifts his silver eyes to me and Wren tilts his head back to look at me from the dining table. Kastian eyes me. They've seen us converse... but how did Moro know?

I hesitate for a second, not really sure if it's okay to share our not-so-secret connection, but I finally give in. "How did you know?" I hold my breath, trying to restrain myself from running to my broken Rune.

Moro pats my Dreadius on the shoulder and lets out a long breath, one filled with so much... memory.

"His scar is finally fading."

I flinch. *What? His scar...* I haven't looked at it in a while, but... Moro's right.

"How?" I say on an exhale. His thick and gruesome scar is nearly gone now, a mere scratch compared to what it used to be.

Rune's eyes widen as well and his hand lifts to his tattooed throat. Shock sinks into his features as he slumps to his knees.

"Dreadiuses hold onto their pain and it keeps their

wounds fresh, unhealed and nearly raw, until they fix whatever trauma it is that they won't let go of." Moro's smile tightens as he takes a seat at the dining table with Wren. Wow, fuck all the books we found, Moro knows *everything*.

I kneel next to Rune. His gaze is distant, but once my hand touches his cheek he's back and staring into my soul as I am his. His trauma makes me want to take his entire past away. I want to take away all his hurt and just see him happy.

Then I feel it too—or rather the absence of it.

I've been so focused on Rune and fixing his hurt that I've almost forgotten about my own. The way he's healed me in return has a lump forming in my throat. It fills my heart with an inexplicable amount of love.

His love.

Moro takes a long sip of his tea and coughs a few times. "I never thought I'd see this one again though. His brother must have saved him."

"Kol?" I say with more venom than I intended.

He nods. "I don't believe anyone to truly be evil. None are born that way anyway, but Kol has goodness in his heart. As does Violet." He leans back in his chair and stares at his living room wall.

Wren frowns. "No, I'm pretty sure Kol and Violet are evil. Don't forget Arulius either."

Kastian chimes in from behind me. "They took everything from us... even our identities. Violet did everything she could to destroy the Rhythm—look how close she got to succeeding."

Moro smiles nostalgically, but it doesn't reach his eyes. "All of them have stories of their own. Just as each of you carry a story, and I do. None of us are *truly* evil."

I flatten my lips. I don't want to admit it, but he has a point—considering Talia was a fucking evil bitch and I'm technically her, so...

Maybe we all can change—we just need guidance and second chances.

Wishes for our former selves. The ones that are so broken by trauma.

"Rune... I'm so sorry you've been hurting for so long. I wish I could take it all away." I press my forehead to his and he quickly shakes his head, looking up at me with tenderness seeping from his soul.

I wonder if he feels the same love that I do for him.

I want it so badly—more than anything in the realms. I want his heart and pain to be shared with me so that we can carry the burden together.

Wren coughs. "We're all still here."

I roll my eyes but rub my nose against Rune's. "My drop of blood in the snow. I guess I helped you heal. You healed me too, so well that I didn't even know it."

Moro stands and walks over to us, helping me and Rune to our feet. "You two were always meant to meet... I see it now." He looks from me to the Dreadius slowly, in thought.

Wren walks over to stand next to Kastian and quirks a brow. "What do you mean?" He studies us as if he's trying to see what Moro does. My dark-winged Eostrix tilts his head with curiosity too.

"Rune is the God of Peace. He keeps the harmony of the realms and is a vital part of the Rhythm."

We all gasp in unison.

I've been wondering what other gods are a part of the Rhythm since reading about it. I never fathomed Rune could be one.

Here in front of me. We are harmony itself together, blending perfectly like two sides of the same wing. The pull I've been feeling for him has been our Rhythm, desperately wanting to join and rekindle the realms.

Rune is my equal—Kastian my opposite. Each holding significance beyond my understanding.

The God of Peace. Hidden so well, but against all odds we managed to find one another. I wonder if this is the first time we've met. I think of all the lifetimes we've left behind us, how many more we'll share.

"Is he... Are we..." I'm at a total loss for fucking words.

"You two are the single most important parts of the Rhythm. Yes, death has his part to play, but you two keep the humans alive, keep them happy and at peace. Without life and peace, there is only death and war."

Goosebumps shiver across my skin. *War.* Bruno's words slither from my mind and wrap my consciousness in their darkness.

You are cursed. Run. Run. Run. Run.

"Then... that means North is a Rhythm God too."

Moro nods grimly. Wren and Kastian share a confused look.

I clench my fists. "We think that Violet has North's bones in her dungeon and she's been doing some sort of possession curse on me. She was draining my blood the entire time I was there." Moro's eyes fill with horror but I press on. "She wants Lucius, and the only thing that makes sense to me is that she's trying to get North to possess me so he can tell her what's in my head."

Kastian's eyes widen and he opens his mouth a few times before actually getting anything out. "No."

Rune lifts his head and his crimson eyes flicker with the embers from the fire that warms Moro's cottage.

"No, what?" I ask slowly. At this point I don't even want to know.

Kastian stares into a dark corner of the room. The blank expression on his face is beginning to worry me. His hands shake.

"No... I think it's much worse than that."

Great.

That's exactly what we need—something *much worse.*

"She was taking my blood too... I didn't know this is

what she was doing with it though." Kastian stares off into the living room as he sorts through what this means.

Moro hums in agreement. "North can only take over a vessel, he doesn't get access to your mind. The host stays dormant, but very much their own being. Aware." Kastian stands and a blue fury fills his eyes, like he's prepared for war this very second.

I bite my lower lip. "Why is Violet trying to bring him back?"

"She wants him to tell her where Lucius is," Wren chimes in.

I shake my head. "How would someone who's been dead since the last war, four hundred years ago, even know where Lucius is?"

Rune sits next to me on the couch and rests his elbows on his knees, leaning forward as if he's taking in something hard. I furrow my brows and nudge him.

"What? What do you know?"

My spine tattoo warms. *"What are the chances she needs all the Rhythm Gods' blood to bring him back fully?"*

My bones chill. "Moro... does she need the blood from all the Rhythm Gods to complete the possession?" Kastian runs a hand through his white hair like this all is making sense. His ebony horns absorb the light that the flames cast toward them.

Moro looks me dead in the eye. "Lucius was resurrected four hundred years ago. That's when the Fernestian War waged across the human realm. The timeline is so similar... It can't be a coincidence. They knew one another... perhaps even once arriving back here after regaining their memories." His mouth presses into a flat line. "Yes... she'll need all four in order to complete the curse. She mustn't find out about Rune."

We all look at my precious Dreadius and I hug him a little tighter at the thought.

Fuck. This *is* so much worse.

"But there's a big chance we can escape this, right?"

Moro's silver eyes narrow with sorrow. "I'd say a *small* chance."

26

Elodie

I nestle into Wren's chest as the morning chill settles over us. The summer months were warm, but now that it's winter I'm realizing how cold Moro's cottage is. Rune's sleeping soundly on my other side, his slow breaths telling me he's still dreaming.

Wren wraps his arms around me and pulls me in tight to his bare chest. I take a deep breath of his pine scent and it helps calm my thoughts a bit. I didn't sleep well after the wisdom dump from Moro yesterday. The information flooded my dreams.

Rune and I both being Rhythm Gods... that part

338

was a dream come true, but North being one too sends ice through my veins. Kastian isn't evil even though he's the God of Death, and Moro seems to think that nothing is born *bad*, so maybe there's a way we can get the War God on our side. I think we'll have to. The book said *all* four Rhythms must be in sync for the realms to flow.

My insides twist at the thought of the possession that Rune spoke of weeks ago. It's been a few nights since my last nightmare. Maybe there's still time. I don't know how we can stop it, but I'm also not sure how far into this Violet is.

Rune stirs behind me and starts to stroke my hair softly. He squishes my fluffy ear to get my attention. These males are obsessed with the damn things. I guess they are pretty cute.

"What are you thinking about, pup?" My spine warms as his voice enters me. I can hear the deepness of his true voice and it fucking breaks my heart that no one but me can hear such a beautiful voice.

I shake my head into Wren's neck and he chuckles lightly, the vibration in his chest making me smile even though I feel impending doom about our entire situation. Rune presses in closer from behind, his lips brushing against my ear, but his voice stays in my mind.

"Don't worry about North. We'll figure this out, I promise."

My stomach turns. "Don't make promises you can't keep."

He leans back, turning me to look at him as he sets his crimson eyes on me. His dark hair is sexy as fuck in the morning as it falls over his forehead.

"Who says I can't keep my promises?"

"I do. You can't keep promises if you don't have control of the situation. This is all really out of our hands." I hold his gaze and he frowns, brushing my hair back and pressing his lips to my forehead. Wren's hands trail up and down my arm soothingly before he presses a kiss to the back of my head and wraps his arms around me tighter.

"You're so stubborn, pup. Fine, how about this then—we will call them wishes. They're my promises to you, but you can call them wishes if it makes you feel better." He pulls his head down so our foreheads meet and our eyes dance together in the dim light. "And my wish is that we will make it out of this. I'll keep you safe and you're going to ruin Violet."

My heart fills with so much warmth and tears are begging to fall.

"My wish is... to be with you forever."

"Forever is a long time, pup."

I stare into his soul with a hunger unlike any I've ever felt. "Can we kiss forever?"

His lips crash into mine and we hold one another's

faces like we'll lose each other if we don't. His voice swirls in my mind.

"There's no better wish than that."

Moro takes us all out to the Pine Hollow Grove.

It's the first time I've seen it filled with Hollows like it should have been the first time. There are so many of them, their winter coats thick and each one with their own characteristics. They seem so happy, and when Moro walks in they all swarm him eagerly.

I'm looking for one in particular.

My soul leaves my body when I spot the white fur with gold tips, deep eyes set on me as she runs right for me.

"Margo!" I cry as she crashes into me. She's licking my face and whimpering happy cries as she greets me. Tears are already streaming down my cheeks but she quickly laps them up.

The males laugh behind me and Marley rushes up to meet my Hollow.

"Whoa, she's beautiful!" The Moss Sparrow's eyes widen with awe. "I've never seen one this majestic. She's like light itself." He buries his face into her fur and she hums low in greeting.

"Yeah, she's pretty great, isn't she?" I watch with so much pride at my sweet Margo. Finally... we're together properly, with so many other Hollows in the grove all wagging their tails and waiting their turn for love.

Wren pats her on the head and moves to help Moro with the feeding buckets he brought along. Rune and Kastian join me and pet Margo. The fear in Rune's eyes from his first encounter with the Hollows is long gone. Kastian laughs as my Hollow barks at him to throw her a stick.

"Let's start by breaking out the Hollows," I blurt out. Not entirely sure what first step we should be taking toward regaining the Rhythm, but this is important to me.

Moro and Wren smile wide, their breaths curling in the air as Marley jumps up and down with his fist in the air.

"Yeah! In Murph's honor!" the boy shouts into the sky as if Wren's lost friend can hear him.

Wren smiles and his eyes follow the boy's enthusiasm into the sky above as he murmurs, "For Murph."

I echo him. "For Murph." Tears brim in my eyes but I keep them there. I'll bring him back—I'll bring everyone back, and then there won't be any reason for us to shed tears anymore. I'll fix this...

"For Murph." Kastian's ocean eyes flicker respectfully to the Cypress and they share a hopeful smile.

Rune raises a brow. He doesn't know Murph or what the beautiful beast sacrificed for us, but he lifts his head nonetheless, willing to join in our battle.

Moro finishes tossing the feed into the large bowls on the ground. "Well, we'd better make a plan then. I want no Hollow left behind."

"I wouldn't have it any other way." I meet the Keeper's silver gaze and he grins.

I've missed my family so fucking much.

27

Elodie

Time seems fickle when everything's at stake.

I know we could easily lose one of us like in the past... but with the bond edging on breaking, I can feel my powers thrumming through me stronger than it ever has.

We didn't waste time that morning in the grove. We make plans that evening about what's in store for the Nesbrim raid. Rune and I know the city in and out so we have the perfect path to the Hollow's Atrium lined up.

Wren makes Marley stay behind. "Someone needs to watch the Hollows," he tells him. The boy is reluctant at first, but Moro assures him it's a duty above all else, so the Moss Sparrow eventually becomes compliant and happy to stay behind.

The suns are already peeking above the mountains and the walls of Nesbrim cast long dark shadows across the plains on the west side.

"That guard was an *asshole*."

Wren spits blood off to his side as he complains. The Dreadius that punched him in the face got torn to shreds by the thorns Wren summoned from the ground. I'm still impressed as fuck at his magic and how easily he commands it.

We push through the west gate and move toward the atrium. Town is still pretty quiet this early in the morning, but the shopkeepers are already setting up their signs and turning on lights for the day.

No one even bats an eye at us as we walk casually. I know many of them recognize me and Rune so they probably don't see anything wrong with this picture.

"Did Violet not tell anyone about you peacing out?" Wren leans in and whispers in my ear.

I shrug. "I haven't felt anything through the bond that would suggest Arulius being pissed or worried, but then again it's been more difficult to feel—"

I stop, my feet freezing to the cobblestones beneath. A wave of hatred and anger washes through me. Not through the bond, it's not Arulius... This is that feeling I got when I nearly tore my heart out over Rune.

North.

"Elodie, what the fuck?"

I turn and meet Wren's horrified gaze.

My eyes dip down to my hands. It looks like I rolled in soot and ashes. My wings are growing longer and darker, like blood is dripping from their roots and straight into the feathers.

"S-something's wrong!" I choke out, feeling my consciousness starting to slip.

Rune catches me as I slump to my knees and holds my face in his hands desperately. The flash of fear across his gaze has me curling inward.

But when I hear his eerie voice ring out, I'm more afraid for him than myself.

"Elodie!"

I watch helplessly as Wren and Moro's eyes shift to black. The curse falls over them and I know they're hearing that ghost-like voice that whispers for them to harm Rune.

My Rune.

"Get out of here, Rune!" I shove him away but he just scoops me up and charges toward the atrium. Kastian is hot on our heels.

"What the fuck is going on?!"

I look over his shoulder, watching our friends chase us

with murder in their eyes. "They can't hear Rune's voice like you and I can—it's cursed!"

The Eostrix's eyes flash with shock. "Why is this the first I'm hearing of it?!"

Holy fucking shit, Rune wasn't bluffing when he said his voice is cursed.

"How do we snap them out of it?" I clench Rune's shoulders as he carries me, not letting my eyes leave our friends. He shakes his head and keeps his gaze trained on the streets ahead.

Of course he doesn't know how. "Let me guess, you have to kill anyone who hears you?" He ignores me for a few blocks but then finally nods curtly, pain flaring across his red eyes.

"Godsdamn it!" Kastian growls.

Fucking shit—there goes our plan.

Rune shifts on his feet and dives into an alley. I crash into the ground and roll a few times before he snatches me and pulls me close in the corner of the building and some crates. Kastian is a step behind us and effortlessly swoops over us with his black wings, hiding us all in the shadows.

Our breaths are sharp and we hold them as we hear footsteps run by. We remain silent for a few more minutes before breathing again.

"Why did you talk out loud?" I hiss at him, knowing it was an accident and that it was because something super fucking weird is going on with me, but I can't fight back the bite in my tone.

"Because you look like the scariest goddess I've ever seen," Kastian snaps back on Rune's behalf.

Rune glares at me and the tattoo on my spine heats. *"You look like a fucking god of carnage right now. Your wings, horns, and ears are red, eyes are black, your skin looks like you rolled in soot, and your hair is white. That's why."* I don't miss the attitude he's throwing back at me but I'm too stunned by all the shit he and Kastian just said.

I scramble toward the back door of the café we are tucked behind and look at the half window on the door. My jaw drops.

Everything he said is true... but he left out how truly horrifying I look. Kastian nailed that part.

I'm disturbingly spine-chilling.

I turn back to them and Rune's already giving me a worried look. I know he knows I hate pity but fuck, I'll take it right now.

"What's happening to me?" I crumble to the ground, digging my sharp claws into the snow and shaking at the thought of North taking over my body.

Rune dips down and rubs my back soothingly. *"It's North. He's getting closer. We need to stop Violet now. We'll save the Hollows on the way out."*

I shake my head. "No, we can't—we had a plan—"

He cuts me off by covering my mouth and presses us close to the wall. Wren and Moro run by again, back the way they came, eyes still just as dark and cursed.

After a few seconds he releases me and gives me a stern look. *"We don't have a choice. The plan is fucked and I'm about to lose you too. We're stopping her first."* He grips my wrist and pulls me toward the alley opening.

Kastian checks to make sure the coast is clear before nodding at us.

I bite my tongue. I'm so fucking mad. Our plans *never* work out.

I keep pace with them as we dash through the streets, up to the High Court. I'm sweating from the thought of walking back in there for many reasons.

Facing Arulius, Violet, and her entire army. How are we going to stop them with just us three? Fuck, how did things get so twisted?

We come up to the shrubs that line the walls of the castle and pause to catch our breath. I nudge Rune and he looks back at me, his dark hair messy and the veins beneath his tattooed skin raised.

"The torture chamber, it's that skull... I can feel it."

Rune nods and leads the way through the main doors as Kastian and I follow.

I glance at the gods reaching for one another as I do every time I pass them—only now I'm wondering what court holds the Gods of Harmony and Ruin. Everything is so twisted and all I can feel is anger... It's building and welling in my chest, burning hotter than Arulius's ever did.

The corridors are quiet and cold.

The guards are still chatting before they switch shifts and we walk easily by them all. I have a horrible feeling. This has all been much too simple, and if there's one thing that Violet isn't, it's stupid. She's played me like a fool since I've met her... so I know she's up to something.

"It's almost as if she knew we were coming back," I whisper from behind Kastian. He peeks around a corner and continues to move toward the torture chamber. I poke his back to get his attention but he ignores me. My other hand is tightly gripped in his. Sweat beads down his sun-kissed neck and I can feel the tension in the air.

Rune stops at the double doors and turns to us, looking us each up and down to make sure we're ready. I grab his hand. He pauses and stares at me with his deep crimson eyes.

"My wish... is to love you for eternity."

I want to say it. I want to tell him how I really feel just in case North possesses me and I'm not here anymore.

He considers me with heavy eyes before looking away. His jaw flexes and his hand tightens over mine.

My heart fucking hurts watching him.

My heart is mine again, after everything—but it's not really mine anymore, is it? It's his. He fixed it, put me back together, and I did the same to him. My eyes flick to the place where the scar used to reside on his neck.

Our wishes to save one another, they will always hold true—because no matter what, here... right now... our wishes came true. We saved one another from ourselves.

His beautiful crimson horns tilt as he finally looks at me. There's so much pain in his eyes, fear of losing me, and I understand it because I feel it too, burning brighter than anything in the realms.

"You don't have to say it—"

His lips press against mine and time seems to still. This moment matters and I'll hold onto it for the rest of eternity.

"I love you too, pup." My heart throbs and for a second the anger and hatred from North dissipates. I cup his cheeks and let my fingers intertwine with his hair. *"I promise I'll always love you."* He dots my forehead with a few last kisses as he straightens his stance.

I blink the tears from my eyes, meeting Kastian's gaze beside me. Pain flickers there but he smiles wearily at me anyway. He looks so fucking tired—we all do.

My dark-winged Eostrix hugs me tightly. Even my wings get scooped up in his embrace. He lets a relieved sigh roll from his lips as he presses kisses to the top of my head.

"We can do this—we have to." He looks from me to

Rune and back to me. His ocean eyes are steady and brimming. "Do you trust him?"

I hesitate—a smile forming across my lips.

"Nope."

My eyes meet Rune's and they flicker with amusement.

Kastian catches on and smirks. "Do you trust her?" Rune keeps his eyes connected with mine and shakes his head easily as my back warms and his voice rolls through me.

"*Never.*"

"And neither of us trust you either." I nudge my Eostrix and we all share a hushed laugh.

I never want to leave this hall, but we have to. There are so many things in this life that I wish I could just ignore to live in peace. But the chances of me walking out of this unscathed are really low.

So I should be entirely honest. I look at my somber Kastian, perfectly sculpted and ready for bloodshed.

"I love you, Kastian."

28

Elodie

Rune and Kastian push the doors open and I look ahead into the chamber as all hope slips from me.

I'm not surprised to find Arulius here waiting for us.

His perfect gilded bone armor is polished and his amethyst eyes bore into my soul. I'm lost on how I feel about all this. I can't even think of emotions right now, staying focused is the only option.

There's only Violet's side or my side—no in-between.

"Hello, love."

The three of us stand at the entrance and don't move

as we try to feel out the situation. He's alone—I'll ask him once to give him the benefit of the doubt, but that's it. That's all his kindness has earned him.

"We're destroying North's bones, stopping Violet's reign, and taking back the Hollows. I don't need you to break the bond anymore, I've figured it out. So tell us which side you're on, Arulius. This is your last chance."

He keeps his face impassive and considers me. His beautiful amethyst eyes falter for a second with pain. "I'm sorry, love. There's no choice in the matter, not for me... I'm sorry for all the blood that will be spilled today."

I'm fighting the urge to slap him to bring him to his senses, but I let out a sigh regardless. I was really fucking hoping he would come with us.

Kastian steps forward and his black wings stretch out slowly, looking larger than even Arulius's. He holds his hand out and a blade as dark as a void of nothingness cuts through the air. His death aura lashes out ominously.

A true God of Death. He's much stronger than he's ever been and it fills my heart with pride.

He won't *ever* fall again.

Arulius smiles but it doesn't reach his eyes. Being this close to him, I can feel the last remnants of our bond. It's faded and just a whisper against my skin. It fills my chest with anguish. He really believes he's doing what's right. Protecting me from *her* wrath. But he's wrong. I'm not Talia and I'm not alone.

Rune, Wren, Moro, Kastian. We've built a better realm this time. I just need to prove it to him.

I cut the last threads of the bond. I can feel them as they slip weightlessly into the air between us. Arulius feels it too. His brows furrow at the sensation of me letting him go, and just like that... the bond is gone.

"Kastian, I won't go easy on you and I'm not letting her go," Arulius says dully. His eyes are sunken and he looks like he's given up on everything. No longer the shiny and perfect god he was. He looks miserable.

My dark-winged Eostrix grips his aura blade tighter, his muscles flexing beneath his tight, long-sleeved black shirt. "Perfect—I intend to kill you after what you've done."

Arulius opens his own hand and his golden aura blade lights the room as he lashes it out and points it at Kastian.

The gods don't waste another second. They're flying at impossible speeds at one another and their blades meet. The entire castle quakes at the ripples their auras send through the floors.

Their swords clash faster than I can keep up with but the waves of power that shatter the glass and ring in my ears are indisputable. Kastian lands a small cut on Arulius's arm and flicks his eyes to me to see if I felt it—I didn't.

I nod to confirm that the bond's been severed.

Their fight can get as violent as they want and I won't

be scathed. Kastian smirks and his aura surges with a fresh wave of pure dark power shrouded with shadows.

They really are trying to kill each other...

I shake my head, trying not to picture either of them dead, and look at Rune. "Let's go!"

Rubble falls from the ceiling and crashes around us as we bolt for the basement.

I look back at my Eostrixes and Kastian catches Arulius on a hard left swing, his blade sending the gilded warrior straight out the windows. Blood and darkness whirl through the air like a parade of death. His black wings dart him out the windows in chase and I send a helpless prayer to any gods that will show me mercy to keep both of them alive.

Please.

The staircase is crumbling and Rune stands above me, taking a few hard hits from large blocks of stone.

"Hurry!" he growls as blood curls down his forehead. My heart hammers through my chest and I feel like I'm going to be sick.

We burst through the door and I charge for the blanket, throwing it off, relieved to find the skull and bones still here.

Thank the gods.

I focus my powers into my palm and my blade forms without trouble, but it's tainted now. The once pure gold aura is now half crimson, wild and filled with hatred. I can feel it trying to keep me from shattering the bones but I grit my teeth.

"Fuck you, North!" I shout as I bring my blade down and destroy everything in that disgusting bowl. Blood sprays in every direction and across my cheek. Thank fuck my mouth was closed.

The skull shatters and the veins on its temples cease pulsing.

We did it—we fucking did it!

Rune grabs my wrist and races for the exit. *"Okay, now just Violet and the Hollows!"* I can hear the smile in his voice.

"I'm going to punch her in her face!" I shout-laugh. Rune laughs ahead of me as we take two steps at a time.

We get halfway up the staircase before the rubble gives and crashes down on us.

I don't even have a chance to scream because floors' worth of stones are pelting us and burying us alive.

I can't hear anything.

I can't see anything.

Rune?

29

Elodie

"Rune!" I rasp, coughing violently as dust curls around my face. I don't know where I am, but it's dark. It's so dark here and I'm in so much fucking agony. My legs are crushed and my wings—I can't feel my wings.

"Hey, pup... You okay?"

His eerie voice is right above me but I can't see him.

I can't see anything. It's so dark. I'm scared.

"Rune," I sob. The pain and emotions flare through me and I can't fucking breathe. "Rune, a-are you okay? Where are you? It's d-dark... I can't—I can't see."

I feel his breath curl on my forehead and hot liquid is dripping on my neck and chest. Blood... I start to breathe harder. Am I hyperventilating? Oh gods. Oh gods, please.

"I'm okay. Can you move?"

I hesitate, checking in with myself, and when I can feel my toes I murmur, "Y-yeah. I th-think so."

"Perfect. I need you to ball yourself up and use your aura as a shield. Focus it around your body. Can you do that for me, baby?"

I don't like how he's talking... It's too soft and comforting.

Something's wrong.

"R-rune, what's wrong? I—I can't see you! Are you o-okay? What's wr-wrong?!" I wail, shaking uncontrollably with tears streaming down my cheeks. I gain mobility in my arms and shakily reach above my face. I'm instantly met with his chin and neck. His skin is slick with hot liquid and he's trembling uncontrollably.

He's holding all the stones off of us.

No. I can't... Please don't let this be happening.

Not real, not real, not real.

"Rune... W-we're okay... We're okay, right? Tell me... p-please!"

He keeps trembling and his voice is a mere whisper now. I can feel his jaw clenching so hard his teeth are cracking.

"J-just do as I say. Use your aura as a shield and close

your eyes, pup. Close your eyes for me." Cool drops trickle onto my face from his and my heart is drowning in that deep dark lake in my chest, sinking farther away from his, reaching so desperately.

Tears stream down the sides of my face and I do as he says, curling into a ball and casting my aura over my skin like a shell.

"Tell me you're... y-you're g-going... to be okay. P-promise me," I cry, my consciousness being robbed from me as the air thins in this small pocket beneath the rubble.

"*I wish we could be together forever. That's my wish, pup. I wanted it more than anything. But we can't make that promise.*"

My eyes snap open and I look up where his face should be. The little light coming from my aura lights his face enough for me to see. He's smiling at me with the crushing weight of love. His entire face is covered in crimson, tears streaming down his cheeks and onto mine.

"N-no—Rune, y-you promised," I rasp, sobbing, but he shuts his eyes and roars as a bright red light emanates from his body, blinding me. All I can do is shut my eyes. The weight lifts from us and a cool breeze brings new air into my lungs.

I force my body to push past the pain and sit up quickly. My now-white hair drifts over my face, blurring the carnage around me.

"Rune?"

I fight the light from the winter suns, beaming hard and reflecting off the snow. Rubble from the castle is everywhere and there's blood... so much blood everywhere, bodies of so many guards and citizens buried beneath stone. Their bones are jagged and are still very much bleeding. The screams tell me that many of them are still alive but dying.

My jaw's trembling and I can't breathe. I can't fucking breathe.

I catch eyes with Naminé. She's with Greysil... and they're both dead. Hugging one another. The Dreadius is leaning over my sweet Cypress friend in an attempt to protect her like Rune did me... but they were both crushed. Naminé's amber eyes are hazing as the last light leaves them.

My heart sinks.

My stomach wrenches and I catch my mouth in a dry heave.

I look down at my hands. They're shaking so violently and covered in crimson. I can hardly feel the pain of my own body anymore as the will to search for my drop of blood in the snow consumes everything I am.

Where is he... Where is—

Three crimson horns peek out of a pile of debris. I force my legs and arms to crawl to him.

Please. I'll do anything. *Anything.*

Just let him be alive.

361

"Rune!"

My scream echoes through the many cries and shouts. I muster up the strength to move the stones covering him and pull his body until he's as free as I am.

I land on my back and he falls beside me. I roll him over and—

He's smiling. It's subtle but it's there. Dried tears run through the crimson covering his cheeks.

His red eyes gaze endlessly into the somber sky above us.

And a piece of my soul goes with him.

30

Elodie

I've felt loss.

I've survived so much.

But I won't survive without him—not without Rune. I stare into his glazed eyes and can feel the blank nothingness that I watch him with.

This *isn't* happening. I won't let it happen.

It may be real... but I won't let it stay this way.

I stand, my shattered legs cracking—bone slitting through my flesh—but I don't as much as wince at the pain. My broken shin bones *clack* against the stones beneath.

I watch him like he watched me so many times. I watch him.

And then I let go.

My wings snap and crack back into place with the burst of power I release. My legs morph back to normal as well with sloshy snaps.

I'm not the same goddess as I was when I lost Kastian.

I look across the faces of the dead—the aftermath of *our* plan, my precious Rune among them.

I blink and can feel the shift beneath my lids. When I reopen them I can see all their souls resting beside their bodies. The world around me is shrouded in a dark red mist, like blood sprayed into the air, creating a haze of rot. They all look like they're sleeping next to their destroyed bodies.

I let my instincts run wild and lift my arms into the sky. I hear Rune's voice in my head, the song he hummed to me the first night that he showed me kindness. I bite down on my tongue and force myself to focus.

The world around me hushes.

Quiet.

Silence and light. The red mist blows away with one thrust of my wings.

I smile and open my heart, leaving it vulnerable to the souls I welcome. I feel every single soul pass through me as they reenter their bodies. My eyes widen at my power.

I've never seen it actually work. Their bodies are sewn back together like time itself has been turned back. Flesh and bone mend until they're all perfect again, healthy, and not a single death remains on the cold stones of Nesbrim.

One soul lingers, caressing mine, and I let myself fall to my knees, wrapping my arms around myself in an attempt to hold onto the feeling of Rune's heart within mine. I let out a choked cry. It's the warmest caress against my weary soul.

"I knew you could do it, pup. You just needed a little push."

I flinch at his voice.

His voice. No eerie, ghostly curse wrapped around it.

I look up and his eyes are crimson once more, staring deeply into mine with the life of a million suns.

I cry and leap into his arms, squeezing the hell out of him.

"I thought I lost you!" I wail and he clutches onto me just as desperately. "You said. Y-you said you couldn't promise me you'd be with me forever." I pound my fists angrily into his chest.

His red eyes are so soft and gentle as he laughs—actually laughs—and the sound of it makes me cry harder because I've never wanted anything so desperately.

"Don't ever do that again. *Ever*. I won't survive

without you, Rune." I stop hitting his chest and slump with the emotions.

He leans up and presses his forehead against mine. "Forever. A million wishes that we will make together and more."

"You promise?"

He nuzzles his beautiful face into my shoulder. "I promise."

"Your voice—the eerie curse isn't there anymore," I mumble into his shoulder.

He pulls away and looks at me, surprise filling his beautiful face. "Really?"

Sharp waves of aura rain down on us, ruining our perfect moment, and all I can see when I look up are flashes of black and gold feathers. Blood colors everything that remains of the castle.

Nesbrim is a ghost of its former self, but at least everyone who perished moments ago is back. They all look around, confused, while their friends who survived hug them dearly.

Naminé and Greysil are hugging desperately and sobbing. I let out a sigh of relief. I'll never regret being the Goddess of Life again, not when I can grant such beautiful wishes.

Rune stands and offers me his hand to help me up. His dark hair is illuminated by the dusted-out orange suns behind him, his shirt lost in the rubble somewhere. My

God of Peace and I intertwine our fingers and stand together as one.

"I don't think we will have luck finding Violet in this mess. Let's get the Hollows and pray to the gods that Wren and Moro have snapped out of their curse." I jump on the largest pieces of stone slabs with Rune at my side.

I try not to glance up at my two Eostrixes destroying the beautiful city as we sprint through the snow-filled streets. After several blocks, the rubble finally clears and we can run a bit easier. All the creatures who live here have fled to their homes, and thank gods for it.

"There!" Rune shouts as he points to the atrium. Wren and Moro stand with horror written all over their faces. Their eyes are tracked on Arulius and Kastian as they war in the sky.

We approach them with caution but I relax once I see their normal eye colors.

"Where the fuck have you two been? What's going on!" Wren stalks toward me and eyes my shredded clothes, which are covered in crimson. Moro gives us an equally questioning look.

"Well, okay, here's what happened. You two went crazy and tried to kill Rune because you heard him talk... and you can clearly see Kastian is fighting. We managed to destroy the skull and now we just need to get the Hollows out!"

The two look at each other incredulously. Rune

remains silent at my side. I'm sure he's still nervous about talking since it's been so long since he's been able to speak without being attacked.

"I suppose that explains why I'm missing some memories about how we ended up here... and why you look like that." Moro rubs his eyes like he's stressed out—fuck, we all are.

Wren doesn't look so convinced but he drops it. "Okay, we can sort this out when we get back home. Let's hurry up here," the Cypress snaps as we enter the atrium.

Home. I want to be home with all my males and family, warming by the fire, safe and sound with the Rhythm intact.

It's so close.

The Hollows are all frenzied by the energy in the air and the destruction that wages outside the glass dome. I try to calm them as much as I can but it's Moro who handles them like the master he is. I don't miss the gleam and admiration in Wren's eyes as he watches the Keeper calm them all with one hum and cast a beautiful silver dust across them. That must be his power, and it works instantly.

"Let's go!"

Rune and I charge through the atrium to shatter the glass. I lash out a few arcs of my now-crimson aura while Rune summons his fire aura—I'm entirely in awe of it.

Fire engulfs his hands, the center heated with crimson

but the tips licking the sky with ebony flames. He gives me a cocky glance and smirks because I'm gawking at him like a love-drunk Eostrix.

His flames devour the glass and all the shattered pieces that fall, making them disappear into nothing. It's as if the fire itself is a beast that eats anything the caster wishes.

Moro doesn't wait to stare in awe like I do—he's on the largest Hollow in the group and leads the way as every single last one charges out behind him. Wren leaps and grabs the scruff of one like he's making a grand escape and he shouts with excitement. My heart is pounding out of my chest with adrenaline and I can't help but shout with the rush of this too.

"We did it! Oh my gods!" I leap into Rune's arms and he smiles wide at me. I can feel his heart hammering in his chest too as we embrace. We manage to catch the last two Hollows in the group.

The wall is just a few leagues ahead of us and I'm worried some of the smaller Pine Hollows can't jump the wall like Brevik could, but Moro is already on it.

He raises his hand and makes a vertical slashing motion at the wall. For a second nothing happens, but then an enormous sword made of light from the fucking gods crashes down from the sky.

"What the *fuck,* you crazy asshole!" Wren shout-laughs.

The sword is entirely made of glowing, light blue aura, and I would bet my life it's bigger than the court that Arulius and Kastian just destroyed.

Moro flicks his fingers like he wants the sword gone and the wall just obliterates into nothingness, creating a large opening for all of us to escape through.

I laugh and inhale deeply, spreading my arms out as I feel the cold air rush through me. I've never felt so fucking alive.

The beasts all howl and grunt as they realize they're free and my heart couldn't be fuller. Margo and Brevik are at the top of the hill, at the tree line, waiting for us.

We dismount and I instantly return my attention to the skies. I don't see either of my gods and it makes me nervous, but I have to trust Kastian can hold his own until we get there to help.

We still need to take care of Violet.

"Moro, I didn't know you had that kind of magic! Where was all that power when we got our asses whooped the first time?" Wren pats him on the back roughly and Moro smiles weakly.

"I didn't have them until I visited Liasium." I raise a brow and Rune narrows his eyes. "I met with the God of Memories."

It takes me a second but I remember Kastian telling me about him. He resides in Liasium. We were going to go there to get the Vernovian Thorn taken off before Arulius and Wren attacked us in the tree.

"And you were able to recall your abilities? What about who your past life was?" I don't think I'll ever want my full memories back... Talia isn't someone I want to become and the thought of it makes me queasy.

Moro nods, running his hand through his short silver hair. His dark skin is humming with the power he exerted to break the wall and I'm still in shock he has reserves.

"I did... The memory god is wise. You and Kastian need to see him as well. You may have visions and pieces of who you once were slipping back to you in small waves, but you'll never fully be your true selves until you regain them."

I frown and am about to shake my head but Wren cuts in.

"We can chat about memories later. Kastian needs us —Margo, take the Hollows to the grove and keep Marley safe in case anything happens to us."

He's right, we need to put an end to Violet's reign. It's the last step before I can resurrect everyone. I give Margo a kiss on her forehead and promise to see her soon.

Margo and Brevik lead the Pine Hollows through the forest and we watch until the last tail disappears in the shadows. The wind picks up and goosebumps spread up my arms. I'm not cold, but something about this all being over is surreal.

Months of suffering and losing myself... just to rebuild who I am and what I stand for. I've never been more ready to take my place here. To become the Goddess of the Rhythm.

To fix everything.

31

Elodie

The streets are filled with cries and it's really hard not to stop and make sure everyone is okay, but we have to finish this. I look from side to side as we pass many injured creatures—Moss Sparrows trying to heal wounds on Dreadiuses, Eostrixes flying younger creatures away to safer parts of Nesbrim.

It's amazing to see them all working together.

We reach the rubble of the castle and find Kastian and Arulius depleted of their auras and now fighting with their bare fists.

A lump gets caught in my throat as I watch them tear

at each other, their bloody faces and arms, their wings ruffled and feathers missing. I want them to stop but I know they can't. We have to find Violet and end her.

"Where the fuck is Violet?" I glance at Rune. It's been utter chaos since the fighting started but I haven't seen her anywhere. It's like she left the city. "Where's Kol?"

He clenches his jaw and then flinches, eyes widening, as a thought clearly pops into his head. He immediately turns around and draws his aura flames. They blaze hot as he cuts into something invisible behind us.

Oh my fucking gods.

I forgot Kol has invisibility just like Rune.

A horrible, gut-wrenching thought twists through me. *How many times has he been watching us under the cover of his invisibility? How long has he been watching... and with who?*

No, no, no, no.

"Fuck!" Wren spits as blood gushes from the soldier Rune just slashed into. Their crimson liquid spurts out and coats us all. I summon my aura into my palms and two crimson blades form.

"Rune, you fucking idiot." Kol's hot breath curls in the air as he lifts his blanket of magic.

Beneath it is himself, Violet, and Willow. My marrow thickens and I'm trying to stay in the moment rather than letting my mind trickle through every not-private moment they've seen us have...

Please, gods... don't let Violet know what Rune is. If she followed us to Moro's cottage... If she heard what Moro said about him...

My Dreadius flashes his teeth at his brother as he growls, "You'd let the Rhythm die? For what, brother—for a lost ruler to find her loved one?"

Kol's eyes widen with disbelief at Rune's voice. He's clutching his chest as tears of blood drip from his sharp jaw and onto his wound, healing it almost immediately. "Rune... When did you... You can talk." Tears brim his black eyes and his stance falters for a moment. Even Violet looks distraught by the sound of my Rune's perfect voice but she quickly grips her wits again.

"Elodie, this is your last chance. Don't make me do this," she hisses at me. I can see the pain tearing her soul apart. She clearly doesn't want to do whatever it is she's planning, but her determination to regain Lucius burns hotter. Her fists are shaking and she looks like she's about to shatter.

She has nothing left. Her court is in ruins and her own guards' loyalties are constantly in question.

When you've given everything, done things that can't be forgiven, you think there's no way to go back. Perhaps for her this is true.

I furrow my brows and tighten my jaw. "Violet. I don't know where or who he is. It's time to give up. I already destroyed the skull. You're finished."

Her crimson eyes hold mine hostage and she pulls out a long, black aura blade from her hand, pointing it at me and smiling like a crazy bitch. There's something jagged in her other hand and she's clutching it tightly.

"You were too late, *Talia*... I'm sorry." A tear falls from her eyes and she lunges at Rune, slicing his forearm before any of us can react.

I thought she'd be after me.

No. She knows.

She's found the final god to complete the curse.

His blood shines on the ebony blade and she presses the fragment of bone in her hand against his blood. We were fools to think we could get ahead of her...

The fragment of bone glows red and I feel a dark spirit within me rise to meet it.

I'm plunged into darkness.

32

Kastian

Arulius's eyes are furiously blinking out the blood that relentlessly spills into them. I'm blocking as many of his tight punches as I can, but gods, I'm fucking spent. My jaw feels like hell and my core is on fire with the amount of aura I've expended. He's clearly at his end too.

"What are you even fighting for at this point, Arulius?" I growl at him and I land a perfect blow to his cheek, sending him to the ground. I pant and spit out blood while I try to steady my legs beneath me.

Arulius glares at me, shutting one eye as blood spills

into it from his forehead. "You wouldn't fucking understand. You've never lost her like I have... You never had to... had to rip her heart out and watch her die at your hands." His remaining purple eye blazes with fury.

He's a mess. Traumatized like we all are, but twisted into thinking he is doing what's right for her. Such a fucking idiot.

"That's your own fault for following Violet's orders like a blind dog. You can't pretend like you're the one I should pity." I kneel on his chest, setting my knee heavy on his bone armor. He rasps in a few tight breaths as I wrap my ruthless hands around his throat. "Because at the end of the day, *you* killed her twice."

His eyes round with pain as he chokes out, "I didn't have a godsdamn choice, Death God."

I squeeze tighter and he wriggles beneath me. "There's *always* a choice."

He goes limp, his arms falling to his side in defeat. He stares up into the dust clouds we've created. His purple eyes flicker with acceptance and then he smiles weakly into the sky.

"Not when you're born of this realm by wrath," he whispers and I wrinkle my nose at his words because he's not making any sense.

"What do you mean, *born of this realm?*"

He flicks his gaze to me. He looks so fucking tired and I'm at my limit too. "I was born of Violet's wrath. Her hatred and pain for Talia created me. There was no place for a God of Wrath before such pain was endured... I am her darkling, her shadow, her *puppet*."

I flinch and my marrow chills. Loosening my grip on him, I murmur, "You... You're the god that was created after all else." My mind whirls and a lump forms in my throat. He's been her puppet all along. By his actions and feelings, he obviously has his own heart and soul, but he can't disobey Violet... she controls everything.

He looks back to the sky, a frown cresting his lips, and nods. "I'm the odd sheep. The piece of this world that's never truly belonged. That's why I fight. I'll never let her die at my hands again. Violet can control me if she wills it. I'll never be truly *free*."

"You've never lived as a human in the other realm."

He shuts his eyes and nods slowly.

I stare at him for another second before cracking and gasps catch our attention. We both snap our heads toward Elodie and the others. Looks like Wren and Moro are back to normal, and Violet... What did she do?!

Elodie hunches over and screams. It's so eerie and hollow that it rings through my entire being. It's as if two voices scream as one and she clutches her head tightly, fisting her hair as if her mind is on fire.

"Elodie!" I shout and push off of Arulius.

I run to her. Her wings double in size and drip with steaming blood. Her once-beautiful feathers have gone red and when she looks at me, her eyes are black—like a dark, starless sky, void of any light.

"Elodie... what the fuck did she do to you?!" I shout as I turn to Violet and clutch my dear Eostrix in my arms. Wren and Moro are stunned and stare at her in horror. Rune's eyes are desolate, like he's lost the one thing he lives for.

Violet stands, shaking as she gives an uncertain smile. "*North*, I've brought you back from the plains of the endless rest. Now tell me where Lucius is!"

A sinister laugh rumbles from Elodie and my bones seize with the sound of it. *No. She didn't... She wouldn't. Not to my precious Elodie.*

She completed the possession.

An eerie and haunting voice pierces my ears as Elodie speaks. "Violet, you're as simpleminded as you've always been. So shattered by a little loss, are you?"

I release Elodie and fly backwards. She's gone now... North can kill more easily than any god. I've seen his carnage on the plains of the human realm. There's a reason he's been dead for centuries. Is that why Borvon shared those images with me when Elodie and I had our argument? It was a warning of what he's seen...

Violet's red eyes heat with rage and fear. She looks to Kol in case she needs him, but he's as frightened as the rest of us. We all know that only the Goddess of Life can bring down North. But Violet put him *in her*.

"I brought you back! Now tell me where he is—"

Elodie stands and points, her skin devoured by ash and soot and her hair as white as the snow around us. We all follow her hand, which is pointed straight at Moro.

It's quiet. No one dares speak and the wicked smile on Elodie's face has me trembling.

Moro slowly closes his silver eyes. He doesn't seem shocked. As he opens his eyes back up, he looks at Violet with tangible sorrow.

"Is... Is that you, Lucius?" Violet falls to her knees against the stones, keeping her eyes trained on Moro desperately.

He watches her for a moment and then nods. "Yes... It's me, Vi."

She smiles and gasps as tears fall down her cheeks, but when she tries to reach for him he turns coldly away from her. "Lucius?" I can see her soul hardly holding on. She's so far gone with madness. Is this what love looks like when it's been corrupted? Twisted into such a desperate and saddened state?

When it's been poisoned.

Moro looks back at her from the corner of his eyes. He looks miserable, like his heart can't take what he's going to say. "Look at what you've done, Vi... Look at the chaos and pain you've created for such selfish reasons."

She hangs her head low and sobs, covering her mouth

to keep the pain-filled cries at her lover's words. "B-but I did it for us! I—I couldn't l-live without you any longer!"

My heart clenches... What would I do if I were in her situation? I'd do anything for Elodie.

His silver eyes narrow on her with pity and his own anguish burns through, but he holds strong. "I would have *found you,* Vi. I would've come for you just like I did the first time, and if you'd just left everything alone... we could have been together again." He hesitates and takes a steadying breath. "I'll never love you. You're not the woman I fell in love with. You're not even a shell of her."

Ouch.

The goddess slumps to the ground, her eyes wide with the horror of what her actions have reaped. It's hard to not feel bad for her, but with Elodie now under North's possession I'm indifferent as fuck.

Elodie tips her head back and laughs at the pain that fills the air. "War. Blood. Ruin. I want it all, every bit of emotion and agony that it sows. *More*, more, I want it all!" she sings into the sky.

Rune grips her wrist. "Elodie, you need to fight it!" I'm shocked to hear him speak but that's the least of my concerns right now.

Elodie snaps her head to him and lashes out with her aura. It's unrecognizable, it's a beast of blood and terror, boiling with the anger of the God of War himself.

"Rune, get back!" Wren tackles him to the ground as

Elodie releases an arsenal of curved blades around her. *Holy shit, that would have cut them in half.* I clench my teeth as sweat beads down my temples.

"Elodie is gone. The true Rhythm God is here now, and you will all bow to me. A purge is in order. Wouldn't you agree, Death God?" Her black eyes flick to me and I hold my breath.

"North... Borvon still sleeps within me. I don't know what kind of man I was, but I'm not a monster. I don't enjoy taking life." I glare at her.

Elodie narrows her eyes at me and stretches her large crimson wings out.

"Hmm. Too bad. Borvon and I had too much fun once upon a time." She cracks her neck as she rolls it and then takes the fighting stance I vaguely remember North using long ago. Fuck. "And you're going to have to destroy the goddess's body if you wish to defeat me. I won't stop until war is heavy on the human realm, their bones and blood seeping into the soil, my taste buds, and their screams deeply engraved in my soul. Oh, how I miss it."

I clench my fists and try to tap into the last of my aura. I'm running on fumes at this point but I won't die that easily. Not with everything on the line.

The stones shift beside me as Arulius stands at my side. I raise my brow at him. He gives me a curt nod and rests his good eye on Elodie. Relief floods me, seeing that he's finally come to his fucking senses.

Our friendship was strained when we first met, ruined by his betrayal, and then we were enemies. But perhaps now we can stand together for our one cause.

For our precious Elodie.

"Hope you didn't waste all your pathetic aura on me," he hisses as he wipes his bloody face with his torn sleeve.

I scoff at him. "I haven't even gotten started yet."

Elodie's smile is wicked as she lunges forward at us, her wings carrying her faster than I can fly. I hardly dodge in time and Arulius barely deflects her viscous crimson arc. It shatters his bone armor like it's nothing and he curses as he takes to the sky after her.

"Fuck!" Wren shouts as he chases after them on foot. His Cypress vines tremble from the ground and it vibrates beneath my feet with his rage. I dart into the sky after them just as I hear Violet scream and Moro trying to gather warriors below.

What a fucking mess.

A godsdamn mess.

33

Kastian

The clouds are turning red as drops of blood start to pelt down on me from the sky. The God of War truly has returned. My skin's crawling with goosebumps but I ignore it as I try to find any trace of Arulius and Elodie.

It doesn't take long because I hear their aura blades clashing against each other before I even reach the clouds.

Shit, how are we going to get her back—how can we undo *this*?

I break through the clouds and am surrounded by golden bolts of lightning rippling through the air space.

Every hair on the back of my neck rises and my skin feels charged.

Arulius moves at speeds that I can hardly track and Elodie evades every bolt, punch, and cut he throws at her. My teeth are hot with fear and my heart's pounding out of my chest. She's going to beat him.

We don't even stand a chance. We never stood a chance—not against *this*.

Arulius roars, blood spilling from his mouth as Elodie plunges her blades deep into his chest cavity.

"Arulius!" I shout but he pulls away from her swiftly and coughs through ragged breaths as his wild purple gaze finds mine. He's done... If he doesn't heal he'll fucking die.

He raises his hand in the sky and all the bolts of electricity connect with it as one giant force of his golden aura. "You have to get her back... You have to, Kastian!" Tears spill from the golden god and he throws his lightning in her direction. A million beams of light and static roar through the airspace at her. "I'm so fucking sorry!" he wails as the streams of electric yellow and white hit their target. The heat from the attack hangs in the air and the scent of flesh fills me, making me nearly vomit.

Arulius tilts his head back as the last of his energy is spent and then falls to the earth below. I catch his glimmering golden feathers from the corner of my eye but don't dare let my gaze lift from Elodie.

Fuck. Wren, I hope you fucking catch him.

This is far from over. I can feel it in my feathers.

"That was it? Weak, *so* weak. Please tell me you're not that pathetic too, Borvon." Elodie's dual voice haunts me. She's unscathed by the largest attack I've ever seen and the only burn she has is on her right hand, where she focused his attack.

I swallow. I don't want to fight her, I really don't want to fucking fight her, but... maybe Wren and Moro can aid me if I can lure her to the ground.

My wings press tightly to my back as I dive into the clouds and plummet toward the ground. The south field is nearly empty and I know the others will see us over here. I need to get her away from Nesbrim. There are so many citizens that can't protect themselves. I turn back to see if Arulius landed okay and find him secured between Wren and a group of Nesbrim Eostrixes.

Cowards. Of course they won't join the fight. They won't do anything unless Violet leads them, and she's in shambles.

I duck and roll as I meet the ground and I'm fucking glad I do. Elodie is right above me and would have stomped my brains in with the way she crashes into the ground behind me. Her crimson aura dissipates as she charges at me.

I pull a black blade from the earth and thank the dead creatures below for lending me their aura. I whip it in an upward slice and it slashes the entire right side of her face.

I wince and my heart falters, but I fly back until I'm a good ten feet from her.

Elodie laughs maniacally as blood rushes down her torso. I've destroyed her right eye and I'm struggling to hold myself together at the sight of her being ruined like this. I don't want to hurt her.

"Not bad, Borvon, but I'm finished playing now." Her remaining eye dulls with boredom. I flick my attention behind her as Wren, Moro, and Rune appear to help.

I have a horrible feeling in the pit of my stomach.

Elodie turns her attention to them and I take my chance. It's the only one I may get. I wrap one arm around her neck, pinning her arms to her back with the other so she can't use them.

"Moro! Can we bring her back or..." I shout. The words are poison leaving my lips and my chest is heavy as I set my hands, ready to snap her neck.

"You have to do it!" Moro yells, terror flashing in his gaze.

I shut my eyes before I twist my hands.

I try not to think about it as the cracks from her neck shudder up my forearms and a gasp escapes her sweet lips.

"I'm sorry," I whisper as her body slumps in my arms. I sink to the ground with her. A plume of frozen crystals rises around us and my hands tremble. The sobs start to shake my chest as her limp head remains still. "I'm so sorry, Elodie. I—I didn't want to do it."

I don't want to give rest—death—to anything ever again.

I hate being the god of such a horrible thing, and I just killed the one person that I loved more than anything.

Rune's eyes fill with horror and despair. Just like that, I've become Arulius.

The guilt, pain, and endless suffering that I will endure for this... I understand why he never wanted to risk being forced to kill her again. I don't think I will *ever* be the same.

I set her body on the ground softly and we all stand above her. Snow begins to fall softly over our shoulders, sharpening death's grasp.

Her shoulders shake as a laugh erupts from deep within her twisted throat.

A part of me is writhing in fear, but a much larger part is relieved that she's still alive.

"Moro..." Wren mumbles and the Hollow Keeper just shakes his head with terror.

"It's not possible." Moro backs away, Wren following suit. Rune remains on his knees at her side like a shell of himself.

"Borvon, that was a really dirty trick," Elodie mumbles as she stands, her legs trembling. A grotesque bump juts from the side of her neck where I broke it.

"Luckily for you, I have a dirtier one," she coos and wraps her wings around her body briefly before reopening them, revealing her healed body and extended horns that pierce angrily into the sky.

She crosses her arms over her chest and casts out a dark, riveting aura. Blades of hardened blood chase after me. I barely manage to bring up my wing to guard myself before it's blown clean off and agony rips down my back.

Elodie crashes into me feet-first and her hot, bladed hand meets my throat. I stare into her hollow black eyes as we fall to the ground together. A tear forms in the corner of her eye but a horribly evil smile carves her beautiful face.

"Goodbye, Borvon. Take my place on the resting side of Tomorrow, will ya?" She laughs into my face and then—

The world is spinning.

What... just happened?

Blood is twirling in the air with me, a parade of dark drops of death spinning and dancing until I hit the snow. My eyes widen and become blurry as I see Elodie perched on my headless body.

Everything is slow, seconds drawn into minutes. The snow falls slowly, as if time itself has halted.

Am I... No, I'm still conscious. I don't know for how long, but there's nothing left.

We've lost.

War and ruin will reign across the realms and I'll rest forever.

Forever without my love.

Kastian.

Huh? Who is that...

Kastian. It's time to raise them.

Borvon? I've heard his voice a few times before in visions, and the last time I died... What does he mean, *raise them?*

Raise them all. Let me take over—we're running out of time.

I shut my eyes, the tingling in my neck starting to crawl up my jawline until I'm numb, cold, and feeling Borvon rise from my consciousness. His aura brings new strength to our core.

Now—rise, slumbering bones of Tomorrow.

Wake up and fight for your goddess.

34

North

I sever the God of Death's head clean from his body.

What a glorious feeling as his blood sprays at me. I can feel the hot slickness across my skin and I'm thriving in it. I pull my lips tightly in a smile and lick the blood in the corners of my lips and bend down to feast on Borvon's blood. That silly blood-repulsion curse is pathetically easy to break—well, at least for a War God like me. The goddess's body was weak from her lack of Eostrix intake. Stupid girl couldn't even break a simple curse.

I'm doing her a favor by keeping her flesh.

Ruin—let there be *ruin*. Rage, hate, despair, loss. All the things and all the trauma, feed it all to me. I want the humans writhing in it.

I stand, buzzing with the power that's humming in my veins. I glance at the weak gods that have failed the realms. They've failed for centuries. One in particular looks familiar and I kick up my lips.

"Rune, is that you? I swore I heard you talking earlier. What happened to that nasty curse I put on you? *God of Peace*. Peace, my asshole. You live to spite me, don't you." He looks so desperate and broken. Why do all these gods love *her* so much?

No matter—the more pain, the better.

I'm about to kill off the rest of them when the ground beneath me trembles. A fissure splits across the snow-covered fields and black steam bellows out from below.

My eyes widen. What power is this?

Kastian's black aura snakes around his body and head like a shadowy spinal cord, joining them back together in a snap of death's power.

I smile.

There's Borvon, out to play.

"What took so long, Borvon? Such a weak little god you've become," I taunt him, getting ready to use my full powers too, but then I see heads popping up from the crevice in the earth.

Ah, raising them? It won't matter.

Borvon's wings are perfect again. They're coated in glossy black and gold-tipped feathers. His eyes are a darker blue and hold depth only the true God of Death had.

"North, of all the gods, *you* are the only one who won't concede to the Rhythm. We must exist in harmony. Submit to the Life Goddess."

I grit my teeth. What would he know?

"You are death, something that must come to pass. Peace and Life are greeted so easily by all because they are good and happy. What about war? What am I to do? My purpose calls to me, Borvon. Deep in my bones. I hear it ringing in my ears and I've been the only god to suffer the long, forlorn rest of Tomorrow. Never to be awoken again just for being myself."

I shift my attention to the deceased creatures as they gather in the field. Does he really think this will work?

They are nothing, auraless. They're dead.

Borvon smirks at me, reading me like a book as he always has. "They aren't for you. They're to reach her."

Just as his words come out, I feel a sharp pain in my head. I fist my hair and scream as my knees hit the ground. She's fighting, warring against me to regain her body. *No —it's mine. I've gone for centuries without one and I won't give it back!*

"Elodie!" Her friends call for her and she hears them. She's angry with me for everything I did here today. But I won't let go. I push her down as far as I can and stand, shaking my head and laughing.

"She's gone! It's just North now—you hear me?! She's fucking gone and you'll never get her back!"

Goosebumps crawl across my skin as I lock eyes with a large deceased Hollow. His fur is decayed but I can see the dark tufts that were no doubt once glorious. His eyes are yellow and deep, and he has translucent leaves scattered throughout his coat.

Murph.

She surges through me and throws me back into the darkness, into the deep nothingness to watch alone again.

Alone—and filled with so much hate.

35

Elodie

Murph.

He's here.

He's here and he saved me again. Even from the second death, he came back to save me.

I crash into the ground before the great Hollow that I left in the Moss Forest so long ago. My heart cries out and my body's in so much fucking agony. Murph walks up to me, humming low in greeting, and I wrap my arms around his bony corpse tightly.

I never want to let go. I never want to say goodbye

again, but I know I have to. He can't stay this way. None of them can.

I'm sobbing too hard to get any words out but my old friend seems to understand. He lifts his head and turns back to look at Kastian.

The Death God stands like a stone. He's not Kastian, not right now. That's how he was able to do this... to bring me back. He knew what would call out to me, the desire to save all those I've let down.

"Borvon."

"Elodie." He speaks evenly and his tone is deeper than Kastian's. "You need to channel Talia."

I shake my head. Maybe it's because I'm so distraught and I'm still fighting back the other god trying to possess me right now, but I just want to stay... I don't want to disappear again.

"Elodie," he snaps, bringing me from my thoughts.

"Yes?"

His eyes soften on me, sad and weary. "She will give you the knowledge to resurrect them. To take them all to the other side."

My breath hitches and my heart soars with the thought of sending all the dead back to the human realm. I nod slowly.

I'm not sure how long I'll be here before North takes over again. I look to the side and Wren and Rune are already crashing into me, hugging me and pressing kisses to my head. Moro narrows his eyes at me. Our time must be short by the way he tightens his lips.

Fuck.

Wren cries as he wraps his arms around Murph. His Hollow nuzzles his hair and licks his cheek. My soul is fading by the second and there's nothing I can do but say goodbye.

I hold Rune's face in both my hands, caressing him as tears flow from his eyes. "I'm going to sleep now... I don't know if I'll come back."

His crimson eyes widen. "No—no, you're not going anywhere. We have a million wishes to make. You can't go. You can't," he chokes out as he sets his head on my shoulder. I lean my head against his and let a few of my own tears fall.

"After I resurrect them... if North comes back, I want you to kill me." I tilt Rune's face up. He's hardly holding himself together. My once so steeled and emotionless guard—he's crumbling with them now because of me.

I'm sorry I'm breaking you—I hope you'll heal again someday.

I feel Talia reaching up against my skull. *It's time.*

Wren looks back at me and he nods, smiling easily at me like nothing's wrong, like we will all be okay.

Talia's spirit connects with mine and it's... surprisingly warm.

Elodie, are you ready?

I guess so... I don't know what I'm ready for but there's no choice.

We'll save them all and then there will be a moment, just one. Tell them to kill you. Lucius will do it if Rune cannot.

My chest is so fucking heavy with the thought of dying again. I know as the Goddess of Life I will be resurrected, but to live another lifetime without them? To forget and not be *me* anymore...

I watch as my hands rise. A beautiful bright yellow light emanates from all the bones Borvon raised. Their faces all animate with life once more. Hollows of all sizes and shapes, Moss Sparrows, Dreadiuses, Eostrixes. All the dead. All the sleeping creatures of Tomorrow.

Awaken.

Murph's fur fills like time has reversed and he looks just as he should, with beautiful fur. The translucent leaves that once caught my heart now fill Wren's short hair once more as his Hollow touches noses with him.

I catch my breath as the lights begin to orb like fireflies against the winter snow. It's the most beautiful thing I've ever seen.

The bodies of the dead shift into spirits and they begin to float into the sky. Wren breaks out laughing and crying as Murph dances around him happily. The Pine Hollow is going back to the human realm to serve his true purpose and bring happiness to the other side.

Murph licks Wren's face one last time before trotting into the sky, chasing the Hollows that came before him as they wait, and together they all ascend into the universe above us.

My heart fills with so much sadness that they can't stay, but this is the cycle. They aren't meant to stay and Wren's painful smile tells me he feels the same way. I try to hold onto what he told me.

His words from the forest reach into my heart and wrap me safely. *We will all chase one another until we meet, again and again, in an endless cycle until we can all be together.*

They will meet again. In another life.

36

Arulius

My body is surging with pain and my aura is completely depleted. The Eostrixes trying to heal me aren't healing as fast as the damage is spreading. Fuck.

North... the War God that I thought was long dead. What the hell was Violet doing with his bones and why didn't I know about it? Obviously my loyalty is in question.

I grit my teeth and groan as a fresh wave of hell rolls through me.

A Dreadius sprints up to the group of Eostrixes

surrounding me, fucking manic as her legs tremble violently.

"The G-goddess of Life just severed the Death God's h-head!"

What?!

Everyone starts to panic around me and gods—I do too.

I bite back all my agony and force myself to my feet. My flesh is burning from the inside but I can't let Kastian die like this... Fuck, what if he's already gone?

Godsdamn it!

I stumble through the debris and rubble until I see Moro, Violet, and the others. Kol's eyes meet mine and he's at my side in a second, helping me along.

"What the fuck's happening out there?" I cough and a few drops of blood splatter across my chest.

Kol curses under his breath at my state and walks faster, as if I'll die on the way over. "Borvon took over right before Kastian died and he raised the dead. Elodie resurrected them and last I heard they're going to kill her to get rid of North."

My soul shatters with the very mention of them even considering killing her.

"No—no, I'm not letting that happen." I shove him away, draw what strength I have left to my wings, and fly the rest of the distance.

They can't take her away. Not again. I've waited

endlessly for her... only her. There's no one else in the fucking realms that can bring me peace like she does.

The resurrected creatures are still ascending into the sky in a beautiful and heart-wrenching display of the Rhythm.

I see Elodie and everything seems to slow as I land next to her, crashing to the ground with no energy left to spare. She looks at me with her soft brown eyes and that timeless flicker of affection passes through her gaze.

Tears spill from my eyes as I take her appearance in. She looks like corrupted love—poisoned and taken by the malice of the realms. Her wings are crimson and though her skin is back to normal she looks like she's fighting with everything she has to keep him at bay inside her.

North.

"Elodie... I-I'm so fucking sorry." I shatter like I was even whole to begin with—there are pieces of myself that I'll never find in the shadows of the grief we've been dealt. None of this is fair for any of us.

She drops to her knees and clutches my face desperately, sobbing as she studies my face like it will be the last time we ever fucking look at each other.

My throat is tight and I feel sick.

Don't go. Please, gods, don't go. We've only just begun to fix things.

"Don't go, l-love," I choke out as she presses kisses to

my forehead and lips. "Please don't fucking go. I—I can't lose you again."

She lets out a wail that breaks me more than any man in the realms has the right to be broken. I can't see her clearly through my blurry eyes but I can tell she's smiling at me painfully.

I reach a shaky hand to her cheek and she instinctively leans into it as she murmurs, "I have to g-go... I can't stay."

"*No...* I love you, Elodie. Please..." I beg and it comes out as a guttural cry.

She clutches my hand to her lips and shakes her head. "I love you, Arulius... so much." She sobs and presses her quivering lips against mine. "I forgive you."

My love.

My everything.

Don't leave me behind.

37

Elodie

Arulius's amethyst eyes caress me and I fully believe they'll hold my heart for eternity. He's hurting as much as I am and I bite back the pain that wells in my heart. His own wounds finally get the better of him and his head drops to the ground.

Kol kneels next to him and starts healing him with his blood tears.

I look back to the sky with a heavy heart.

The orbs are vanishing and the universe above darkens as the world hushes around me.

The snow falls in thick waves of powder. My lashes

are becoming heavy with the weight of my weariness. I've exerted all my aura and all that's left is the evil within me.

Talia's presence grows stronger for a moment and I open my arms to my God of Death. Borvon's eyes fill with emotion and he meets me, our bodies molding against the cold air and our blood sticky between us.

His hand reaches for me and he rubs his thumb softly over my cheek. He dips down and our eyes connect with the deepest waves of love flooding over me. Talia does love him, more than anything. Her emotions flow through me and they match the love I carry for Kastian.

"Talia, I'll love you till the end," he whispers against my lips and then kisses me. I bring my hands to his beautiful face and press into him more. Our tears fall together.

"Borvon, my darling. Our love will always be endless." I smile somberly against his lips. Turning to look at Rune with anguish in my heart, I say, "The Rhythm Gods will always chase each other. Forever. Until the cycle is corrected."

Rune looks empty, like the entire world has been stolen, but his eyes meet mine slowly.

Then I feel it, Talia fades from me and Kastian's eyes turn back to a light blue. Our ghosts are gone and we're all that's left.

"I love you," I whisper to Kastian. My healed organ is holding together, but barely. I meet Rune's sad gaze and repeat, "I love you all... I'll always be a part of you, and you a part of me. Even if I won't remember."

Kastian hugs me and lets out a low whisper. "It's not fair. *It's not fair.* I can't let you go again. I fucking can't." I lean against him and let my tears fall.

No—It's not fair. None of this was *ever* fair.

Rune finally stands, wrapping his finger in his crimson aura. He walks toward me and I know this is my end. Not forever—maybe I'll live on as Talia does in someone's consciousness. I steel my legs as he stops in front of me.

Wren reaches out and wraps his arms around me. He's still sobbing and trembling but I know he'll be okay. I know he will bring me back from the human realm again someday.

"We can find another way." His amber eyes rove my face and when I shake my head he covers his face and curses. There's no time.

"I know you'll find me again someday, Wren. Chase me down and drag me back here kicking if you have to."

He looks up at me, surprised, and for a second his tears stop and he laughs. "I promise."

Moro sighs with grief and embraces me quickly, pressing a kiss to my forehead. "Tomorrow will be brighter when it sees you again."

I blink back tears. That's all I can do with his kind words.

Rune steps forward and presses his forehead to mine. I gaze into his crimson eyes and make a final wish.

"I wish... that we can all be happy one day. For Violet to find her heart again, for the fighting to cease, for the Rhythm to be restored. For Wren to reunite with Murph, Arulius to forgive himself, and Kastian to never be alone again."

I pause and look into his eyes for a few moments.

"But most of all, I wish I could stay with you." I keep my eyes on his. He clenches his jaw and then brings his flame blade to my throat.

This is it. I brace myself for death. For the dreary rest I hope to find in another life.

"I love you, pup. More than words can say—more than there are stars in the sky and pebbles beneath my feet." I sob and close my eyes. He tilts my head back, pressing his finger tighter against my throat to slit it. "Look at me, Elodie. One more time—I just want to see your eyes one last time."

I swallow the lump in my throat but it's still thick as I open my blurry eyes. His own tears are streaming down his cheeks too and he smiles hopelessly at me, leaning in and pressing a bruising kiss against my lips.

"You made beautiful wishes, pup... I hope every single one comes true."

He cuts my neck and my blood coats his hand. His

eyes turn black and he whispers. "*North*, I give you my vessel."

My eyes widen and before any of us can even blink, North's malicious aura flows from the wound in my neck and into my drop of blood in the snow.

Into my precious.

Irreplaceable.

Rune.

Acknowledgments

I would like to thank my readers first and foremost. Thank you for all the support and love you've showered me and my story with. I know it's been a really heart wrenching ride and I love that I can share it with you.

I would also like to thank my husband. He has been here for me every step of the way. Whether it be helping me plan the story or crying with me at the sad scenes.

Thank you to my beta readers and editor. I couldn't make all my ideas work without your input!

Huge thank you to all my lovely ARC readers. You are such an important part of my books and help spread the love. I couldn't imagine my author journey without each and every one of you.

About the Author

K. M. Moronova has always loved telling stories. She adores reading and writing dark fantasy with a hint of dread and romance. Often, she is found drying flowers and drinking coffee while relaxing in her garden. She loves spending her time with her partner exploring in the forest.

Visit my website for updates on what I'm currently working on and signed copies!
https://www.kmmoronova.com/

Made in the USA
Las Vegas, NV
07 August 2024

58707740-abc5-43ea-9e25-7efd1a38b023R01